The Silent A

CONTRIBUTIONS TO SOUTHERN APPALACHIAN STUDIES

1. *Memoirs of Grassy Creek: Growing Up in the Mountains on the Virginia–North Carolina Line.* Zetta Barker Hamby. 1998

2. *The Pond Mountain Chronicle: Self-Portrait of a Southern Appalachian Community.* Edited by Leland R. Cooper and Mary Lee Cooper. 1998

3. *Traditional Musicians of the Central Blue Ridge: Old Time, Early Country, Folk and Bluegrass Label Recording Artists, with Discographies.* Marty McGee. 2000

4. *W.R. Trivett, Appalachian Pictureman: Photographs of a Bygone Time.* Ralph E. Lentz II. 2001

5. *The People of the New River: Oral Histories from the Ashe, Alleghany and Watauga Counties of North Carolina.* Edited by Leland R. Cooper and Mary Lee Cooper. 2001

6. *John Fox, Jr., Appalachian Author.* Bill York. 2003

7. *The Thistle and the Brier: Historical Links and Cultural Parallels Between Scotland and Appalachia.* Richard Blaustein. 2003

8. *Tales from Sacred Wind: Coming of Age in Appalachia. The Cratis Williams Chronicles.* Cratis D. Williams. Edited by David Cratis Williams and Patricia D. Beaver. 2003

9. *Willard Gayheart, Appalachian Artist.* Willard Gayheart and Donia S. Eley. 2003

10. *The Forest City Lynching of 1900: Populism, Racism, and White Supremacy in Rutherford County, North Carolina.* J. Timothy Cole. 2003

11. *The Brevard Rosenwald School: Black Education and Community Building in a Southern Appalachian Town, 1920–1966.* Betty J. Reed. 2004

12. *The Bristol Sessions: Writings About the Big Bang of Country Music.* Edited by Charles K. Wolfe and Ted Olson. 2005

13. *Community and Change in the North Carolina Mountains: Oral Histories and Profiles of People from Western Watauga County.* Compiled by Nannie Greene and Catherine Stokes Sheppard. 2006

14. *Ashe County: A History; A New Edition.* Arthur Lloyd Fletcher. 2009 [2006]

15. *The New River Controversy; A New Edition.* Thomas J. Schoenbaum. Epilogue by R. Seth Woodard. 2007

16. *The Blue Ridge Parkway by Foot: A Park Ranger's Memoir.* Tim Pegram. 2007

17. *James Still: Critical Essays on the Dean of Appalachian Literature.* Edited by Ted Olson and Kathy H. Olson. 2008

18. *Owsley County, Kentucky, and the Perpetuation of Poverty.* John R. Burch, Jr. 2008

19. *Asheville: A History.* Nan K. Chase. 2007

20. *Southern Appalachian Poetry: An Anthology of Works by 37 Poets.* Edited by Marita Garin. 2008

21. *Ball, Bat and Bitumen: A History of Coalfield Baseball in the Appalachian South.* L.M. Sutter. 2009

22. *The Frontier Nursing Service: America's First Rural Nurse-Midwife Service and School.* Marie Bartlett. 2009

23. *James Still in Interviews, Oral Histories and Memoirs.* Edited by Ted Olson. 2009

24. *The Millstone Quarries of Powell County, Kentucky.* Charles D. Hockensmith. 2009

25. *The Bibliography of Appalachia: More Than 4,700 Books, Articles, Monographsand Dissertations, Topically Arranged and Indexed.* Compiled by John R. Burch, Jr. 2009

The Silent Appalachian

Wordless Mountaineers in Fiction, Film and Television

VICKI SIGMON COLLINS

CONTRIBUTIONS TO SOUTHERN APPALACHIAN STUDIES, 42

McFarland & Company, Inc., Publishers
Jefferson, North Carolina

ISBN (print) 978-1-4766-6768-3
ISBN (ebook) 978-1-4766-2754-0

LIBRARY OF CONGRESS CATALOGUING DATA ARE AVAILABLE

BRITISH LIBRARY CATALOGUING DATA ARE AVAILABLE

Front cover: On the porch of their cabin in a North Carolina
logging camp, Richard James Roberts and his wife
Mabel Gertrude Walker Roberts pose with their first four children:
Clyde, Mary Jo, Norman, and Violet (author's collection)

Printed in the United States of America

*McFarland & Company, Inc., Publishers
Box 611, Jefferson, North Carolina 28640
www.mcfarlandpub.com*

To my maternal grandparents, Richard and Mabel Roberts, who gave me my Appalachian blood.

Table of Contents

Preface

Born in North Carolina, reared in East Tennessee, and blessed with Cherokee ancestry, I am Appalachian. A lifelong writer of both poetry and prose, I earned a degree in English education at East Tennessee State University in Johnson City. I was nurtured toward my place in the teaching profession by mentors Dr. Ambrose Manning, who was generous with encouragement and praise during my semester of student teaching, and Dr. Robert Higgs, who shared his wealth of knowledge about literature but scared the heck out of me in the classroom with his imposing presence and booming voice. My thirty-five-year career as an English teacher includes a brief stint at Northern Kentucky University alongside my late colleague Danny Miller, a well-established, learned scholar of Appalachia. My experiential background and the influence of these three men have greatly contributed to my interest in all aspects of the Appalachian culture, especially literature.

During the course of my teaching English at the University of South Carolina Aiken (USC Aiken), I have had the privilege of teaching Appalachian culture studies for both matriculating students and senior citizens enrolled in the Academy of Lifelong Learning. This topic is so popular that I am often asked to repeat the course—what a delight for me to discover enthusiastic local interest in Appalachia! As a result, I can confidently say that I have played a role in establishing the importance of my heritage and its rich culture to the transplants and lowlanders of the Central Savannah River Area (CSRA).

The origin of this book was my research project "Mute Characters in Appalachian Literature" presented in 2013 at the Appalachian Studies Association Conference, in my opinion the most vital "Appalachian discursive community" (Claybough 18), at Appalachian State University in Boone, North Carolina. USC Aiken awarded me a small stipend to use to hire a research intern, my former student and fellow Appalachian Mary Emily Short, who has been a valuable assistant. In the summer of 2015 on a tour of Scotland, Wales, and England, I met Hal Normand, a writer who shared with me his worthwhile editorial suggestions. Additionally, the pleasure of reading volumes of literature about Appalachia, viewing multiple films and television series set there, and consequently analyzing them for deeper meaning, have been the greatest personal rewards of this project. The only drawback I have encountered is disappointment that there are no characters who are silent or have unusual voices in many of the works I have spent countless hours perusing. It has been like a gamble—unless the literature is specifically known for inclusion of silent characters, it was most often necessary to read the entire work in search of one. Some readers will probably know of works I should have included, but I repeatedly asked authors, book sellers, and academicians for suggestions. Some were helpful, others not so much. Nonetheless, I have gained priceless knowledge of my own Appalachian heritage during this lengthy process, and for that I am most thankful.

Readers should keep in mind that the primary purpose of this book is to narrow the focus on specific literary types: silent, taciturn or unheard characters and those with limited or unusual voices outside the realm of normal spoken language, all found within works set in Appalachia. Secondly, it is to identify the reasons for their manner or lack of communication, and thirdly, it is to analyze their behavior and examine their relationships with other characters who share either their unique form of language or their silence.

The cynosure of Appalachian characters in this book are deaf, mute, pretend to be mute, have lost their ability to speak (either temporarily or permanently), choose not to speak, are apprehensive about their ability to use comprehensible words, are silent for fear of reprisal or as the result of trauma, keep deep secrets hidden, mutter in monosyllabic responses, stutter, grunt and point, communicate with animal-like sounds, are tongue-tied, speak in tongues or develop speech patterns in an enigmatic language such as idioglossia or cryptophasia.

Readers are forewarned that a few of the works contribute to negative stereotyping, a damaging perception of mountain people as ignorant hillbillies that has been widely accepted by some individuals in mainstream America. In no way do I wish to perpetuate this distorted image. Writer and historian Emma Bell Miles acknowledged the work of writers who actually experienced and wrote accurate accounts about mountain life; she believed the "ordinary novel of moonshine and rifles seems merely newspaper twaddle" (Engelhardt 24). Moreover, Henry Shapiro stated that the myths surrounding Appalachia have been "invented and re-invented countless times" (qtd. in Engelhardt 35) for a variety of purposes, most often self-serving ones. With a more hopeful perspective, Casey Clabough believes that contemporary regionalists are exploring our region's "legacy of difference ... a rich milieu" for writers interested in both the "visceral and cultural" (18) features of Appalachia. The works of this treatise simply illuminate the depth and breadth of literature, film, and television programs set in Appalachia, especially those comprised of characters who struggle with language or the ability to speak freely. Attention is drawn mainly to the importance of voice or the lack of it, and how it affects the struggling characters' relationships with others.

While working on this book, I enjoyed returning to areas around my home to visit mountain bookstores in North Carolina, particularly Malaprops in Asheville and City Lights in Sylva, speak to local scholars, and capture photographs of Appalachian people and landscapes. I also had the opportunity to interact with professors of Appalachian Studies programs, such as Pat Beaver at Appalachian State University, and several Appalachian authors, many of whom were so gracious, especially Lee Smith, Wiley Cash, Gurney Norman, Kathryn Stripling Byer, and Dot Jackson. Along my journey, I rediscovered the resilience of mountain people, as well as the undeniable power of our distinct language. Jason Howard, editor of *Appalachian Heritage*, noted that Appalachian literature, indeed an integral part of the American literary tradition, is:

> a living thing, kept alive in the hills and hollers and cities of the region.... Appalachia is a place that can take up residence in the spirits of natives and non-natives alike. It's a region of great complexity, of rural and urban, living and leaving, acceptance and prejudice, wealth and poverty, religion and drug abuse, literacy and dropouts, individualism and homogenization—and everything in between [6].

Much of Connie Jordan Green's YA novel *The War at Home* invoked memories for me. My family lived in a cotton mill town in North Carolina until my father graduated from college and we moved to Oak Ridge. He was hired by Union Carbide and worked at K-25 until he retired. We lived in a Twin Dwelling Unit (TDU), actually a flattop building now referred to as a duplex, when we first arrived in Oak Ridge. I also recognized in Green's narrative the names of the roads and the shopping center we frequented. My elementary school years included trips to the Atomic Energy Museum where I was chosen to place my hand on a large sphere that generated electricity and made my long hair stand on end.

Once my father took a trip to Washington, D.C., to examine NASA-designed space suits for the astronauts. His task was to determine if the suits could also be used as protective gear for workers who handled radioactive materials. He brought a sample suit home and allowed my brother and me to try it on, helmet and all. We were sworn to secrecy, but as soon as we arrived at school the next day, we could not wait to tell our friends. Nevertheless, no harm, no foul, as no one believed us!

It is worthwhile to note the continuing influence of Thomas Wolfe on several Appalachian fiction authors. Wolfe wrote with a style, albeit deemed verbose by his mentors, that has inspired other writers to explore themes, settings and characters similar to those in his literary canon. These elements can be detected specifically in Charles Frazier's *Nightwoods*, Wiley Cash's *A Land More Kind Than Home*, Ron Rash's *The Cove*, and Robert Morgan's *The Truest Pleasure* and *Gap Creek*. It could be said that there is no better Appalachian author to emulate.

Although a few of the writers included in this book are not Appalachian, such as Tennessee Williams, all have written or produced works set in Appalachia that are central to the work. A few of the pieces may even seem a "stretch" to be considered Appalachian, due to the narrow focus, they are included because of relevant characters of silence or unique voices.

Readers will notice that poetry is absent from the book, because of the cost and time involved in securing permission from the poets and the copyright hurdles that must be considered. Otherwise, poetry would certainly be included. I extend my sincere apologies to all the wonderful Appalachian poets whose work I have enjoyed for many years but am unable to include here.

This analytic reference work should be of interest to scholars who are passionate about the complexities and nuances of Appalachian literature, specifically those with characters who fail to find or express their voices, are discursive resistant, or make a conscientious decision to suppress their voices. These individuals mirror personas essential to the diverse and rich culture of the mountains. My hope for this book is that it will be deemed worthy of a place on the shelves of university libraries and find its way into the hands of professors of Appalachian Studies programs and their students. May they find it helpful in research endeavors.

Works Cited

Claybough, Casey. *Inhabiting Contemporary Southern and Appalachian Literature: Region and Place in the Twenty-First Century*. Gainesville: University Press of Florida, 2012. Print.

Engelhardt, Elizabeth S. *The Tangled Roots of Feminism, Environmentalism, and Appalachian Literature*. Athens: Ohio University Press, 2003. Print.

Howard, Jason. Editor's Note. *Appalachian Heritage* 42 (2014): 6. Print.

Introduction

When acknowledging favorite works of literature, film, or television, readers and audiences alike primarily recall and often quote or allude to the remarkable speech of characters and the manners in which they interact with other characters. Just as memorable, perhaps, are the silences of those who do not speak. Noteworthy silent characters across multiple media include Harpo Marx, the silent film pantomime who communicated by blowing a horn or whistling; Clarabell the Clown, the mute, horn-honking partner of Howdy Doody; Chief Bromden in Ken Kesey's *One Flew Over the Cuckoo's Nest*; Mr. Bean, portrayed by British actor Rowan Atkinson; the iconic John Singer, who neither hears nor speaks, in Carson McCuller's *The Heart Is a Lonely Hunter*; Edward Scissorhands, the unfinished titular creature in Tim Burton's Gothic film; mute Scotswoman Ada McGrath in Jane Campion's film *The Piano*; and an entire community in Melinda Haynes' contemporary novel *Chalktown*.

The literary origins of silence trace back to the Old Testament. In Genesis 1:2–3, the earth and firmament are dark, void, and without form until God breaks the silence and speaks creation into existence. Moses, who claims he has uncircumcised lips, is hesitant to do God's bidding in Egypt, but his tongue is equipped with words of warning for the Pharaoh (Exodus 6:10–12). To prove Job's faith, God withdraws in silence and allows Satan to tempt him, yet Job does not curse God or lament his horrendous circumstances. He silences his accusers by his longsuffering patience, for "in all this did not Job sin with his lips" (Job 2:10). Notable women such as "Sarah, Rebecca, Leah, and Rachel, the wives of patriarchs" (Tkacz), as well as Miriam, Esther, Deborah, and Jael, may be perceived as passive victims, but their moments of silence are purposeful. In a New Testament account, Zechariah is struck dumb by Gabriel, for he doubts the angel's news that his wife Elizabeth will bear him a son in light of their advanced ages (Luke 1:17–21). Jesus, using only his hands and spittle, heals a deaf and mute man of Decapolis (Mark 7:31–37). In another miracle story, the father of a mute boy who convulses and foams at the mouth asks for healing of his son. Jesus calls out to the demon, "Thou dumb and deaf spirit, I charge thee, come out of him" (Mark 9:17–25). Jesus also exorcises a tortured man who can speak only through the voices of legions of demons that possess him (Mark 5:1–11). During his journey toward crucifixion, Jesus maintains his silence. He is the lamb who utters no words of rebuttal to the false accusations or severe beatings from the Roman guards (Matthew 27:12–14). While he hangs on the cross, he cries out, "My God, my God, why hast thou forsaken me" (Matthew 27:46), as God once again withdraws in silence, for He cannot look at the sin of mankind which Jesus has taken upon himself. Later in the New Testament, St. Paul proclaims to Timothy that a woman should learn in subjective stillness. She is not "to teach, nor to usurp authority over the man, but to be in silence" (I Timothy 2:11–12).

Similarly, Aristotle wrote, "Silence gives grace to a woman—though that is not the case likewise with a man" (*Politics* 1.5.9). Historically, language has been perceived as power and silence as a limitation or weakness. Nonetheless, Leonardo da Vinci believed that "nothing strengthens authority so much as silence." Lao Tzu echoed those sentiments with his claim that "silence is a source of great strength."

When interrogated by a jury of religious leaders, Protestant reformer Anne Askew replied, "God has given me the gift of knowledge but not of utterance. Solomon says that a woman of few words is a gift of God" (Glenn 2). Defiant literary figure Hester Prynne, in Nathaniel Hawthorne's *The Scarlet Letter*, proves the power of silence by refusing to name the father of her child, even after enduring a prison sentence, public confrontation and humiliation, as well as being forced to wear a shameful red marker of her sin. Her rebellion infuriates religious authorities who cannot break her wall of silence. It is well worth noting that the purpose of her silence is to protect a man, Arthur Dimmesdale, a minister and the father of her child. As a result, she shoulders the entire burden of punishment while he continues to stand unscathed in his pulpit. The purpose of his silence is also to protect a man—himself—so his reputation will remain one of righteousness. Elizabeth Alsop notes that in the literary works of early 19th century writers like Hawthorne, silence is a result of "trauma, crisis or duress, [and] despite the consequences" (84), an intentional act of bold opposition.

George Steiner wrote that people function within the "act of discourse … but there are actions of the spirit" based on quietude (12), for "the election of silence" is the voice most loudly heard (46). Communication is not limited to an oral code. Thus silence should be considered a universal language. Casey and Stephens contend that there are two types of silence: "actual and perceived. Actual silence is easy to understand—no one is communicating. Perceived silence can be more insidious" (26), i.e., when someone is speaking, but no one is hearing.

Cheryl Glenn confirms that the "Western notion of language" is perceived positively but silence negatively, with language in the foreground while silence is relegated to the background. Speaking out signals the freedom and power of an individual or a culture. The "obverse," which is subordinate to speech, suggests nothingness. For women, silence is most often rewarded only when it connotes obedience and subordination (3–5). In fact, the natural order of our society is based on "ambition, competition," confidence, and self-sufficiency, qualities historically associated with men who have an inclination to suppress feminine values such as "emotionality … inclusivity, collaboration, and cooperation" (Young 21).

Robin Patric Clair asserts that from the dawn of patriarchy, women have been "marginalized" and subjected to supportive roles for privileged men (4–5). He points to Charles Courtenay's 1916 treatise, *The Empire of Silence*, in which the author writes that the chatter of women "provides a vent for superfluous energy … much talk cannot be wise talk, and in letting off steam, somebody is apt to be scalded" (183–84). The subjects of female discourse are merely inconsequential. In a similar chauvinistic attitude, Clair suggests that women should not be treated harshly by men but be expected to take the "high road" of silence. Ironically, Courtenay dedicated his book to his wife, "a true comrade and the best of helpers." Clair satirically assumes she must surely have been a silent wife (25).

Elissa Marder, in her article about articulating silence, writes that in response to the suppression of female voices, the gender which needs to address the issue is, ironically, silenced. She claims "feminist discourse" must be examined by the collective feminist "we" for its "parameters" (148), but Kamuf asserts that this approach "engages an attempt to uncover something specific to women that patriarchy has veiled" (qtd. in Marder 152).

In a chapter titled "Indirect Language and the Voices of Silence" in his book *Signs*, Maurice Merleau-Ponty writes that our notion of absolute speech is fatuous, and that "all language is indirect or allusive" (43); in other words, silent. Scholars of linguistics must acknowledge that before a word is spoken, silence is its backdrop, and should strive to determine how that silence is interwoven with speech. The author also points out that no language can ever entirely free itself from the "precariousness of mute forms of expressions" (78), for humans basically express themselves, even before utterance in "silence, gestures, and lived behavior" (back cover).

John Cage, in his "Lecture on Nothing," notes that the "pusher and the pushed" of any thought is discourse, yet silence requires words to help create that silence, and we should not fear it (109). One might believe that silence is an empty void, a gap in oral or written text, but Cage claims that it is an "intensifier" to support what comes before and after it. William Bronk, who suggests that silence offers a multitude of opportunities for nonverbal expression, cited Thoreau, who believed that silence is an "inviolable asylum" (Heller 136).

Traditionally, Americans have mistrusted silence and its partner, stillness. Silence is often suspected as "madness, mooncalfing, woolgathering, laziness, hostility, or stupidity" and "stillness is linked to death" (Baxter 176), notions that originated during the era of Puritanism. A writer and man of great solitude and reflection, Rainer Maria Rilke confided that he longed to speak at a more profound level, but was left with "a mere intimation of the kind of speech that may be possible … where silence reigns" (*Where Silence Reigns*).

Joseph Devito stated that humans communicate "by manipulating words and gestures" (153), yet silence communicates just as deeply as words that may be uttered. He refers to several schools of thought about silence:

> Don Fabun noted, "Holding one's tongue may be prudent, but it is an act of rejection; silence builds walls—and walls are symbols of failure." Thomas Mann, in one of the most often quoted observations on silence, said, "Speech is civilization itself. The word, even the most contradictory word, preserves contact; it is silence which isolates." On the other hand, Karl Jaspers observed that the "ultimate in thinking as in communication is silence," and Max Picard remarked, "silence is nothing merely negative; it is not the mere absence of speech. It is a positive, a complete world in itself" [153].

An important mode of silent communication is American Sign Language, "its history in the South linked to deaf education" in the United States (Lucas and McCaskill 40). Graduates of Gallaudet University in Washington, D.C., came south to establish schools for the deaf in Virginia in 1839 and in North Carolina in 1845. The fundamental forms of American Sign Language—phonology, morphology, and syntax—follow the same basic rules as written and oral language but are expressed using "handshape, location, palm orientation, and nonmanual signals (facial expressions)" (41).

Indirect discourse, especially in African American communities, has included the nonverbal "body language of 'suck-teeth' and 'cut-eye,' both used to show annoyance, disapproval, or hostility" aimed at others. Suck-teeth, inhaling "air between the upper teeth and lower lip," is a meaningful slight or sharp dismissal. With cut-eye, one would look a person directly in the eye but then immediately look down or away, a demonstrative insult. Both means of silent communication were most likely an antebellum "code" for passing messages among the slaves (Johnson 123).

Victorian writers George Eliot and Charles Dickens contemplated the potential of "sound and silence" (1) as profound literary representations. Eliot's belief that silence is as intentional as sound is supported by the numerous silences of her oppressed female characters who are permitted only to listen, not speak. She was especially concerned about the "muffled" voices of women who were silenced by the long-established propriety of "femininity, domesticity, and marriage" (Dupree 11).

Ren Yiming, in her article about the metaphorical uses of silence, avers that silence in postcolonial literature is prescribed according to the characters' gender role expectations and race. She believes the silence of women in postcolonial texts indicates being "denuded of the ability to speak" as well as resistance to displacement from a native culture and against a "marginal life far off the man-dominant center" (4). Silence used as an oppositional ruse is a forethought that "foils and confuses interpretation" (4) by other characters, according to Kathryn Steele and her article about the novel *Clarissa*. However, the silence of the proper, single heroine is obligatory to prevent the peril of unwarranted speech.

In his book *Silence and Subject in Modern Literature,* Ulf Olsson opines that literature is a historical document and as a "textual or written medium, can generate silence that, perhaps paradoxically, speaks" (3). Literature can make apparent the "order of discourse" (20), so the silent character is most often problematic within the social hierarchy. The dichotomy of silence and sound signify conclusive distinctions but are actually wed as a single "binary" character (8), perhaps like a linguistic hybrid (172). Olsson also reminds readers that in certain situations or establishments, silence is properly perceived as a sign of reflection, morality, obeisance, respect, deference, subordination, nobleness, or homage, for it "facilitates solemnity, reverence, recollection, and a sense of mystery" (Teahan 365).

In austere religious institutions such as convents and monasteries, ascetical silence implies the sanctity of prayer, deep meditation, or somber mourning. "Taught to distrust the veil of language ... the holy man, the initiate, withdraws not only from temptations of worldly action; he withdraws from speech" (Steiner 13). Due to his ritual silence, the ascetic buffers "physical quiet from verbal intrusion" (Teahan 365) to direct his thoughts away from worldly disorder and to render a peaceful interior existence.

In libraries and educational institutions, silence is the expected standard of behavior and suggests serious concentration (164).Yet in other instances, silence is deemed unacceptable, for it is a threat to an "order based on the circulation of speech" (2); however, the silent character who does not or cannot participate in verbal expression may be perceived as simpleminded or illiterate.

Katherine Sohn asserts in her book *Talking Appalachian: Voice, Identity, and Community* that "silence, voice, and identity intersect" (11), recognizing that her own voice has been shaped by various silences (126). James Paul Gee believes communication to be the tool used to "integrate words, acts, values, beliefs, attitudes, and social identities" (qtd. in Locklear 5) along with gesticulation, countenance and attire. Charles Baxter claims that silence and stillness run the risk of being misconstrued, but they may also be "powerful intensifier[s] and marker[s]," deserving of our consideration (181–84).

Language is the manner by which we connect with others and reveal our deepest thoughts, a path that permits us to "construct boundaries and accentuate our differences" (Woodside 2). It enriches the soul and defines experience, gives us a sense of identity and grounds us to certain times, places, and people. "Language suggests that there is always more out there, like the mountains in the distance" (Downer 103–04). It makes known the values and beliefs of a specific regional and cultural heritage; consequently, sharing discourse within families, among community members, and across generations is a fundamental and primordial connection to humanity. "Speech is related to societal perceptions of an individual's communal ability, intellect and culture" (Montgomery and Johnson 14).

A major theme of Appalachian poet and novelist Jayne Anne Phillip's work is an inability to communicate (Willis 23), a failure she finds most unfortunate within the family unit. Her characters are at times "anguished, isolated, and frequently misunderstood" (*Listen Here*, 478). All her novels, she states, begin "with a line—this sound, this voice" (Willis 23). Language, at the core of meaning, is fundamental to her work, and that language is Appalachian, especially in her tales of mountain people's lives (24–25).

Speech, the primary and constructive element of literature, has been the focus of numerous discourse theories. The silent character seems to be a type of "shunt" in literature and draws attention to the onset of reflection. Nonetheless, silent characters continue to be "key co-creators of great stories" ("Silent Characters" 2). In contrast, since the early twentieth century, various writers have chosen to forgo customary dialogue to create characters who cannot or choose not to speak. The tradition of Western literature is "shadowed" by the exclusion of speech, specifically how to respect silence and use it for expression without coercing it into language (Olsson 169).

Ironically, "silence always speaks" (164) or we would not be cognizant of it. According to Blundell, interspersed between dialogue, silence is a powerful presence. It is unyielding, "self-conscious, often vexatious. Amidst the clamour of voices and the discursive clatter of self-expression, a character's speechlessness is an incomplete telling" (5). Blundell also observes that "physicality of the damaged body has proved to be a more effective mouthpiece than voice" (6), an observation supported by a variety of Appalachian characters examined in this book.

Nonetheless, not all silent characters are completely voiceless; for those who can hear but do not speak, silence is often insufficient language rather than an absence of utterance. We learn that mute speech, albeit an oxymoron, is of "human interdependency" (Noe 13). In some literary works, readers are not invited into the minds and hearts of silent characters; in others, an "interior monologue" exists. Silent characters emerge in metonymy as a vehicle or an "ellipsis" for situations that challenge the conventional structure of the narrative (Blundell 12–13).

The Latin forms *muttum* and *mutum* signify "a slight sound, both muteness and muttering" (Allen 7). In *The Melodramatic Imagination*, Peter Brooks observes that in the literary "gallery of mutilations and deprivations" mutes have established significant positions:

> Describing melodrama's "text of muteness," he argues that the different kinds of drama have their corresponding sense deprivations: for tragedy, blindness, since tragedy is about insight and illumination; for comedy, deafness, since comedy is concerned with problems in communication, misunderstandings, and their consequences; and for melodrama, muteness, since melodrama is about expression [qtd. in McDonagh].

Minimal utterance, due to a variety of factors such as issues considered taboo, genetic affliction, disease, an absence of understanding or confidence in articulation, a lack of both oral and textual literacy, suspicion of outliers, solidarity in cultural resistance to corporate exploitation, or sacred trust among mountain people in an insular community, occur most often in the reticence of male characters in Appalachian literature, which has traditionally been "written largely by and about men" and their work as farmers or coal miners while women have been "hidden behind bonnets and quilts" (Smith 5) in shadowy roles of support. The inarticulate nature of female Appalachian characters is frequently attributed to isolation, inconsolable grief, a need for privacy and secrecy, deference or submission to others (especially men), hardship, fear of judgment, rejection, oppression, suffering, trauma, lack of empowerment, or a sense of invisibility.

For characters who are not inclined to speak, some authors have instilled in them the traditional mountain notion not to "get above their raisin'" for "to move ahead is to betray the past" (Palencia 202). Reticence demonstrates loyalty to their society, and silence is merely a reflection of the culture and history of Appalachia. There is, in essence, a futility of words. Audiences are required to be acute observers of the demeanor of silent characters—their posture, facial expressions, hand movements, and repetitive gestures. They must also be listeners to what is not said but intended.

Along with the restrained communication shared among characters, music is often a connecting factor. "Silences are essential in shaping noise into music" and interpreting the nuances of sound; for complete comprehension of music, one must "question the silences" (Thompson 67). Some non-vocal characters use musical instruments as their voice boxes, or they are drawn to the Appalachian music played or sung by other characters.

Voiceless humans "signify the magnitude of what remains unsaid" (Blundell 12). These characters lack the commonality of the spoken language with other characters, so they are often perceived as the literary "Other," deviant in their resistance to language, an important social convention. An author's silencing a voice, by means of a character who does not speak, causes readers to wonder why restricted vocalization is necessary. Why would writers, when crafting their work, purposely withhold a character's capacity to speak? In Appalachian literature, perhaps the characters' lack of utterance is merely an echo of the silent mountains they call home, where they spend a great deal of time in solitude and seclusion. The ability of readers and viewers to *hear* occurs only when they *listen* to those who are silenced.

Works Cited

Allen, Paula Gunn. *Grandmothers of the Light: A Medicine Woman's Sourcebook*. Boston: Beacon Press, 1991. Print.

Alsop, Elizabeth. "Refusal to Tell: Withholding Heroines in Hawthorne, Wharton, and Coetzee." *College Literature* 39.3 (2012): 84–105. Literary Reference Center. Web.

Aristotle. *Politics*. Trans. H. Rackham. Cambridge: Loeb/Harvard University Press, 1977.

Baxter, Charles. "Stillness." *Burning Down the House*. Minneapolis: Graywolf Press, 2008. Print.

Blundell, Sally. "The Language of Silence: Speechlessness as a Response to Terror and Trauma in Contemporary Fiction." University of Canterbury, New Zealand, 2009. Web.

Cage, John. *Silence*. 50th Anniversary Edition. Middletown: Wesleyan University Press, 2011. Print.

Casey, Michael, and Michael Stephens. "Measure the Silence." *Library Journal* 134.1 (2009): 26. Literary Reference Center. Web.

Clair, Robin Patric. *Organizing Silence: A World of Possibilities*. New York: State University of New York Press, 1998. Print.

DeVito, Joseph A. "Silence and Paralanguage as Communication." *Et cetera: A Review of General Semantics* 46.2 (1989): 153–57. Literary Reference Center. Web.

Downer, Hilda. "Mutant in Bandana." *Bloodroot: Reflections on Place by Appalachian Women Writers*. Ed. Joyce Dyer. Lexington: University Press of Kentucky, 1998. Print.

Dupree, Catherine. "Victorian Sound, Victorian Silence." *Harvard Magazine* (Nov.-Dec. 2003): 11. Web.

Glenn, Cheryl. *Unspoken: A Rhetoric of Silence*. Carbondale: Southern Illinois University Press, 2004. Print.

Heller, Michael. "A Note on William Bronk's Poetics of Silence." *Chicago Review* 44.3/4 (1998): 136. Literary Reference Center. Web.

Johnson, Ellen. *The New Encyclopedia of Southern Culture: Language*. Volume 5. Chapel Hill: University of North Carolina Press, 2007. Print.

Locklear, Erica Abrams. *Negotiating a Perilous Empowerment: Appalachian Women's Literacies*. Athens: Ohio University Press, 2011. Print.

Marder, Elissa. "Disarticulated Voices: Feminism and Philomela." *Hypatia* 7.2 (1992) 148–65. Literary Reference Center. Web.

McDonagh, Patrick. "The Mute's Voice: The Dramatic Transformations of the Mute and Deaf-Mute in Early-Nineteenth-Century France." *Criticism* 55.4 (2013): 655–75. Academic Search Premier. Web.

Merleau-Ponty, Maurice. "Indirect Language and the Voices of Silence." *Signs*. Chicago: Northwestern University Press, 1964. Print.

Montgomery, Michael, and Ellen Johnson. "Language in the South." *Language: The New Encyclopedia of Southern Culture*. Volume 5. Chapel Hill: University of North Carolina Press, 2007. Print.

Noe, Denise. "The Mute Speak." *Humanist* 56.2 (n.d.). Literary Reference Center, 2013. Web.

Olsson, Ulf. *Silence and Subject in Modern Literature*. Hampshire: Palgrave Macmillan, 2013. Print.

Palencia, Elaine Fowler. "Leaving Pre-Appalachia." *Bloodroot: Reflections on Place by Appalachian Women Writers*. Ed. Joyce Dyer. Lexington: University Press of Kentucky, 1998. Print.

Rilke, Rainer Maria. *Where Silence Reigns: Selected Prose*. New York: New Directions, 1978. Print.

"Silent Characters in Dramatic Literature, on Stage and in Reality." Maribor Theatre Festival, 2015. Web.

Sohn, Katherine. "Silence, Voice, and Identity among Appalachian College Women." *Talking Appalachian: Voice, Identity, and Community*. Ed. Amy Clark and Nancy Hayward. Lexington: University Press of Kentucky, 2013. Print.

Smith, Barbara Ellen. "Walk-Ons in the Third Act: The Role of Women in Appalachian Historiography." *Journal of Appalachian Studies* 4.1 (1998): 5–28. Print.

Steele, Kathryn L. "*Clarissa*'s Silence." *Eighteenth Century Fiction* 23.1 (2010): 1–34. Literary Reference Center. Web.

Steiner, George. "The Retreat from the Word." *Language and Silence*. New York: Atheneum, 1982. Print.

Teahan, John F. "The Place of Silence in Thomas Merton's Life and Thought." *The Journal of Religion* 61.4 (1981): 364–83. JSTOR. Web.

Thompson, Deborah J. "Searching for Silenced Voices in Appalachian Music." *GeoJournal: Geography & Music*. 65.1–2 (2006): 67–78. JSTOR. Web.

Tkacz, Catherine Brown. "Are Old Testament Women Nameless, Silent, Passive Victims?" *Catholic Answers Magazine* 17.10 (2006). Web.

Willis, Meredith Sue. "Seduced into Consciousness: The Art of Jayne Anne Phillips." *Appalachian Heritage* 37.1 (Winter 2009). Print.

Woodside, Jane Harris. "Mother Tongues." *Now & Then: The Appalachian Magazine* 17.2 (2000): 2. Print.

Yiming, Ren. "Three Metaphorical Uses of Silence in Three Female Postcolonial Writers' Works." Literature Institute, Shanghai Academy of Social Sciences. Web.

Young, Stacy L. "When Silenced Voices Speak Out: The Hidden Power of Internal Communication Networks." *Women and Language* 21.2 (1998): 21–30. Literary Reference Center. Web.

PART I

Physical Affliction

1

Austistic Characters

Christopher "Stump" Hall
A Land More Kind Than Home
by Wiley Cash

An attempt at exorcism is the catalyst for the death of Christopher "Stump" Hall, a mute boy in Wiley Cash's debut novel *A Land More Kind Than Home*. The novel plants readers in the Madison County town of Marshall, where "evil has come to preach in a house of worship" ("A Land More Kind" 8). Common to these secluded areas is a pervasive darkness, and the evil that hides under its cloak is "closed to outsiders" (Carson 83). In Cash's book, the dichotomy of human conditions is apparent—the evil that wears a false façade of religious morality ultimately causes the demise of an innocent, silent boy.

The midwife who delivered Stump Hall recalls that he was marked at birth and never cried. His father Ben "saw his own quietness in the boy … figured silence marked Christopher as being his son in a way that blood never could" (Cash 215). The only sounds he now makes are soft hums or grunts to accompany his pointing to an item he wants. A thirteen-year-old autistic mute, Stump is a happy-go-lucky boy who takes comfort in his "quiet box" which holds a personal collection of items he has gathered from around the barn, the woods, and nearby creek. The box has been assembled by Stump's mother Julie, who knows he will need solace when the world is too loud and complex for him to bear. The box is symbolic of Stumps' internal sanctuary, the keepsakes inside representing Stump's private language that no one else shares. Stored on the top shelf of the boys' closet, it is for Stump's eyes only. Even the reader is not privy to its contents until Jess, who wishes his mother had made a quiet box for him, opens it for comfort after Stump dies.

Stump is deemed a vacuous boy by a spiritual community that is allowed to exploit him. When his mother Julie is drawn to the snake-handling church and into the welcoming arms of Pastor Carson Chambliss, she becomes trapped in the twisted terror that awaits an unsuspecting Stump. The River Road Church of Christ in Signs Following ascribes to selective scripture taken out of context. Pastor Chambliss, who aggrandizes himself and runs the church as if he has received a special consecration from God, quotes Matthew 9:33: "And when the demon had been driven out, the man who had been mute spoke" to persuade Julie that demons have bound Stump's tongue, and the only way to loosen it is through exorcism.

In her research about demonic possession, Dr. Betty Stafford reports that "there is mounting evidence today that evil spirits do oppress and occasionally even possess the unwary, the weak, the unprepared, the unlucky or the targeted" (13). These spirits are not selective—they inhabit the souls or minds of people with different religious beliefs around the world. As support for this belief, she notes that there are seven different Gospel accounts when Jesus exorcised evil spirits during his earthly ministry.

Many traditional, fundamental churches, due to their "geographical isolation and autonomy" (Homestead.org), teach that deviating "one jot or tittle" (Matthew 5:18) from The Word could cause a soul to go straight to Hell. Certainly, this conservative congregation would not question the inerrancy of the Bible but accept it literally, word for word. Unfortunately, the church also does not question the tenets of their errant preacher, Carson Chambliss.

Hypocrisy of church leaders is not merely a current phenomenon. In the Old Testament, priests Phinehas and Hophni, the sons of Eli, eat select portions of meat previously designated as sacrificial offerings and lay with female assistants at the entrance of the temple. For their abomination, God strikes them dead as they carry the Ark of the Covenant into battle (1 Samuel 2). Likewise, Chambliss beds Julie and is stricken for his sins as he tries to flee in his ark, an old Chevrolet.

The New Testament contains accounts of the Sadducees, the aristocratic high priests of the Sanhedrin, and the Pharisees, who stand on street corners to loudly proclaim piety, but their ritualistic prayers and public personas consistently belie their darkened hearts (Matthew 23). Readers can easily see the parallel to Carson Chambliss who stands in his pulpit and proclaims the Word, but is unashamedly an adulterer and murderer. Moreover, during the modern era the careers and lucrative lifestyles of many fervent evangelists have been cut short by indiscretions, most often extramarital affairs or fraudulent practices against financial supporters.

In small, remote churches, particularly in the Bible Belt of Southern Appalachia, some preachers claim to have been called to the ministry but are actually self-called and unconscionably self-serving. They frequently quote Scripture to pass judgment on church members, but like Carson Chambliss, are somehow able to justify their own sinful behavior, at least in their own distorted minds. Sadly, this evil preacher has also convinced Julie Hall that their adultery is not a sin because it has been ordained by God.

The Bible warns about false teachers who "hide behind the cloth" and use intimidation to prey on uneducated or unsophisticated congregants who are afraid of committing blasphemy if they speak out against their leaders. They are too meek to oppose or contest the dogma of these counterfeit men of God, and they lack the spiritual discernment to identify them as "wolves in sheep's clothing." Their religious backgrounds are firmly fixed in churches where generations of family members have worshipped, so they see no reason to change their beliefs or traditions, such as testing their faith by speaking in tongues, handling snakes, drinking strychnine, or challenging fire since these same practices had served their ancestors well.

For the members of The River Road Church of Christ in Signs Following, even more menacing than Carson Chambliss are the rattlesnakes he uses to instill fear in those who do not follow his doctrine. The congregation witnesses the repeated snake bites Molly Jameson endures, and then believes that her faith was not strong enough to protect her from the poisonous venom. When Molly's death is investigated, they fear reprisal from their leader, so they remain silent about the actual events that occurred inside the church. Unfortunately, they are oblivious to the real snake in their midst—their preacher—who regularly spews poisonous words from the pulpit. His cavalier attitude about Molly's death and its subsequent cover-up should have raised red flags for the church assembly.

They also seem oblivious to another red flag: the extent of evil Chambliss perpetuates. They accept the windows being completely covered with old newspaper to hide the darkness that occurs inside the church. No other institution should be as welcoming to all people or as transparent, both literally and figuratively, as the church. The darkened windows indicate that outsiders are not welcome. It seems appropriate that this church building is actually a gutted-out former general store, for Carson Chambliss has sold a bill of goods to his gullible congregation.

The author may have been inspired by details from Dennis Covington's book *Salvation on Sand Mountain*, which covers his years of research about snake handling in Appalachia. One of the first churches Covington visited was The Church of Jesus with Signs Following, a converted gas station and country store on Sand Mountain. The members prayed in tongues, anointed each other with holy oil for healing, "and when instructed by the Holy Ghost, drank poison, held fire, and took up poisonous snakes" (Covington 24–25). They were often referred to as Jesus Freaks or Holy Rollers. Like Carson Chambliss, the preacher in Covington's book, a former hoodlum who repented when purportedly called to the ministry, regularly took up snakes, drank strychnine, and even put his fingers inside electrical sockets. When Covington attended this church, former preacher Glenn Summerford was serving ninety-nine years in the penitentiary for trying to kill his pregnant wife. As does Chambliss, he kept seventeen snakes in wooden boxes in a shed behind their house, and while he held a gun to his wife's head, he forced her to reach inside the crate for a snake, just as Chambliss does to Addie. After his wife suffered baneful bites from the snake and fell to the ground, Summerford "unzipped his fly and pissed on her" (30).

After Stump Hall accidentally observes his mother and the preacher together in his parents' bed, Chambliss' decision to ensure their infidelity is kept secret seems unnecessary, since Stump, like many autistics, never speaks, avoids eye contact, and does not initiate or respond to any form of communication other than his normal compliance. There is minimal possibility that he would be able to testify about the sexual encounter he has witnessed, so the reader must surmise that Chambliss has intended all along to kill Stump, thereby removing the boy as an impediment to his ongoing relationship with Julie. Perhaps he wishes to divert Julie's attention away from Stump and channel that devotion solely for him. The preacher, who plants his evil seeds inside Julie's body as well as her mind, convinces her that if church elders lay hands on Stump, he can be delivered from his silence. Julie is, of course, concerned about Stump's lack of speech, understandable since a mother treasures the sound of her child's voice.

When the men wrap him up and hold him down, as if trying to exorcise satanic spirits from his body, and Stump is in great distress, it seems odd that no one in the congregation, including his mother, tries to intervene. This scene iterates their reluctance to question the seemingly cruel practice of their preacher, believing that he is their shepherd and they must trust and follow him.

From outside the church window, Jess' protesting cry of "Mama!"

causes Julie to think that Stump has spoken her name, that God has manifested himself in a miracle. Regrettably, in her desperation to hear Stump speak, Julie chooses to believe a supernatural marvel rather than question the probability of his communication after more than thirteen years of silence. Her unfounded faith and trust in the evil preacher trumps her own sense of natural reasoning.

Sadly, it is Jess Hall who could save his brother's life, but he decides to remain silent. He has several opportunities to tell his father what he and Stump have heard and witnessed, as well as admit that Julie actually head his voice, but each time Jess is snooping where he does not belong, so he fears punishment. He also does not want to disappoint Julie since she is so elated in her belief that Stump can speak. These facts weigh heavy on the young shoulders of Jess Hall. Although others in his family suffer physical pain or death, his emotional burden is the most tragic of all.

It is possible that Chambliss also mistakes Jess' cry as an utterance from Stump and fears the boy may eventually find his voice, so he must finish his malevolence. Chambliss certainly mandates the physical stranglehold on Stump, but he also maintains a spiritual stranglehold on the entire church membership, and while a complicit Julie watches, Stump, who is neither healed nor delivered from demons, smothers to death and is forever silent.

Her son may be mute, but Julie is blind in her obedience to this man, evident by her willingness to leave her husband and son Jess to spend her life with the preacher who is instrumental in Stump's demise. In a Bonnie and Clyde-like shoot-out, Julie's loss of most of her left hand is an uncanny and symmetrical match to Chambliss's right hand, which was burned in a meth lab fire, even though he tells his congregation that God sent down holy fire to anoint him. Their bodies' physical mutations are outward symbols of their tainted souls; they are guilty not only of sexual indiscretion, but also the death of Julie's innocent son. They can neither literally nor figuratively wash their hands of his blood.

Locklear notes that in this narrative of mountain fatalism, "Cash avoids giving readers a sugar-coated ending but instead imbues a dire situation with the possibility—however unlikely—of a better day for his characters" (121). This is evident in Adelaide's final, optimistic thoughts that just as people can be healed and saved, so can a church. For this congregation, it begins with the newspaper being torn off the windows to announce there will be no more dark secrets and everyone is welcome inside.

Works Cited

Carson, Warren J. "Review of A Land More Kind Than Home." *Appalachian Heritage* 41.2 (Spring 2013). Web.

Cash, Wiley. *A Land More Kind Than Home*. New York: William Morrow, 2012. Print.

Covington, Dennis. *Salvation on Sand Mountain: Snake Handling and Redemption in Southern Appalachia*. Cambridge: Da Capo Press, 1995. Print.

Holy Bible. King James Version. Nashville: Thomas Nelson, 1973.

"A Land More Kind Than Home." *Kirkus Reviews*: 8–9. Literary Reference Center, 2012. Web.

Locklear, Erica Abrams. "Mountain Fatalism in Wiley Cash's A Land More Kind Than Home." *Appalachian Heritage* 42.3 (2014): 110–21. Print.

Stafford, Betty. "The Growing Evidence for Demonic Possession: What Should Psychiatry's Response Be?" *Journal of Religion and Health* 44.1 (2005): 13–30. Web.

Jaxon McKenzie
There Are No Words
by Mary Calhoun Brown

A winner of eleven awards, most notably the Outstanding Book for Young People with Disabilities 2011, Mary Calhoun Brown's book *There Are No Words* has chimerical elements of fantasy, but it is categorized as historical fiction since it is based on a true, tragic train derailment in 1918 at Dutchman's Curve near Nashville, Tennessee. The wreck occurred when two passenger trains, owned by Nashville, Chattanooga, and St. Louis Railway, slammed head-on into each other, killing at least 121 people and injuring 57 more.

The silent protagonist is twelve-year-old Jaxon MacKenzie, who recounts a series of events in her young life in Bartlett, Tennessee. She narrates the book in conversational style, but ironically, she is an autistic mute; however, the reader hears her inner voice loud and clear. To add emotional pain to her disability, her mother has relinquished parental responsibilities to Jaxon's grandparents.

Upon learning that a child has a disability, some parents experience emotions similar to the stages of grief: shock, denial, and anger, but at times also guilt and shame. Parenting a child with a disability would be difficult, but to give up parental rights to someone else might seem like a convenient way out, at least in some circumstances. However, some parents are not financially or emotionally stable enough to care for a special needs child. They can suffer excessive distress and depression, especially if they are unaware of their options and resources. In Craig Shulze's *When Snow Turns to Rain: One Family's Struggle to Solve the Riddle of Autism,* he recounts his and his wife's long search to find "appropriate schooling and treatment" for their son. They eventually sent him to Japan, but their decision caused disruptions in the family dynamics, such as absences at work and frequent moves. Beck remarks that it would be even more difficult for "less motivated parents [to] have coped and succeeded" (207).

A qualitative study of the case of Ben, a ten-year-old autistic boy, was conducted regarding perception and reality of friendships for autistic children. Results showed that Ben genuinely wanted friends and believed that he did have them (Potter 210). However, unlike Jaxon, Ben had rudimentary language skills and attended a mainstream school where he had opportunities to develop friendships.

Jaxon displays common traits of autism. She is hyper-sensitive to "the electricity of touch" (Brown 26) from others, able to tolerate it for only a few seconds before she pulls away. When she feels uncomfortable or stressed, such as being around her cold-hearted mother whose voice sounds like "a tornado of words" (25) or shards of jagged glass, thankfully, her grandparents are able to diffuse the harsh demands of her mother, and Jaxon's humming helps to block them out. For comfort, she rocks her body back and forth. She also spends an inordinate amount of time fixating on objects.

According to the Mayo Clinic, autism spectrum disorder "impacts how a child perceives and socializes with others, causing problems in critical areas of development—social interaction, communication, and behavior" (1). Jaxon is most likely functioning at mid-level of the spectrum. Her lack of speech, humming, and repetitive rocking are manifestations of the syndrome, but she does not show signs of severity, such as lack of coordination, lack of cooperation or resistance to change. For children with autism spectrum disorder, the involvement of family is of utmost importance, as well "creating a safe environment" (Jolly 11). Although Jaxon's mother is emotionally detached, Jaxon's grandparents are providing this vital care for her, but they are the only friends she knows.

An introspective girl, Jaxon has not revealed to anyone that she can read, which seems unlikely, for her education consists of secretly borrowing books from her grandfather's shelves. Although Jaxon cannot respond, Dewey Mackenzie carries on a spirited conversation with his granddaughter, reads aloud the newspaper, and sings to her, but this is not commensurate with teaching her to read. While spending time with her grandfather, Jaxon yearns to speak to him. "I practice the words over in my mind…. I move my lips in the shape of an 'O'" (Brown 33), yet she is unable to utter any words. In her internal dialogue, she does relate excessive, detailed descriptions of sights, sounds, and smells of the world around her, suggesting heightened sensory perceptions. This seems more plausible because of the daily walks she takes with her grandfather.

Two separate elements in the book are tied in a mysterious way: a newspaper clipping about the train wreck and the oil painting that hangs above the parlor sofa. In her fixation, Jaxon spends a great deal of time staring at the painting of a boy and girl who are walking along a dirt path. When the girl reaches out to clasp Jaxon's hand and draw her inside the painting, the author uses this scene of fantasy to appeal to young readers' whimsical interests. It also connects the past and present, as Jaxon is transported back to 1918 when she spends time with her grandfather as a young man. The most significant experience for Jaxon is that she is able to speak while in the past. A lifetime of former muteness would be a hindrance, so initially she is reluctant to cross the line between her thoughts and actually verbalizing them.

Jaxon's decision whether to remain in the past where she has found her voice or return to her world of muteness places her in a transitional phase of liminality. While in the past, she is accepted by everyone she meets, finally enjoying friendships she has never known, but understandably, her present life makes it virtually impossible to develop relationships. Not attending school and being isolated in her grandparents' home are the major factors that hinder her socialization. Realizing what she has missed from being caught in a world without language surely makes her decision more difficult. She shares that in her real life beyond the painting, many people think she is stupid or deaf. Even though well intentioned, sometimes they scream at her in order to be heard, a common reaction to the mute by a hearing world. She reveals that some people act as if she is "invisible or they treat me as though I'm contagious" (54). After Jaxon decides to go back, she time travels through another painting, which extends the element of fantasy and brings her liminal rite of passage to a circuitous end.

When she returns home, and begins to learn sign language, her hands become her unique voice. Brenda Seal and John Bonvillain note that elements of American Sign Language are similar to the "phonemes" of oral language. They report that some autistic children who are taught sign language combine their large "lexicon" of signs to form phrases and complete sentences. "Concomitant with their enhanced sign communication," most autistic children show improvement with attention span, willingness to learn, and social skills (438–439).

Works Cited

"Autism Spectrum Disorder Symptoms." Mayo Clinic. Web.

Beck, Linda. "Book Reviews: Social Sciences." *Library Journal* 118.14 (1993): 207. Literary Reference Center. Web.

Brown, Mary Calhoun. *There Are No Words*. New York: Wentworth & Collins, 2010. Print.

Jolly, Adriane A. "Handle with Care: Top Ten Tips a Nurse Should Know before Caring for a Hospitalized Child with Autism Spectrum Disorder." *Pediatric Nursing* 41.1 (2015): 11–22. Health Source: Nursing Academic Edition. Web.

Potter, Carol. "I Didn't Used to Have Much Friends: Exploring the Friendship Concepts and Capabilities of a Boy with Autism and Severe Learning Disabilities." *British Journal of Learning Disabilities* 43.3 (2015): 208–218. Psychology and Behavioral Sciences Collection. Web.

Seal, Brenda C., and John Bonvillain. "Sign Language and Motor Functioning in Students with Autistic Disorder." *Journal of Autism and Developmental Disorders* 27.4 (1997): 43–66. Academic Search Premier. Web.

Lonnie
Deliverance
directed by John Boorman

Both James Dickey's Appalachian novel *Deliverance*, a "metaphoric study of man's potential for violence and salvation" (Inge 13), and the subsequent screen adaptation have earned their rightful place in the popular culture of America. Critics have pointed out the connection between Dickey's work and his "flamboyant public persona" (Havird 261), elements certainly found in *Deliverance*. With a setting of water, it "constitutes an identifying imaginative trope" (Claybough 25), similar to the author's other novels, as it presents "intense explorations of the primal" ("James Dickey" 808) nature of humanity.

The narrative's focus is on four Atlanta businessmen who interact with unsophisticated mountain people as they embark on an odyssey of survival down treacherous rapids. Lewis Medlock, the character portrayed in the film by Burt Reynolds, has goaded his reluctant friends to join him on this adventure, for he "fears nothing and no one on the river, not the ignorant Griner brothers nor the mountain men … he is reckless and wants not only to survive but to prevail" (Bruccoli and Baughman 286). His supercilious verbal jabs and swagger foreshadow the tragedy that lies ahead.

Director John Boorman, who adapted the book to the screen, searched for just the right person to play the character of Lonnie, a mountain boy whose distinctive facial features are suggestive of backwoods inbreeding and mental infirmity. He found Billy Redden, a fifteen-year-old from Rabun County, Georgia. After the Atlanta businessmen arrive in Oree, they meet Lonnie, an autistic mute and child of great poverty. "Despite his apparent retardation, Lonnie surprises the suburbanites with his deft banjo-playing, skillfully picking out a response" (Knepper 17–18) to the chords of the guitar played by the Coca-Cola salesman. Readers should note that James Dickey, known for his "sense of southern place," was also an accomplished bluegrass musician, playing both 6- and 12-string guitars (Hill 242). The author also makes a cameo appearance toward the end of the film.

One important scene allows readers to observe the behavior of the autistic boy. When Drew, played by Ronnie Cox, begins to pluck a few chords on his Martin guitar, each note is perfectly matched by Lonnie, who displays attributes of savant syndrome, manifested in one in ten autistics, normally males, and usually, but not always, accompanied by a low IQ. Lonnie's ability to replicate the notes suggests that he is a duplicative savant. He could also be a creative savant, for whom abilities gradually intensify "on a continuum from duplication, to improvisation, to creation" rather than decrease or cease to exist. Individuals with savant syndrome display "spectacular islands of genius that stand in jarring juxtaposition" (Treffert 564) to disabilities and appear in various talents including music, math, and art. Most often there is a singular, narrow skill, but it is always profound and connected to "massive memory of a habit" (564) or process. This certainly seems apparent in Lonnie's case, for he both duplicates the musical notes and then improvises as the song progresses.

Similar literary examples include the film *Rain Man*, in which Raymond Babbitt, the character played by Dustin Hoffman displays the savant syndrome by his "obsessive preoccupation" (565) and memorization of trivial facts. Matt Damon plays a genius character with hidden mathematical abilities in *Good Will Hunting*. Another portrayal of a savant is Russell Crowe in *A Beautiful Mind*, the autobiographical film about mathematics and economics professor John Nash. These latter two men would be labeled high-functioning prodigious savants; however, both are loners with underdeveloped socialization skills.

As the music becomes more animated, Lonnie, who at first is expressionless, grins broadly, squints his eyes, and bends his tongue back with his teeth. A musical transformation occurs as they play a fast-paced, now well-recognized tune called "Dueling Banjos" while Lonnie's father dances a mountain jig resembling Appalachian flat-foot or buck dancing near the Texaco gasoline pumps. Proving his superiority as a musician, Lonnie quickens his tempo to finish the coda alone, for Drew is unable keep up. When an invigorated Drew walks up to Lonnie to express his appreciation and shake his hand, Lonnie frowns and quickly turns his head to the side. Although Drew asks if he would like to play another tune, Lonnie keeps his faced turned away. He neither speaks nor accepts Drew's outstretched hand.

Drew is perplexed by Lonnie's lack of response, because he does not understand Lonnie's condition. In the midst of playing his banjo, Lonnie is happy and lively, as music is a familiar and safe haven for him and the only way he is capable of connecting with Drew. On the other hand, he loathes being expected to display even the most rudimentary social skills such as direct eye contact and touch, especially with a stranger. His turning away from Drew's attempt at friendliness is a means of protection. Most individuals with autism maintain an inward existence in a world that others know nothing of and are unable to reach, because they are not welcome to enter. External forces are often too difficult for them to bear or process, especially speech, so Lonnie's mannerisms are merely symptomatic of his autism.

About this scene, Don Johnson commented, "If the world of the stereotyped Appalachian is divided into 'strangers' and 'kin,' then the music Drew and Lonnie play breaks down those distinctions" (qtd. in Knepper 24). However, these men *are* strangers to Lonnie, and his mountain upbringing has trained him to be leery of outsiders. He is not an educated boy, but he seems sensitive enough to decipher the snide comments and judging eyes of Drew's companions.

As the men begin to row their canoes through the still water, Lonnie curiously appears above, standing on a footbridge to watch them travel downstream. Although Drew waves and points to both Lonnie and himself in a gesture of musical camaraderie, Lonnie does not acknowledge him. He only stares beyond him at the river, as if he knows, in their haste and folly, these ill-prepared men will soon face unknown pitfalls of the treacherous rapids, as well as find themselves at the mercy of dangerous mountaineers. Lonnie swings his banjo back and forth like the pendulum of a grandfather clock, a motion marking time and indicating the men's numbered days on the river, as unfortunately they are for Drew. Even though the men perceive Lonnie as a fool, once again, he proves his superiority, this time for his perceptions about the river and the mountains he knows well and calls home.

Many critics assert that *Deliverance* offers "debased stereotypes" of Appalachians (Knepper 18), but James Dickey denied any intentions to characterize mountain people in an unflattering manner. His work suggests the "kind of precarious deliverance" that can quickly turn to "brutal confrontation and entrapment" ("James Dickey" 808). The final scene of a bloated hand rising from the river is symbolic according to Boorman, of "a force of unconscious rising to the conscious world" (qtd. in Davis). The hand might also represent a cry of help for a savior, as the men attempt, during their three-day journey, to navigate and master the labyrinth of nature, but they have encroached on Lonnie's neck of the woods, and as a result, they are ultimately the ones in need of deliverance.

Works Cited

Bruccoli, Matthew J., and Judith S. Baughman. "Lewis Medlock." *Student's Encyclopedia of American Literary Characters.* New York: Facts on File, 2008. Print.

Claybough, Casey. *Inhabiting Contemporary Southern and Appalachian Literature: Region and Place in the Twenty-First Century.* Gainesville: University Press of Florida, 2012. Print.

Davis, Cindy. "Mindhole Blowers: 20 Facts about Deliverance That'll Make You … Well You Know." Pajiba. 2 July 2012. Web.

Deliverance. Dir. John Boorman. Perf. Jon Voight, Burt Reynolds, Ned Beatty, and Ronny Cox. Warner Bros., 1972. DVD.

Havird, David. "Dickey, James." *Benet's Reader's Encyclopedia of American Literature.* New York: HarperCollins, 1991. Print.

Hill, Robert W. "James Dickey." *Literature: The New Encyclopedia of Southern Culture.* Chapel Hill: University of North Carolina Press, 2008. Print.

Inge, M. Thomas. "Southern Literary Renaissance." *Literature: The New Encyclopedia of Southern Culture.* Chapel Hill: University of North Carolina Press, 2008. Print.

"James Dickey." *The Literature of the American South.* Ed. William L. Andrews et al. New York: W. W. Norton, 1998. Print.

Knepper, Steven. "Do You Know What the 'Hail' You're Talking About? Deliverance, Stereotypes and the Lost Voice of the Rural Poor." *James Dickey Newsletter* 25.1 (2008): 17–29. Literary Reference Center. Web.

Treffert, Darold A. "Savant Syndrome: Realities, Myths, and Misconceptions." *Journal of Autism and Developmental Disorders* 44.3 (2014): 564–71. Psychology and Behavioral Sciences. Web.

Raymond Babbitt
Rain Man
directed by Peter Guber and Jon Peters

The 1988 movie *Rain Man*, directed by Peter Guber and Jon Peters, won four Academy Awards. The film is a both an emotional and literal journey of two brothers, Charlie Babbitt, portrayed by Tom Cruise, and his autistic brother Raymond, portrayed by Dustin Hoffman. The brothers meet in Ohio, take an extended road trip to California, and then Raymond returns to his home in an institution for special needs individuals. The character of Raymond Babbitt was based on savant Kim Peek, who "couldn't operate a light switch or button his shirt" ("Man Who Inspired") but his memory was profound. In fact, he was compared to a computer, and NASA even studied his extraordinary abilities.

Raymond is a middle-level functioning autistic savant who displays "splinter" skills, such as "obsessive preoccupation with and memorization of music & sports trivia, birthdays, license plate numbers, historical facts, and train or bus schedules" (Treffert "Savant" 565). In Raymond's type of savant syndrome, individuals are "endowed" from childhood with "extra-ordinary" abilities (Treffert "Accidental" 52) that are in stark contrast to their limitations. Many theories exist about the origins of these amazing talents; a popular one is genetic memory, for the savants know things they have never studied or learned.

Raymond's autistic traits include a strict routine, such as his repeated reminder of "lights out at eleven" and his ritual of reciting "who's on first" when he becomes nervous. He also can calendar count, a typical ability of savants. His behavior aligns with the symptoms of autism spectrum disorder (ASD):

> persistent deficits in social communication and interaction … restrictive, repetitive pattern of behavior, interests, or activities as manifested by, but not exclusively, simple motor stereotypies such as lining up toys, echolalia, idiosyncratic words or phrases, insistence on sameness, inflexible adherence to routines, highly restricted fixated interests and hyper- or hypo-activity to sensory input such as specific sounds, textures, fascination with lights or excessive smelling of objects [Stoppelbein et al. 251].

While he insists on watching *Judge Wampner*, *Wheel of Fortune* and *Jeopardy*, Raymond's eyes do not focus on the television screen; however, his hearing is acute, another trait of his syndrome. Comic moments in the film that are also indicative of his autism include demanding that boxer shorts be bought at K Mart and that maple syrup is on the table *before* pancakes are served, as well as his echoing sounds, such as the moans made by Charlie and his girlfriend during lovemaking. Additional manifestations occur when he hums, rocks his body back and forth, and immediately withdraws from human touch. Trying to converse with Raymond is frustrating at best, for his answers are monosyllabic words ("Yeah"), phrases ("I don't know"), or irrelevant responses ("I'm a very good driver"). He loses control of his emotions by screaming and violently slapping his head during perceived or actual threatening situations, such as boarding an airplane; hearing a fire alarm; and running water in the bathtub, a deeply embedded and frightening memory from his childhood which resulted in his placement in the institution. The bathtub scene provides an epiphany for Charlie, who begins to understand the dynamics of his dysfunctional family history.

Raymond's savant aptitude is shown by his memory of baseball statistics, important dates, and a telephone directory. He also can correctly determine the number of toothpicks in a box and solve difficult mathematical equations for which the doctor who tests him must use a calculator. Conversely, Raymond is unable to discern common logic, such as how much a candy bar costs.

Although Charlie's motive for "kidnapping" Raymond is greed, and he becomes repeatedly exasperated by his brother's behavior, Raymond's ability to memorize and "count cards" leads to Charlie's low point in the film. To remedy his desperate need for money, he unconscionably uses his brother's genius at the gaming tables in Las Vegas. Sadly, his selfishness puts both himself and an oblivious Raymond at risk with casino officials

At some point during the road trip, Charlie's feelings toward Raymond begin to soften. This is most evident by the poignant scene in which he teaches his brother to dance. His refusal of the inheritance check and his sadness over his inability to clearly express his love for Raymond support this fact. Even though he considers allowing his brother to live with him, he must admit that he cannot provide the consistency Raymond needs and has grown accustomed to at the institution. As the road trip comes to an end, Charlie's rite of passage is complete when he realizes the importance of family from the valuable life lessons his older brother has taught him.

In *The Screening of America: Movies and Values from Rocky to Rain Man,* Tom O'Brien addresses the importance of "works that broaden conversation about our culture and values" (qtd. in Kelly 552). He stresses that rather than watching movies only for entertainment, viewers should reflect on the themes and messages presented. Many film critics refrain from using this approach lest they seem "narrowly moralistic" (552), but O'Brien wishes to explore how American culture has evolved. His choice to examine these issues in *Rain Man,* which is "accurately and sensitively" (Treffert 565) dramatized, is certainly relevant, as a plethora of individuals—some kind, some judgmental—are touched by their interactions with "Rain Man" Babbitt.

Works Cited

Kelly, Mary Pat. "Broadening the Conversation." *Commonweal* 117.16 (1990): 552. Literary Reference Center. Web.

"Man Who Inspired *Rain Man* Dies at 58." *All Things Considered.* 2009. Literary Reference Center. Web.

Rain Man. Dir. Peter Guber and Jon Peters. Perf. Tom Cruise and Dustin Hoffman. 20th Century Fox, 1988. DVD.

Stoppelbein, Laura, et al. "Predicting Internalizing and Externalizing Symptoms Among Children Diagnosed with Autism Spectrum Disorder: The Role of Routines." *Journal of Child & Family Studies* 25.1 (2016): 251–71. Psychology and Behavioral Sciences Collection. Web.

Treffert, Darold A. "Savant Syndrome: Realities, Myths, and Misconceptions." *Journal of Autism and Developmental Disorders* 44.3 (2014): 564–71. Psychology and Behavioral Sciences. Web.

Aunt Jo
Creeker by Linda Scott DeRosier

Linda Scott DeRosier's memoir *Creeker: A Woman's Journey* is a "study in the creation of female identity" (Johnson lvii). The novel's timeframe is the beginning of World War II in the remote community of Two-Mile Creek in eastern Kentucky, a "hillbilly settlement which revered kinship, practiced open-door hospitality, and possessed a strong sense of community" (Hazucha 52). DeRosier describes the poverty and adversity of living in Appalachia during that time, but also the proud, independent, and "can do" spirit that allowed families to endure. Nonetheless, a woman was expected to "step away from the center of her life in order to make room for a man to occupy it" (Johnson lvii), a profound statement about gender role perceptions during that time period.

DeRosier writes about her father's younger sister Aunt Jo. Although the author refers to her aunt as severely retarded, her symptoms seem to align with those of autism. She also reveals stories that abound about Aunt Jo, which help readers to better understand the circumstances surrounding her aunt as well as the language and mindset of the community. Some family legends are of Jo's being "sharper'n ary tack" until age three when she developed a high fever that "burnt up" her brain and caused her to have "spinalmengitis" (DeRosier 29–30). No doctor was in attendance during her illness, so there are no documents to prove or disprove these claims. DeRosier believes that the medical explanation is her family's way of covering up the shame of having a child who does meet society's standards of normality. She also acknowledges that when tales are told over and over, true or not, people eventually find it difficult to separate fact from fiction; this is truly an overall reflection of the human condition.

Jo's behavior includes fits of laughter, stomping her feet, and biting her own fist, indicating frustration over her inability to verbally communicate her feelings or express her needs. The family is protective of this vulnerable young girl, especially after her encounter, at age thirteen with the Fannin boys, and "nobody ever specified how that sexual assault took place" (30). The author does not indicate how family members knew the Fannin boys were the perpetrators since Jo could not report the rape to her family. Perhaps there was physical evidence or someone saw the boys as they ran away. Morally void and cowardly, these boys took advantage of a young disabled girl who could neither consent nor attest to what happened to her. They may have spent years mocking her and then realized when she became a teenager that they could have their way with this silent girl, who appears quite lovely in the photo included by the author.

In 1875, the first nongovernmental agency devoted entirely to child protection was established: the New York Society for the Prevention of Cruelty to Children. However, during most of the 1900's, "many cities and nearly all rural areas had little or no access to formal child-protective services. For most abused and neglected children, help came—if it came—from family and neighbors" (Myers 452), and this was true for Aunt Jo, whose family chose to administer her care in their home.

A literary parallel is the Greek mythological story of Philomela who is also raped by a family member, her brother-in-law King Tereus of Thrace. Overcome by lust as he escorts her to visit her sister, he forces Philomela into the woods where he rapes her. He is adamant that she tell no one, but her defiance enrages him until he cuts out her tongue to ensure her silence. As a result, the "rape is both symbolic violation and physical mutilation" (Marder 159) as the text "establishes a relationship between the experience of violation and access to language" (157). Determined to recount her story, Philomela weaves her words in a tapestry and gives it to her sister Procne. Philomela is eventually turned into a nightingale, symbolically fitting since the female of the species is mute. Unfortunately, Aunt Jo had no access to language. Since her brain is purported to have "burnt up," it is quite unlikely that she would have been able to write down an account of her rape.

Another similar literary example is the 1948 movie *Johnny Belinda*, for which Jane Wyman won an Academy Award for her portrayal of the titular character. Adapted from a play by Elmer Harris and thrice remade for television, the focus is on a "drab and shabby deaf mute" under the care of a doctor who teaches her sign language. Belinda is raped by an "unscrupulous villager" and later gives birth to his child (IMDb).

Although DeRosier's grandfather was unable to obtain justice about the incident, the family did not speak of it again, and there was forever bad blood beneath the surface of this secret. Psychologist Dr. Judith Herman reports that the rationalization to excuse or gloss over such victimization "in the interests of preserving peace and family harmony" is perceived as a need to "draw a veil over" matters that should not be mentioned again but forgotten entirely (qtd. in Jensen 348), like "sweeping dirt under the rug" and keeping family matters behind closed doors.

The entire extended family allowed these two boys to escape the consequences. The clear and rigorous laws pertaining to rape had not been established at that time, and the terms "pedophile" and "sexual offender" were not widely used, if they had even been coined yet, so rather than try to prosecute the boys, which would have been difficult in the 1920's especially since Jo did not speak, the family chose to handle the situation internally. It is likely that widespread reports of this incident would also have caused the family additional shame; nevertheless, it was a grave injustice to Aunt Jo.

Works Cited

DeRosier, Linda Scott. *Creeker: A Woman's Journey*. Lexington: University Press of Kentucky, 1999. Print.

Hazucha, Winifred. "Creeker: A Woman's Journey." *Now & Then: The Appalachian Magazine* 17.2 (2000): 52. Print.

Jensen, Derrick. *A Language Older than Words*. New York: Context Books, 2000. Print.

Johnson, Nancy Revelle. "Creeker: A Woman's Journey." *The Sewanee Review* 111.2 (2003): lvii–lix. Web.

Marder, Elissa. "Disarticulated Voices: Feminism and Philomela." *Hypatia* 7.2 (1992): 148–68. Literary Reference Center. Web.

Myers, John E.B. "A Short History of Child Protection in America." americanbar.org. Web.

Characters with Congenital Hydrocephalous

Juney Hall
On Agate Hill by Lee Smith

In Lee Smith's novel *On Agate Hill*, narrator Molly Petree, after many years away, returns to Agate Hill and tends to Juney, whom she calls her "little man." Juney, the literary "other" of the novel and son of the deceased owner of the estate, has an oversized head, stocky arms and legs, and is almost blind. He responds to people with a sweet smile, a nodding head, or clapping hands. Though reluctant to speak, he does sometimes sing and play an old harmonica that belonged to his half-brother Spence, also a quiet character in the book but from a previous marriage over twenty years before Juney is born.

In the past, Juney lived temporarily on the plantation by himself or in the woods like an animal, and the Negroes called him the "Big-Headed Boy." In spite of his unusual physical attributes, Molly believes Juney has been blessed with the uncanny gifts of healing and prophesying. The mothers of the community believe it as well, for they bring their colicky babies to Juney. He quiets their cries by placing them on their tummies across his knees. He cures thrush by blowing down their throats and their earaches by whispering into their ears, though his touch seems to be the greatest healing power he possesses.

Juney's gifts of healing by breath and touch are rooted in Appalachian tradition. Early European colonists from Scotland and Ireland who settled in the Appalachian Mountains were said to have brought these skills with them and passed on their secrets to others. Other gifts were talking out, drawing out, or blowing out fire from burns, stopping blood, and removing warts. Some of the faith healers chanted nonsensical syllables or recited

Scripture and waved their hands across the patient's afflicted area. Related folklore claims that these gifts could be performed only by individuals who had never seen their fathers; they must be passed on to an unrelated person of the opposite sex; and once the secrets had been revealed, the healers would no longer possess those gifts (*Health and Healing in North Carolina*). Juney never saw his father, so he is eligible to receive these gifts.

Molly has appointed herself as Juney's protector from a cynical world. Those who do not know that Juney is harmless sometimes respond in fear. For example, when he tries to play marbles with other boys, their mothers snatch their sons away. Although Juney is harmless, these mothers fear what they do not understand. Older boys who dump him on the porch after a party see an opportunity for mean-spirited fun at Juney's expense. He is not wise enough to realize how some individuals perceive him, so initially he trusts outsiders, but he eventually understands when they finish their tomfoolery with him. Their behavior is commonplace among individuals who respond inappropriately to someone who is different. They are sometimes hesitant to approach someone like Juney, so they taunt or make fun of him to make themselves feel superior in their normalcy, but too often their curiosity ends in cruelty.

Juney is a happy boy as long as someone pays him attention and gives him the love he craves. The author's description of Juney's behavior and his physicality—an increased head circumference, blurred vision, delay in speech, and a decline in thinking—suggest that he was afflicted with congenital hydrocephalus at birth. The reader can see that in spite of his limitations, Juney does indeed share with the community his capabilities to heal.

Works Cited

Health and Healing in North Carolina. An Interactive Timeline. North Carolina Museum of History. Web.

Smith, Lee. *On Agate Hill*. Chapel Hill: Algonquin Books, 2007. Print.

Termite
Lark and Termite
by Jayne Anne Phillips

Jayne Anne Phillips' national bestseller *Lark and Termite* is set in the author's home state of West Virginia during the 1950s. The narrative is structured by the voices of the four main characters. Each tells his or her own version, sometimes in a stream of consciousness, of the same events. Their accounts parallel historical place and time and are full of details about two totally different landscapes: the North Chungchong Province of South Korea and Winfield, West Virginia. Thomas Douglass describes the novel as a "search for lost and confused origins ... the genesis and consequence of family" (248). Like many Appalachian works, Phillips' book is about being lured away but ultimately being drawn back home. Common among Appalachians, who are either forced or are anxious to leave and find their own path in the world, is their eventual return to the mountains.

Termite, who suffers from congenital hydrocephalous, tells his story through the omnipotent narrator, as readers are pulled inside his world of acute aural awareness. When asked about Termite's characterization, Phillips confessed that he is based on children she knew "who were supposedly disabled and surely challenged, but whose perceptions seemed perhaps wholly, dimensionally, deeper than ours" (Johnson 21).

Of Termite's response to his environment, she added, "sensory compensation is sensory invention, and sound is inside language" (21). This is interesting to note, for even though Termite cannot speak, he does make sounds that mimic phrases spoken to him, his own "quiet, tonal code" (Phillips 153). His sister Lark, a devoted caretaker and protector, remarks that the "water in his head never got in the way of his listening" (98). He croons and purrs like human onomatopoeia. His responses to a variety of sounds—the hum of a lawn mower, the whirr of a fan, the whisper of a pencil, the sound of a ragged cat dragging its belly, the wind ruffling blades of grass, the rumble of a distant train—indicate a heightened sense of hearing. To most individuals, these background noises are rarely noticed.

Termite was born with an enlarged head and diminished use of his lower limbs, common symptoms of hydrocephalous, which is caused by an "imbalance of cerebrospinal" production and absorption that affects the central nervous system (Mayo Foundation 4). Difficulty in feeding is another symptom, and his mother had to initially coax him to latch on to her breasts. For the year that Lola cared for him, she continually whispered soothing words and sang to him, which most likely was the onset of his sensitivity to sound, especially the human voice. She also noted that he was unusually quiet, for he never cried, and when he was scared, his skin would flush and his body would become rigid. In spite of these hydrocephalic symptoms, Termite retains a loving disposition.

Because he is so responsive to sound, Lark places a bell on her brother's favorite chair so that he can alert her and Nonie when he has needs. He also responds to different stimuli of touch. Even though he is unusually quiet and still, his hands and fingers are constantly moving. Some of his favorite items to hold are fat crayons—easily grasped by unskilled hands—that Lark uses to teach him to draw. With underdeveloped muscular skills, he feels a sense of accomplishment to be able to use the crayons independently. Most of all, he loves to wrap a blue plastic strip around his fingers and hold it up to his eyes, even though his disease has diminished his sight. For some individuals with disabilities, using a blue clear overlay on top of an item somehow increases their ability to see or read clearly. Termite is mesmerized as he looks at the world through the lens of a blue, shimmery strip of plastic, although his cheerful nature would suggest "rose-colored glasses" instead.

Lark acknowledges that she will never fully understand his sense of wonder, but she enhances it by pulling him around in a wagon and exposing him to their Appalachian environment. Lark denies herself the usual pleasures and experiences of being a healthy, intelligent teenager. Her commitment to her brother is indeed unusual for someone so young, but the fact that she has been his primary caregiver all his life is a testament to her level of maturity. At the end of the novel, she even risks her own well-being to ensure that she and Termite are not separated.

An interesting character that Phillips includes in her novel is Mr. Stamble. With a head capped with an aura of white hair, like a guardian angel, and a person seen only by Lark, like a ghostly figure, his presence is enigmatic. Although she is suspicious when he arrives at their doorstep, he proves an interest only in Termite's comfort and well-being. With a hint of magical realism which "integrates realistic elements with supernatural or fantastic experiences" (Quinn) Stamble disappears just as mysteriously as he appears.

Works Cited

Douglass, Thomas. "No More Appalachian Ghosts: Jayne Anne Phillips' New Novel *Lark and Termite.*" *Appalachian Journal* 36.3/4 (2009): 248–55. Literary Reference Center. Web.

Johnson, Sarah Anne. "The Sound of a Novel: Jayne Anne Phillips, Author of 'Lark and Termite,' Painstakingly Writes by Ear—Finding a Way into a Story through a Voice Not an Idea." *Writer* 122.11 (2009): 18–21. *Literary Reference Center*. Web.

Mayo Clinic Foundation. "Diseases and Conditions: Hydrocephalus." Web.

Phillips, Jayne Anne. *Lark and Termite*. New York: Vintage, 2009. Print.

Quinn, Edward. "Magical Realism." *A Dictionary of Literary and Thematic Terms*. New York: Facts on File, 2006. Bloom's Literature. Web.

3

Characters
Afflicted with Dyslalia
(Apraxia or Aphasia)

Millie Floyd and Frankie and
Verdie Pennybacker
Tales of Chinkapin Creek by Jean Ayer

In Jean Ayer's memoir *Tales of Chinkapin Creek,* she channels the voice and life story of her mother, Nellie Wister, who grows up on a large farmstead in West Virginia. The book relates tales of the diverse individuals whose lives intermingle with the Wisters in their community of Chinkapin Creek. Despite her pleasant outward appearance, twenty-nine-year-old mute Millie Floyd has a mind that is a confusing and wrongly wired network, which prevents her ability to speak. Her mouth "[hangs] open as if she were on the verge" of speech, but she can utter no words. "What ailed her was a birth defect that affected the roof of her mouth" (Ayers 51). The author's description of Millie's symptoms seems to indicate fetal damage to the brain or dyslalia, impairment of the speech organs, or dysarthria, "defective or deranged articulation in speaking" (OED). The few breathy sounds she is able to emit are unintelligible, due to her difficulty with respiration; her repetitive, pointless movements back and forth also suggest autism.

Both her parents and siblings are annoyed by her presence and ashamed for others to know Millie exists, so she is confined in the house. Lack of knowledge, a pervasive societal stigma, and misguided guilt most likely cause the Floods to neglect their daughter. Nellie Wister's compassionate attempts to speak with her are not successful. Every response from Millie is "Haangh, haangh, haangh, haangh" a sound made as if "blowing air across the top of a glass bottle" (52). Nellie also witnesses Mollie's habit of constant motion, taking one step forward and then immediately moving back, her repeated steps accomplishing nothing except a comforting routine for Millie.

Nellie's father was the Guthrie County Commissioner in charge of the poor, so when he discovered that Sally Pennybacker's home was to be sold to pay for back taxes, he placed her children Frankie and Verdie in a cabin on the poor farm and brought her, with a goiter "as big as a goose egg" (91), to their home as a housekeeper. He also secured her two normal children with private families. Frankie, a "small dumpy figure" lumbered to the homestead where his mother took his "chubby hand" to help him up to the porch, for she never allowed him inside. On the porch of their cabin, Verdie "sat in a heap, with her mouth open. She never went anywhere" (89). Mr. Wister's lack of prejudice and good-hearted benevolence speak well of his integrity.

In early America, "concepts of insanity were fluid and not medical," basically viewed as an imbalance of the humors and were perceived as problems for families, not the state. This memoir is set in the early 1900s when communities were small and scattered. In the rural mountainous area of West Virginia, few medical resources would have been available, so mentally infirm individuals were usually kept at home, and family members cared for them the best they could. The only other options were repositories such as almshouses or workhouses or even the streets. Asylums were established for the wealthy, but these institutions were located in larger cities, and the treatments were often experimental ("A Brief History of Mental Illness").

Works Cited

Ayer, Jean. *Tales of Chinkapin Creek*. Lexington, Kentucky, 2011. Print.
"A Brief History of Mental Illness and the U.S. Mental Health Care System." Unite for Sight. Web.
"Dysarthria." *Oxford English Dictionary* (OED). Web.

Lonnie Spikes
Icy Sparks by Gwyn Hyman Rubio

Gwyn Hyman Rubio writes about Lonnie Spikes, a twenty-year-old simpleton in her novel *Icy Sparks*. When Lonnie emits clucking sounds and swings his head back and forth, the townsfolk of Ginseng feel only pity as they comment to each other what a blessing it is that he is unaware of his own condition. They slow their pace and step aside to allow Lonnie to stumble by them on his way to the post office, where he sits on the front porch for hours on end "with his pants unzipped, his tongue lolling from his mouth, his eyes enameled over like those of a corpse" (Rubio 10). His lack of intelligible speech and inability to control his motor movements indicate possible dyslalia or Broca's aphasia, "in which intelligence is impaired" (OED) due to damage of the anterior parts of the brain.

Speech sound disorders (SSDs) "result from a variety of etiologies and represent impairment at a number of different levels of speech production" (Strand et al. 505). The difficulties of diagnosing this type of disorder is determining the level of "motor speech impairment" in individuals who struggle with apraxia of speech, including the modes of articulation for "volitional speech" (505–06). Although Lonnie might wish to speak, his disabilities prohibit verbalization of intelligible words.

Although the citizens of Ginseng do not understand Lonnie's affliction, they do accept him as one of their own and accommodate him when he appears in town. There is no mention of disgust, mockery or teasing—only compassion—as Lonnie has become a regular fixture among their midst, and they feel a sense of obligation to protect him. Lonnie must have an inkling of what it means to be part of a community, especially since he regularly comes to downtown Ginseng. Not only the townspeople, but his family members as well, permit him the freedom to explore his surroundings. Rather than hide him behind closed doors, they allow him his independence, perhaps knowing it will add quality to the limited life Lonnie already lives.

Works Cited

"Aphasia of Broca." *Oxford English Dictionary* (OED). Web.

Rubio, Gwyn Hyman. *Icy Sparks*. New York: Penguin, 1998.

Strand, Edith A., et al. "A Motor Speech Assessment for Children with Severe Speech Disorders: Reliability and Evidence." *Journal of Speech, Language & Hearing Research* 56.2 (2013): 505–20. Web.

Celestine
Refuge by Dot Jackson

Winner of the Appalachian Book of the Year Award, Dot Jackson's novel *Refuge* is set in the late 1920s in the Appalachian Mountains of North Carolina. The historical fiction describes the severity of mountain life for the "strong Southern woman survivor" (Fisher 11). Mary Seneca Steele

(Sen), the protagonist and narrator who feels displaced, can no longer tolerate her abusive husband, so she leaves Charleston and rushes headlong with her children to find the paternal family homestead and to search for her identity among kinfolk she has heard stories about but has never met. In Caney Forks, she meets a stream of family members, most married within the family tree, who are also curious about her.

Humor during potentially dangerous circumstances occurs when Sen, who does not know how to drive, steals her husband's car, and heads north with no map or knowledge of how to reach her destination. One adversity after another is met until they reach the abandoned Steele family plantation. Sen's intense desire to return to her roots is common among mountain people who often leave Appalachia to pursue financial opportunities or in the folly of their youth think "the grass is greener" elsewhere. The appeal of family, a simple life, and the beauty of the mountains is more than they can resist, for many wayward mountain folk often find life difficult as flatlanders.

The silent character in the novel is Celestine, the daughter of Ben Aaron and his despicable wife whom the locals call "Sophier" and the children call "Sofa," a fitting moniker for the pasty, bloated woman. Knowing this family tends to mate with each other, Sophia arrives in a fancy carriage to get a good look at Seneca, establish her spousal position, and subtly urge Sen to return home. A wealthy Boston snob, her whole being is incongruous to the mountain way of life, which she abhors, for she is unable to adjust to the rugged life and unwilling to "lower herself" to mountain standards. Sophia will forever be an outlier.

Celestine, a seventeen-year-old replica of her mother's physicality, sits in the carriage fidgeting and making grunting sounds. Celestine "scooted across the seat, working her mouth sideways, trying to speak" (134). With sagging eyelids and jerking face, Celestine reaches her arms out to Seneca for a welcome hug but struggles to answer her kind inquiries. "Her jaw worked, but the words could not quite form" (135), indicating dyslalia associated with speech problems caused by fetal damage. Another possibility is dysarthria, "lesions of articulation which depend clearly on gross mechanical defects in the external apparatus of speech and motor nerves" (OED. Her symptoms are similar to Millie Floyd's in Jean Ayer's *Chinkapin Creek*.

Celestine's brain was damaged at birth. During delivery, Sophia had help only from Cleone, a Steele cousin she calls an "ignorant servant girl" (36) and incriminates for almost drowning the baby. After Sophia developed "a fearsome case o' the trots" (154), Celestine plopped out while her mother was crouched over the chamber pot, and before Cleone could fish her out, Celestine had apparently inhaled and perhaps ingested fecal material. At that point, Celestine most likely stopped breathing, and the lack of oxygen affected her brain, thus her mental and motor abilities were compromised. Even after Celestine was bathed, a detached Sophia refused to place the silent baby at her breast, so no maternal bond was ever formed between mother and child.

Sophia revels in her motherhood of Celestine as a marker of martyrdom. She enjoys telling the tragic story over and over to draw sympathy from listeners. While she selfishly focuses on her own suffering, Ben Aaron is loving and kind to his daughter. "Bouncing on her chair" (217) in anticipation of a hug, this child hungers for genuine affection from others since Sophia perceives her as a cross to bear. Once Celestine "clapped her hands and laughed a great coarse laugh, out loud" (265), perhaps one of the few times her father ever heard her voice. She may be brain-damaged, but she is aware of her mother's egoism and indifference to her needs. During Ben Aaron's funeral, when Patience "turned loose a screech and wail to raise the dead" (274), the loud, unfamiliar sound frightens Celestine who joins in the cacophony. Unaware that her father is dead, she merely reacts to the auditory stimuli with echolalia, a common symptom of those with disabilities of limited speech.

Works Cited

"Dysarthria." *Oxford English Dictionary* (OED). Web.
Fisher, Ann H. "Refuge." *Library Journal* 131.11 (2006). Literary Reference Center. Web.
Jackson, Dot. *Refuge*. Charlotte: Novello Festival Press, 2006. Print

4

The Mute

Henry and Melvin
Amy directed by Vincent McEveety

One of Disney's Generations Collection, the film *Amy* is set in the early 1900s at The Parker School for the Deaf & Blind. Forty deaf and twenty blind children from the coal mining area reside at the institution. A sign in the foyer of the school reads "Training of the Hand Corresponds with Training of the Mind," indicating that the school's traditional instruction for hearing-impaired students has been through sign language. Now, the Board of Directors has shown a slight interest in teaching deaf children to speak, so Amy Medford is hired with that mission.

The staff welcomes her to the school except for Malvina, the sign language teacher, although her icy greeting and resentment of Amy is understandable. Amy is young and enthusiastic about exposing the children to an innovative mode of learning. She showers her students with genuine compassion and love, and they respond likewise. Malvina, older and "old school," feels threatened by Amy's presence. She maintains a sober demeanor in the classroom, where the children are neither motivated to learn nor do they react positively to her archaic methods, which have not improved student achievement over the many years of her tenure. She fears that her services will no longer be needed if Amy successfully teaches the children to speak, so she is critical of Amy and highly vocal about her doubts for the new teacher's enterprise.

In the nineteenth century, a dispute arose between educators who "favored teaching oral methods of communication" to deaf children and those who still regarded sign language equally effective, as does Malvina. In the following century, sign language was not only discouraged but was not even considered a language at all. This controversy abated when an English professor at Gallaudet University was captivated by ASL. His journal articles argued that ASL is indeed a "rule-governed" language of grammatical and syntactical features. The main distinction of ASL is a "visual three-dimensional rather than a one-dimensional spoken language" ("American Sign Language").

Likewise, Amy's teaching style is a three-prong method using both visual and tactile standards. After she writes a word on the chalk board, students read her lips as she pronounces it, and then she places the children's hands along her cheek and throat to feel the vibrations as she speaks. Her system has similarities to the one Anne Sullivan used to teach Helen Keller to speak, their incredibly successful story depicted in *The Miracle Worker*. Amy also uses a feather in front of her mouth to indicate a puffing "p" sound. Her first success is with a precocious boy named Henry, who gives her the sign language nickname "Amy-on-the-lips." A poignant moment takes place when his parents visit him for the first time and Henry says "mother" as he wraps his arms around her. She weeps, for in her own blindness, she has never seen her son, and because of his deafness and lack of oral language, she has never before heard his voice.

This important scene illustrates the fact that speech is more than just words. It allows individuals to be fully engaged with the rest of humanity (Moog and Stein 133). Historically, teaching deaf children to talk was a reality only for those with partial hearing impairment. Before the late 1900's, hearing aids were not advanced enough to give profoundly deaf children "access to sound" (134). Oral deaf education necessitated well-trained tutors and long stretches of time; "conversing often required considerable effort on the part of the listener as well as the speaker" (133). Today, the greatest successes require early detection and the use of innovative hearing aids or sophisticated cochlear implants.

Heretofore, the general public of the mountains has shunned the impaired children, as if they have a contagious disease. One boorish man tells Amy, "Our people don't mix with them kids." A football game against a neighborhood team dispels the earlier attitudes of hearing children and is the beginning of a blended community. It is also an opportunity for the Parker School students to participate as part of a team and to socialize among children outside of their silent world.

Days later, another poignant situation occurs. When Melvin runs away and is killed on the railroad tracks, his parents arrive to claim his body. Viewers expect his parents to be indignant and perhaps threaten to sue the school, but instead they leave their six-year-old deaf daughter in Amy's care, an indication that they realize she might not have a future in society without being taught to communicate.

Works Cited

"American Sign Language." *The Gale Encyclopedia of Childhood and Adolescence*. Ed. Jerome Kagan and Susan B. Gall. Online Edition. Detroit: Gale, 2007. Health and Wellness Resource Center. Web.

Amy. Dir. Vincent McEveety. Perf. Jenny Agutter, Barry Newman, and Nanette Fabray. Walt Disney Studios, 1981. DVD.

Moog, Jean S., and Karen K. Stein. "Teaching Deaf Children to Talk." *Contemporary Issues in Communication Science and Disorders* 35 (2008): 133–42. Web.

Holly
The Waltons directed
by Earl Hamner

Earl Hamner's beloved television series *The Waltons* won five Emmy Awards during its first season although the drama enjoyed nine years of popularity. The show is set in Appalachia atop Virginia's Walton Mountain. Earl Hamner is the unseen narrator who speaks as an adult John Boy, reminiscing about his childhood experiences on the mountain.

In the first season's premier episode, "The Foundling," viewers meet the large Walton family and learn of its conservative values. The episode is aptly named, for the family find outside a bundle wrapped in a patchwork blanket, and in its folds a child's dirty and frightened face appears.

No amount of questioning fazes the young girl; she remains silent and indifferent, and the Waltons are uncertain what to do with her. Because she has already been left behind once, and although the Depression has made life difficult for the Walton family, Grandpa declares, "In our house, there's always room for more." Depression or not, his mindset is typical of mountain people who like the Walton family, eked out a living from the often stubborn land but did not turn away strangers who needed a meal and bed for the night. They seriously followed Christ's command to "do unto others" and responded in Good Samaritan fashion.

The local doctor confirms Olivia's hunch that Holly is deaf and dumb. He gives John a pamphlet illustrating "finger talking" so they might learn to communicate with Holly, but John tells him their daily work does not leave time for other activities. Nonetheless, when John Boy takes on the task, both he and Holly are delighted with their accomplishments, and in deference to the homeless waif, the entire family eventually learns to "talk" with their fingers.

American Sign Language (ASL), which uses hand gestures and symbols of expression, often uses a single gesture to communicate multiple concepts. Reproducing every word of the spoken language is not required. "Beginning signers often use ASL signs in the same order as they would words in an English sentence; this usage is known as pidgin signing" ("American Sign Language"), and most signers can understand communication in this manner.

Holly's newly-learned skill becomes crucial when Elizabeth, who is jealous of the attention Holly receives, runs away and becomes trapped in an old trunk in an abandoned shack. Fortunately, Holly had silently followed Elizabeth, and because she has been taught to sign, she can communicate to the Waltons Elizabeth's location.

The irony of this episode is the contrast between Holly's father, who believes she can never learn to communicate and wants to institutionalize her, and the Waltons, complete strangers who do not hesitate to take her into their home and help her the best way they can. They would never consider giving up one of their children, no matter the obstacles to overcome. Holly's father observes the fear in John Walton's eyes and hears it in his voice when he cannot find Elizabeth, yet Holly's father was determined to send his own daughter away. In the end, two families are reunited and whole again. The Waltons have Elizabeth back among their fold, and Holly's estranged parents reconcile and promise to learn sign language, exchanging their former obstinate monologue for dialogue.

Works Cited

"American Sign Language (ASL)." *The Gale Encyclopedia of Childhood and Adolescence.* Ed. Jerome Kagan and Susan B. Gall. Online Edition. Detroit: Gale, 2007. Health & Wellness Resource Center. Web.

"The Foundling." *The Waltons.* Perf. Richard Thomas, Ralph Waite, Michael Learned. Dir. Earl Hamner. Warner Bros., 1972. DVD.

Mountie O'Teale
Christy directed by Tom Blomquist

Through character Christy Huddleston, Catherine Marshall recounts her mother's life as a young teacher in the Smoky Mountains. Tom Blomquist directed the television series *Christy*, which was later made into a full-length film. In 1912, Christy Huddleston, a naïve young woman from Asheville, North Carolina, has accepted a teaching position in Cutter Gap, a remote mountaintop community. Her seven-mile walk up the mountain in pouring rain would cause misgivings in the strongest of hearts, but a stubborn Christy is determined to disprove her parents' lack of faith in her and to dedicate her life to the teaching profession.

The structure which will serve as a school during the week and a church on Sundays has almost been finished. This arrangement was common in rural and remote mountaintop communities where townspeople were accustomed to multiple uses of all available resources. This practice is often enacted in the popular television series *Little House on the Prairie*, in which the schoolhouse also functions as a church. Christy is surprised at the number of children and the wide range of their ages and levels of education, although in 1902, a one-room schoolhouse was standard. She is also amazed to see that every child is dirty, unkempt, and barefoot. Coming from a life of plenty in Asheville, Christy is unaware of how poor the mountain people can be. She is especially drawn to little Mountie O'Teale who wears a ragged coat with no buttons. When Christy asks for information about each child for her records, Mountie does not respond. The other students inform Christy that Mountie has never spoken, but they do not know why, so Christy, most likely encouraged by her college professors to make regular home visits, decides to speak to Mountie's mother, Swannie O'Teale.

Christy is understandably shocked, for she has never seen the level of poverty at the O'Teales' place where all the children are standing outside in a filthy, trash-strewn yard, and inside the ramshackle house the stench is overwhelming. When she explains that she has come to find out why Mountie does not speak, Swannie is immediately suspicious of the teacher's intentions and says her husband Tom, who comes by only occasionally, would not like Christy being there asking personal questions.

Gender role expectations in the early 1900s are highlighted in the film. Because Tom O'Teale is a man, he is allowed to come and go as he pleases with no questions or complaints from his wife. Although he leaves Swannie and the children hungry and alone, he receives no condemnation from the community. This casual marriage arrangement is similar to the one shared by Alice and Reese Kincaid in *Songcatcher*, written by Sharyn McCrumb and adapted to film by Maggie Greenwald. Reese comes home long enough to see his children and to impregnate Alice again, and then leaves them to spend the majority of his time with a woman named Josie who lives high up in the mountains. The neighboring families prevent Alice and the children from starving, but no one challenges Reese or his moral obligations until an outsider arrives. The male protagonist claims to the female outsider that "a woman's lot is to suffer." That might be true for Alice, but not for Josie. In an ironic twist of fate, when Reese returns to his wife Alice, Josie—who believes he has betrayed *her*—confronts Reese at a church service and blows the breath out of him with a shotgun. She feels justified in her actions, with no concern for the fate of his wife and children. Josie certainly exemplifies the cliché "hell hath no fury like a woman scorned," for she must defend her place in Reese's life, even though it is a tarnished one.

Taking matters into their own hands is another commonality among mountain people, especially in areas where there is no official law enforcement. In *Songcatcher*, two cowardly men of the community burn down the schoolhouse when they discover the teachers are lesbians. Similarly, in *Christy*, the men of the community resent her attempts to dictate their morals when she insists they stop moonshining, but she does not realize that the illegal liquor is their means of livelihood. Eventually, several irate men burn most of the school building, hoping to quiet the unwelcome educator and send her home. They will not kowtow to a prissy little city girl who neither understands nor appreciates their lifestyle, and they are primed for a fight to defend it. However, they prefer to react rather than to reason.

Tom O'Teale does not like to fuss over girls and is unwilling to allow Dr. MacNeill's examination of Mountie to determine the cause of her muteness. His refusal is probably two-fold. Boys are more revered because they can work on the farms with their fathers, and asking for help makes independent mountain people feel beholden to others. Denying assistance is easier than being unable or unwilling to reciprocate in like kind.

Swannie has no explanation for Mountie's muteness, for she believes they must wait on the Lord to reveal the reason or to heal her daughter. Distrust of outliers, especially a prim and proper teacher like Christy, was prevalent by mountain people who did not appreciate strangers contesting or judging the way they thought or lived. Christy does not understand why the O'Teales refuse to seek help for their silent daughter, but she is unaware of their pride in taking care of their own without interference from outsiders. She also does not understand their preference to wait on the Lord to intervene on their behalf because she is used to consulting doctors for her own health care. Although perplexed by the mountaineer mindset, Christy must remember that she is encroaching on their homeland and should accept their ways—hogs, moonshine, and blood feuds— if she expects them to accept her.

She is mentored and encouraged by a Quaker missionary who has silently suffered her own tragedy and injustice but remains committed to her task of improving the lives of the people of Cutter Gap. Upon meeting

Christy she remarks that the "mountains are beautiful, frightening, even deadly," a lesson Christy will soon learn. Always in the back of Christy's mind is her desire to reach Mountie and help her find her voice. When she tears off the buttons from her own expensive coat and stitches them onto Mountie's worn one, this simple act of kindness tears down the little girl's wall of silence. Mountie speaks for the first time when she repeats Christy's word, "buttons."

Works Cited

Christy. Perf. Kellie Martin, Tyne Daly, Tess Harper. Dir. Tom Blomquist. MTM Enterprises, CBS, 1994–1995. Twentieth Century–Fox Home Entertainment, DVD.

Cletus Gentry
Signs in the Blood by Vicki Lane

Set in the deep hollers of the mountains of North Carolina, Vicki Lane's suspenseful novel *Signs in the Blood* is "an exotic and colorful picture of Appalachia from an outsider's perspective—through a glass darkly" according to Sharyn McCrumb (book jacket), prolific Appalachian novelist. Cletus, the innocent, middle-aged son of Birdie Gentry, is merely called "simple." He has a limited ability to speak but rarely does. Birdie and Cletus live together in a small log house where they take care of each other and make a living by farming tobacco and tending a vegetable garden.

As so often happens in communities with a special needs individual, Cletus is loved and protected by the people around Ridley Branch. He enjoys nothing more than hunting game and searching for ginseng—common interests of mountain men—and attending tent revivals.

> When his work was done and the crop laid by, he would wander through the woods for days, camping out in all weathers and living off the hard-baked cornbread he carried with him, now and then shooting and cooking a rabbit or squirrel. Eventually he would fetch up at some remote cabin where the inhabitants would give him a meal and call Miss Birdie to come get him [Lane 12].

Although he is incapable of higher learning, Cletus feels a sense of accomplishment with the game he provides for others since he can provide little else. He cannot read a map, but he knows well the mountains and coves around the holler. Although neighbors watch out for Cletus, he watches out for his mother who compares him to an old hound that can be restrained for only a short time—then he has to run. This "pull" of nature is the same for Clayt Stargill in Sharyn McCrumb's *The Rosewood Casket.* Tramping around the woods is blissful for both men.

"There is something quare goin' on" (16) about Cletus' whereabouts, so Elizabeth Goodweather, the protagonist of the novel and a recurring character in Vicki Lane's work, volunteers to search for him. The remainder of the novel is, for Elizabeth, a journey with many distractions to deter her from finding important clues, for she is sidetracked by three distinctive groups that have become indigenous to rural America.

In the mountains surrounding the holler, a snake-handling preacher called John the Baptizer, tries to ingratiate himself with Elizabeth, who is surprised by her attraction to him. Her interest is further piqued when she attends the tent revival at The Holiness Church of Jesus Love Anointed with Signs Following. Churches with names ending in "Signs Following" are common in remote mountainous areas and are grounded in Mark 16: 17–18, "And these signs shall follow them that believe; in my name shall they cast out devils; they shall speak with new tongues; they shall take up serpents; and if they drink any deadly thing, it shall not hurt them; they shall lay hands on the sick, and they shall recover."

The emotionally charged services appeal to soul-searching individuals who yearn to be filled with the Holy Spirit and have assurance of Heaven. When the Holy Ghost is on them, they speak in tongues, feel led to handle snakes, and are slain in the Spirit—manifestations that their faith is indeed acceptable to and blessed by God. Some may be attracted to the church out of reserved curiosity, as is Elizabeth, but once they become members, worshipers revel in the spiritual joy of communion.

Another group that is a hindrance to Elizabeth's objective is a cosmic cult. The prophet Polaris and the disciples of Starshine Community are isolated within a large domed structure where insiders are brainwashed and trained while outsiders are denied entrance by armed guards. This insular mountainside cult's focus is black-market baby selling, so young, fertile girls are targeted and lured to the compound. Commonly, people who join cults come from dysfunctional families and suffer from low self-esteem or a lack of attachment bond. Many are old hippies accustomed to living communally, sharing love and all accoutrements with those who view themselves as societal misfits. Established cult members welcome initiates "as is," to provide a missing need in their unfulfilled existence. Neophytes willingly relinquish control of their lives to a leader who offers security and Heavenly rewards.

The character of Polaris might be fashioned after Marshall Applewhite, former guru of the California Heaven's Gate cult, who controlled the minds, clothing, hairstyles, and diet of his believers. He also promised them "new, more beautiful bodies and a boarding pass to a 'Kingdom of Heaven' among the stars and planets" through a collective suicide that would save them "from impending world disaster" (Woodward and Stone 40). They eagerly awaited the arrival of Comet Halle-Bopp, a sign that their souls would be transported to a new level, and in 1997, thirty-nine androgynous members ended their own lives by ingesting phenobarbital (Miller).

In training farther up the mountain is a radical militia group, Aryans who believe they have been singled out to fight the battle of Armageddon. The boundaries of their fortress are less defined, but the Sons of Adam are no less dangerous. Various unexplained "warnings" are sent to those who come too close or ask too many questions about their purpose or activities. Nearby neighbors are often startled by sounds of gunfire or explosions from a well-stocked arsenal of guns and ammunition. Because their movements are clandestine, domestic terrorism is widely rumored, and the mountain populace lives in fear.

Young recruits of militia groups are often fascinated by video games like *Dungeons & Dragons* and are eager to learn the real application of weapons. Adults in this organization are normally disgruntled by threats of governmental restrictions, especially as they pertain to Second Amendment rights, and willingly join this brotherhood of defiance. The Southern Poverty Law Center, a civil rights advocacy organization, reported that in 2012, the number of mostly non- violent militias "galvanized against gun control," reached 1,360 in the U.S. (Leger 3).

In the past, each of the three cohorts has welcomed the guileless Cletus to join them for meals, so Elizabeth believes they have insight about his death. All three groups also have common attributes. They are often predatory in their search for disillusioned people who desire acceptance and a sense of belonging, people who may not be well-educated (unlike the literati of Heaven's Gate) so they are easily manipulated by the notion of unity. As a rule, the newly enlisted are merely ordinary people from all walks of life, but their lives change dramatically once they are part of the inner circle. Because these groups thrive better if they are hidden from mainstream society, they often establish compounds in remote, wooded areas to lessen intrusion and interference from outsiders.

Woven throughout the novel is an endearing subplot—the mystery of Little Sylvie, who tells her story from the grave. As Elizabeth concludes her search, she uncovers information that reveals Little Sylvie's secrets about her forced marriage, her forbidden love, and her baby Malindy who now sleeps in her mother's cold arms.

Works Cited

The King James Study Bible. Nashville: Thomas Nelson, 1983. Print.

Lane, Vicki. *Signs in the Blood.* New York: Dell, 2005. Print.

Leger, Donna Leinwand, "Patriot Militias Swell in Numbers." *USA Today,* March 6, 2013. Academic Search Premier. Web.

Miller, Mark, and Thomas Evan. "Secrets of the Cult." *Newsweek* 129.15 (1997): 28. Academic Search Premier. Web.

Woodward, Kenneth, and Brad Stone. "Christ and Comets." *Newsweek* 129.14 (1997): 40. Academic Search Premier. Web.

Clive
Tragedy in Tin Can Holler
by Rozetta Mowery

In an impoverished community in Tennessee, illiteracy, illegitimacy, and infidelity abound in *Tragedy in Tin Can Holler,* the memoir of Rozetta Mowery, who returned home at age fifty-three to uncover the tragic secrets of her childhood. Unashamedly, Mowery shares with readers the stories of her murderous grandmother, numerous family members in and out of prison, and her father stamping her mother to death when Rozetta was only seven years old.

The most heinous crimes revealed in the book are committed by her grandmother Grace, who as a child was both physically and sexually abused by her father in front of her bedridden mother. As is often true of mountain kin who choose to keep their problems and sins to themselves, "family secrets, no matter how terrible, were never spoken ... those remained within the family" (Mowery 3). In adulthood, Grace was an unconscionable woman—promiscuous, addicted to moonshine, and guilty of both infanticide and murder. Horrors that Grace had seen and experienced in childhood made her completely insensitive to love or compassion for others. She had no attachment bond with her parents; neither did she seek one with her own children.

Being reared by an abusive father, Grace had no moral code. She fed meals laced with arsenic to unsuspecting men, just like fictional Miss Emily Grierson does in William Faulkner's short story "A Rose for Emily." Miss Emily, who yearns for a husband to share her life and bed, lures Homer Barron inside her antebellum home, and when he succumbs to the poison in his food, she sleeps with his decomposing corpse, a morbid act of necrophilia. Neither Homer nor the men Grace lured to her farm were ever seen again.

To dispose of the bodies, Grace secretly enlisted the help of her distant cousin Clive "a large man with the mentality of a small child who could not speak" (18). With smiles and giggles, Grace conveyed to Clive that they were merely playing a game when she told him to drag the bodies outside and help her throw them into a deep pit on a nearby ridge. Because of Clive's lack of speech and intelligence, Grace knew she could manipulate him to help in her unconscionable depravity because he could not report what they had done.

Drinking moonshine (DIY alcohol) was common among the residents of Tin Can Holler. It was easy to make and overhead costs were low, but the potency was high. Because it was "stilled" illegally, there were no safety regulations, hence no quality control. No wonder it was often referred to as "rot gut." It initially affects the central nervous system as a stimulant, but later as a depressant, causing impairment of cognitive abilities.

The author surmises that her grandmother may have had a chemical imbalance. Several causal factors were present in Grace's life: "loss of a loved one or loss of a nurturing relationship in childhood, cultural background, sexual assault, and substance abuse" (Baker and Proctor 442–443). The abuse from her father most likely led to her promiscuity and the physical abuse of her own children. Daily imbibing of moonshine would have exacerbated her mood swings, and genetic abnormalities probably led to brain dysfunction and irrational reasoning. Her addiction caused her to commit horrific crimes, yet she remained unremorseful. Not surprisingly, "her three sons showed no emotion" when she was lowered into the grave (Mowery 29). All factors point to both environment and heredity. Grace Sims, unable or unwilling to break that cycle, was in dire need of medical attention, specifically a detox regimen. In this community, there was limited access to and money for doctors, but plenty of opportunities to secure moonshine. However, day-to-day survival was foremost in the minds of the poor individuals who lived in Tin Can Holler.

Works Cited

Baker, A.E.Z., and N.G. Proctor. "A Qualitative Inquiry into Consumer Beliefs about the Causes of Mental Illness." *Journal of Psychiatric and Mental Health Nursing* 33.7 (2013): 846–61. Science Direct. Web.

Mowery, Rozetta. *Tragedy in Tin Can Holler*. Global Authors Publications, 2007. Print.

Herbert Mullens and Belton Light
Billy Creekmore by Tracey Porter

Set in West Virginia in 1905, Tracey Porter's YA novel *Billy Creekmore* is told in first person by the titular character. Billy's bildungsroman takes him from an orphanage near Morgantown; to the coal mines at Holly Glen, along the Paint River near Charleston; to the travels of circus life. All three experiences highlight the injustice of child labor at the turn of the century, and Billy's circumstances draw attention to the plight of children abandoned by their parents, followed by ill-treatment at orphanages.

The author readily admits that her characters are based on the boys in Charles Dickens' *Oliver Twist, David Copperfield,* and *Great Expectations,* as well as Mark Twain's *Huckleberry Finn*. Additionally, the characters in her book, except for Billy, are named after boys who died in the coal mines, information Porter found during her research at the West Virginia State Museum. She infuses historical elements in her work, including the United Mine Workers and the Baldwin-Felts agents, who flushed out and killed miners who were union sympathizers.

The reader meets the first mute character at the Guardian Angels Home for Boys, a specious name for a disreputable institution. The headmaster, Mr. Beadle, has an overseer's hand with a hickory switch he wields indiscriminately. Six-year-old Herbert Mullens, a "sparrow of a boy, slight and twitchy" (Porter 5), drops a basket of eggs for which he receives a beating so severe that he ceases to speak. Judging that the boy has lost his mind, Beadle sends him to a home for deaf and blind children, where he certainly will be a lost soul.

The scenes at the orphanage expose hypocrisy of the self-righteous. Besides the unwarranted thrashings he administers, Beadle and his wife "hide behind religion" (Hayn 690) and constantly browbeat the boys into submission with threats of Hell. The chapel preacher adds his own damnation of the young souls, telling them they are "halfway to the Devil" (Porter 15), but the real evil resides in the preacher with rattlesnakes hanging from his neck. The greed of immoral individuals with authority over children is also revealed by the Beadles, who when entertaining guests, dine on the finest delicacies, but serve the gaunt, starving boys, exhausted from laboring all day on the farm, a scant meal of hard bread and watery soup. The boys live in a drafty, leaky dormitory with only a thin sheet for cover. Of course, the Beadles are considered saints by the community and the institution's financial sponsors.

The second mute character is Belton Light, a boy of five who lives in the coal mining community of Holly Glen. He actually displays traits of autism, for when addressed, he does not make eye contact; his only response is to twirl around with outstretched arms, "talking to himself in a language all his own" (101). His brother Clyde informs Billy, "He can hear fine. He just don't understand words. Don't use them either" (101).

Belton is both emotionally and physically attached to his brother. When Clyde leaves for school each morning, Belton clings to him, and at the school doorstep, Belton begins to moan and must be peeled from his brother's side. He often covers his brother's mouth, for he dislikes it if Clyde speaks or is attentive to anyone else. When Clyde is forced to work in the mines, Belton becomes frantic: kicking, screaming, and flapping his hands, actions which suggest that he cannot tolerate a change in his routine, a threatening situation for most autistics.

At the coal company's annual Christmas celebration, Belton receives a train whistle, which he blows incessantly. After his mother takes it away from him, a tantrum ensues. He pulls the drapes off the windows and throws coal ashes all over the floor, all the while crying uncontrollably. Nothing consoles him until Clyde gives him his own toy top, a symbolic parallel to Belton's own routine of body spinning.

Within the section about the coal mines is an interesting notion about progeny among both the haves and have-nots. During the Christmas party, Billy observes the company owner, store manager, superintendent, and doctor sitting with their families at the head table on a raised platform. He notes that the children look like miniature versions of their parents— the daughters wear large satin bows in their hair to mimic the dangling earrings of their mothers, and the sons "wear waistcoats with starched collars" (121) just like their fathers. Billy is amused by this sight until he realizes that he and the other boys sitting below the platform, a symbolic reference to their social class, look like little miners.

One theme related to Billy's rite of passage is disillusionment. Billy's father, whom he has never seen, intermittently sends him postcards from a variety of locations. As a result, he imagines Billy Creekmore, Sr., as an impor-tant man whose job requires travel. However, when he finally meets his father, he encounters an alcoholic grifter who has attached himself to a small, run-down circus troupe. Billy joins his father only long enough to discover he is not a real father, and the scam-artist showmen are not real family.

Works Cited

Hayn, Judith A. "Billy Creekmore: A Novel." *Journal of Adolescent and Adult Literacy* 50.8 (2007): 690–91. Literary Reference Center. Web.

Porter, Tracey. *Billy Creekmore: A Novel*. New York: HarperCollins, 2007. Print.

Least
The Day of Small Things
by Vicki Lane

"It'll allus be the least un, fer there won't be no more" (Lane 5). Thus, due to the circumstances of her birth, Fronie names her daughter Least, an adjective meaning lowest in importance, as if she is the runt of a litter. Her childhood in Dark Holler is harrowing, for she is described by her bitter, abusive mother as "a hindrance and a worry, quare, simpleminded, ain't right." Her intermittent spells suggest that she might be epileptic, but her mother's ostracizing Least—no school, no friends, no visitors—cause her temporary muteness. Nine years old the first time she is allowed in the presence of company, Least eventually finds her voice through love and affirmation from her grandmother.

Her mother maintains a cruel demeanor toward Least, but a clue to Fronie's aggressiveness is the elixir she buys from the peddler. Cordelia Ledbetter's Herbal Mixture (18 percent alcohol), is a "popular nostrum" (12) for various female maladies. From ancient civilizations, the "idea of female hysteria as emotional excess" (Haaken 209) and the treatments to alleviate it were established by men who thought they had the right to control women's sexual urges. Hippocrates coined the term from the Greek "hyster" for uterus. The condition, sometimes called "furor of the womb" (Lane 12) or wandering womb, was treated by external-assisted paroxysm, massaging of the pelvis, or clitoridectomy, removal of the clitoris. Fronie's hatefulness might stem from a hormonal imbalance due to the onset of menopause, for she has birthed a full baseball team. She has no other resources, so her bottles from the peddler must do.

Fronie isolates Least to secure for herself a slave with no opportunities to leave the farm. Her insistence that the unnamed dog remain tied up in the yard 24/7 is a parallel to her treatment of her daughter, who without a real name of her own, is whistled for when her mother bids her to come. The dog initially resists fleeing when Least unlocks the chains because it is unaware of its prison, knowing no other life; so too is Least until she discovers the medical papers which inform Fronie that through a government eugenics program she has the authority to prevent her young simpleton from procreating, because she "ain't fit to marry" or "breed" (119).

Beginning in 1929, the "North Carolina Eugenics Board authorized over eight thousand eugenic sterilizations" (Schoen 132), some through coercion but many for poor and minority women without their permission. A statute allowed the procedure for "mentally diseased, feebleminded, or epileptic" (132) individuals, especially those in "custodial institutions (Castles 854).

An element of fantasy, a running motif throughout the novel, is seen in the shared "Gifts" of Least and Granny Beck. Both know the habitat and habits of the Little People, in the Cherokee tradition called *Yunwi Tsunsdi* and the legend of the fairy crosses (Lane 54). A most benevolent man named Aaron, like an earthly god, seems both omnipotent and omnipresent, appearing at times of need or placing others at the right time and place to help the protagonist. The calling song, which causes the little People to appear for safety and protection, is an element similar to the "trajectory" of the plots of "prototypical restoration tales" (Bottigheimer 212), set in agrarian societies and with suspenseful but happy endings. Of course, fairy tales must have villains, and two raven mockers, in Cherokee mythology evil ones who "suck the life" from their prey (Coldsmith 264) and then eat their hearts, play that role in Lane's narrative.

One of the more interesting sections of the book centers on the tale about John Goingsnake who is helped by the Little People during his travails on The Trail of Tears, when approximately "13,000 Cherokee walked from their homes in the Appalachian Mountains to a new government-mandated homeland in Oklahoma" (Blackburn 53). Unlike travelers who eagerly anticipated a new life in the West, the Cherokees were escorted by the military and forced to leave behind "coveted land … divided up among white land speculators" (53). Their tribes were also divided since groups left at staggered times and took different routes. The Little People assist Goingsnake and his baby daughter by hiding them in the laurels from the armed guards.

Glossolalia is another factor in Lane's book. Lilah Bel receives a "licking of the tongues of fire" (Lane 40) at a brush arbor revival when she is only ten years old. She speaks in tongues, quotes Scripture, prophesies, points out a fellow congregant as a sinful drunk, and then with eyes rolled back in her head, hits the floor (41). None of this she remembers. Silver-haired prophetess Belvy returns to the book's storyline in her church, its tenets founded on Mark 16:17–18. The Holiness Church of JESUS Love Anointed with Signs Following relocates to Tennessee when North Carolina outlawed snake handling. Aunt Belvy handles snakes when the "Spirit called her" (263), even though she has been bitten several times and her son died from snake bites. The "building rock[s] in a Babel of tongues" as the Elvis-lookalike preacher works the attendees into an emotional frenzy. Lifting the largest rattler, he intones tongues (268) while others kneel in prayer, wave their arms in the air, and one woman "danc[es] a little two-step out in the aisle. Belvy, considered the "cornerstone" of the church, is not allowed to preach but prophesies when she is "full of the spirit" (275) and has a message for someone in attendance.

Several of the characters receive new names as they mature and take on new roles. Like the snake she observes shedding its outer skin, Least changes her name to Redbird Ray when she dances like a limberjack at Gudger's Stand. After marriage, she "buries" her former personas in the cemetery and becomes Birdsong (Birdie). She calls her lover Young David after the Biblical shepherd but then Luther Gentry when he becomes her husband. Dalilah Belva becomes Lilah Bel, and in her old age, Aunt Belvy. All of these name changes indicate a search for and "trying on" new identities, but Least's is the most significant, as her names suggest flight, most likely from her smothering childhood silence.

Vicki Lane's characterization and storytelling skills are exemplary, but the abrupt jump from a newlywed Little Bird in 1939 to an elderly widow Miss Birdie in 2007 is surprising. However, the last half of the book, although set in modern day, will eventually capture the reader's attention again, for the Little People are eternal creatures still at work.

Works Cited

Blackburn, Marion. "Return to the Trail of Tears." *Archaeology march/April* (2012): 53–64. *Academic Search Premier*. Web.

Bottigheimer, Ruth B. "Fairy-Tale Origins, Fairy-Tale Dissemination, and Folk Narrative Theory." *Fabula* 47 (2006): 211–214. *Literary Reference Center*. Web.

Castles, Katherine. "Quiet Eugenics: Sterilization in North Carolina's Institutions for the Mentally Retarded, 1945–1965." *Southern Historical Association* 68.4 (2002): 849–878. *JSTOR*. Web.

Coldsmith, Don. *Raven Mocker*. University of Oklahoma, 2001. *Biography in Context*. Web.

Haaken, Janice. "Pleasures and Perils in Looking Back." *Studies in Gender and Sexuality* 4.2 (2003): 208–225. *Academic Search Premier*. Web.

Lane, Vicki. *The Day of Small Things*. New York: Dell Books, 2010. Print.

Schoen, Johanna. "Between choice and Coercion: Women and the Politics of Sterilization in North Carolina, 1929–1975." *Journal of Women's History* 13.1 (2001): 132–157. *Academic Journal*. Web.

Mr. and Mrs. Hawkins
"Hawkins' Boy" by Charles Dodd White

"Hawkins' Boy," by Charles Dodd White, is included in *Sinners of Sanction County*, a collection of short stories that "examine[s] the dark edges of the human heart" and "issue[s] the primal scream" (Price 132–134) of Appalachian literature. Even though it is a story of silence, the author infuses many words about sound. George Brosi claims that the stories in White's collection "arise from an intimate and absolute understanding of the landscape" (107). This tale might shock readers with its macabre details surrounding a shallow burial and exhumation by dogs (literary symbols of death) that eat parts of a corpse. Set in the mountains above Sylva, North Carolina, White's story opens with an interesting hook: "Hawkins buried his son more than once that summer" (7).

Surprising to the reader, rather than secure the gravesite so the scavenging dogs cannot disturb it, instead Hawkins stares out the window at what the dogs have done and once again gleans from the ground his son's hands with grey fingertips, a hip joint, and other "hunks of cadaver" (11) before he reburies them in the croaker sacks he uses as burial cloths. These details of White's story bear an uncanny similitude to a Biblical story.

The ancient scenario is of Jezebel, Queen of Israel, whose "unwavering allegiance" (Everhart 688) to the Phoenician gods merits her reputation as a harlot, thus today her name connotes wantonness and temptation. Prior to her death, she stands at her window with eunuchs, liminal "boundary crossers" (689) between life and death, gender, and the transfer of power. Her presence at the window has earned her a place in the "woman-at-the-window" (690) literary motif. After the eunuchs are commanded to throw her out the window, horses trample her body, which is then eaten by dogs as Elijah had prophesied. However, when servants are ordered to bury her, they find only her skull, the palms of her hands, and her feet (2 Kings 9:10). These specific parts of Jezebel's body, like the hands of Hawkins' son, lead to speculation about the placement of the mark of the beast, who "causeth all, both small and great, rich and poor, free and bond, to receive a mark in their right hand or in their foreheads" (Revelation 13:16).

Hawkins' unnamed wife has lost her hearing. She communicates with her husband by using sign language, but when neighbors come to join in mourning the loss of her son, they write chalked words on her slate, "passing condolences like grammar school lessons" (White 8), a paradoxically nostalgic image of childhood innocence evoked by the author in this gruesome tale. White also contrasts the loud noises Hawkins' son made at birth to the silence of the house since his death. A hymn the deaf woman hums is described in a tender simile as "a sound not without beauty" (14). Hawkins has grown accustomed to silence since his wife became mute; as a result, he uses his voice only on rare occasions, preferring an "odd habitual quiet" (16).

The narrative has a significant focus on hands, traditionally used as literary symbols, among them strength, protection, guilt or murder. In addition to the reference to the son's hands, Hawkins examines his own hands that are "ugly weights pinned" to his body but in his youth, they had been "trustworthy tools" (16). "All civilizations employ the languages of hands and gestures" (Chevalier and Gheerbrant 470), for symbolically, the hand can be either passive or active (470). White also incorporates a sewing motif when he describes the silent woman's hands as deftly "stitching words" (13). However, Hawkins' hands that were once strong are now weak and useless for "threading words" (16), for he acknowledges "without easy language" (16), his relationship with his wife has diminished.

At the end of the short story, Hawkins, with a pistol in his hands, walks onto the dark field where his son had played baseball. The author, who is skillful at "identifying what the reader assumes will happen, and delivering the unexpected" (Jordan 30), misleads the reader with this scene of foreshadowing. No spoiler alert here, but at the end of the tale, Hawkins senses the "warm, leaky silence take him" (White 17).

Works Cited

Brosi, George. "Charles Dodd White." *Appalachian Heritage* 40.1 (2012): 107. Print.

Chevalier, Jean, and Alain Gheerbrant, eds. *Dictionary of Symbols*. New York: Penguin, 1996. Print.

Everhart, Janet S. "Jezebel: Framed by Eunuchs?" *Catholic Bible Quarterly* 72.4 (2010): 688–98. Academic Search Premier. Web.

Jordan, Jason. "Not Mayberry." *American Book Review* 33.4 (2012): 30. Project Muse. Web.

The King James Study Bible. Nashville: Thomas Nelson, 1988. Print.

Price, Sharon. "Sinners of Sanction County: Stories." *Appalachian Journal* 40.1/2 (2012–2013): 132–34. Print.

White, Charles Dodd. "Hawkins' Boy." *Sinners of Sanction County: Stories*. Huron: Bottom Dog Press, 2011. Print.

Peter
The Good Dream
by Donna VanLiere

The mute character in Donna VanLiere's novel *The Good Dream* is a starving seven-year-old boy who comes down from the mountain to steal food from Ivorie Walker's garden. The boy is an "orphan with a cleft palate and no speech" (*Kirkus* 1), and Ivorie, who lives in Morgan Hill, Tennessee, is an unmarried woman who longs for someone to love and reciprocate that love. The boy lives with an evil man who beats him unmercifully, forces the boy to perform oral sex, and sodomizes him. The man is a stereotype of the uneducated, backwoods mountain hillbilly who points a gun at strangers who encroach on his territory and has a bit of pleasure with them. He is similar to the mountaineers in James Dickey's *Deliverance* who tie one naïve character to a tree with his own belt in order to perform oral sex on him while the other character is sodomized and made to squeal like a pig.

In her "layered, character-driven tale" (Milone 213), the author includes superstitions such as hanging bottles from tree branches to trap evil spirits and infuses humor with Ivorie's descriptions of potential suitors, such as the man whose ugly face fronts a head "big as a hippocampus" (VanLiere 5), but her mother had declared him tolerable. The chapters of the novel are divided by the voices of several characters as well as an unknown third-person narrator.

It is 1950, and thirty-year-old Ivorie is still mourning the loss of her mother, for now the silence permeates throughout the house and has settled into a cold sadness that Ivorie compares to granite. (7). When she finally catches the unresponsive boy, she cannot imagine why he is so leery of adults. After she gains his trust, she is appalled to discover his condition—urine-stained overalls, filthy skin and hair, and a body covered with bruises and lacerations. Unresponsive to her questions except for shrugging and nodding or shaking his head, Ivorie realizes that he is mute.

Desperate to rescue the boy from his appalling existence, she loads her fathers' gun and rides Kitty Wells, her brother's mule, up the mountain during a torrential downpour until she reaches the shack. This event in the novel is too unrealistic to believe. Why would a seemingly sane woman go alone to an isolated place high in the mountains on the back of an unpredictable animal in a rainstorm to face a monstrous fiend without telling anyone else her plans? I know … it is fiction.

The vile drunk with a dangerous leer and putrid smell is "tucked away from the world of enemies below—none who are scarier than he in this pit of hell he's created, where he beats the flesh off a little boy's back— in this secret place of horror that slithers with puke and filth and evil" (116). At this point, another unbelievable situation occurs. Why would this ogre of a man, who is afraid of nothing and no one, back off from a small, rain-soaked woman on a mule who wants to take away his object of sick pleasure? Again … it is fiction, and thankfully so, for it is hard to stomach.

After the doctor examines the boy, he reveals the sexual abuse he has suffered from the contemptible monster. Most pedophiles are males who prey on prepubescent victims "because they are available and vulnerable" (Murray 221) as well as fearful of reprisal if they tell someone about the molestation. The abuse usually takes place in the victims' homes when no one else is present. Of course, this boy is trapped on the mountain because he has never known any other home, and since his mother died, he has had no one to protect him. Pedophiles normally have "reduced values, a lower IQ, and cognitive impairment" (Kruger and Schiffer 1650). Often friends or family members, they are "pathologically unable to control [their] insatiable sexual desire" (Chenier 172). The evil man, the only male in the boy's life, obviously has no morals, no heart, and no soul, or he would not subject the child to such repulsive acts. Of course Peter is mute, so the bestial man is assured that he can tell no one about the abuse, and one wonders if the repeated fellatio worsens the condition of his cleft palate.

The severe abuse the boy has suffered is subtly hinted at in two specific scenes. Each night, the man orders the boy to come to him, and as he lowers the boy's overalls, he says, "You only bleed a little" (VanLiere 29), an act as vile as the earliest accounts of sodomy in reference to Sodom and Gomorrah "where the Lord's messengers could not find even ten decent people ... due to the sin of nefarious intercourse fell from heaven fire and brimstone" (Hawkins) that destroyed the two cities of haughty sodomites. The second clue occurs on the farm when Ivorie demonstrates how to milk her cow. When the boy looks at the cow's pink teat hanging down, "the walls of the shack are closing in and the man's voice is loud and full of venom, 'Take it! Take it, dammit'" (201)!

By process of elimination, Ivorie finally discovers Peter's name and the cause of his muteness. He has a cleft palate, a split or opening in "the roof of the mouth composed of two anatomical structures, the soft and hard palate" ("Cleft Lip" 361). Surgery to repair cleft palates is usually performed when the child is between three and eighteen months old, and the goals of the repair are "normal speech, normal face growth, and hearing. Prognosis is good, and approximately 80% will develop normal speech" (Gulli etal.). Although Peter is much older than most patients, his surgery is successful and he learns to speak. However, the rapid rate at which he finds his voice is another difficult prospect for the reader to accept.

The title of the novel alludes to the recurring nightmares Peter has of gasping for air while drowning, for the man had often pushed his face down in water. The author hints to his fear on several occasions in the book: in the bathtub and at the lake. However, at the end of the nightmares, he is saved by his mother's hands, thus he decides instead that they are actually good dreams.

Works Cited

Chenier, Elise. "The Natural Order of Disorder: Pedophilia, Stranger Danger, and the Normalizing Family." *Sexuality and Culture* 16.2 (2012): 172–86. Academic Search Premier. Web.

"The Good Dream." *Kirkus Reviews* 80.12 (2012): 1213. Literary Resource Center. Web.

Gulli, Farris Farid, etal. "Cleft Lip and Palate." *The Gale Encyclopedia of Medicine.* 4th ed. Detroit: Gale, 2011. Web.

Hawkins, Philip Colin. "New World Sodom: Biblical Tales of Conquest and Acculturation." *Electronic Journal of Human Sexuality* 15, Annual 2012. Health and Wellness Resource Center. Web.

Kruger, Tillmann H.C. and Boris Schiffer. "Neurocognitive and Personality Factors in Homo- and Heterosexual Pedophiles and Controls." *The Journal of Sexual Medicine.* 8.6 (2011): 1650–1659. *EBSCO.* Web

Milone, Nanci. "The Good Dream," *Library Journal.* 137.11 (2012): 213. *Literary Resource Center.* Web.

Murray, John B. "Psychological Profile of Pedophiles and Child Molesters." *Journal of Psychology.* 134.2 (2000): 211–225. *Academic Search Premier.* Web.

VanLiere, Donna. *The Good Dream.* New York: St. Martin's, 2012. Print

5

Silenced by Stroke

Roy Luther
Where the Lilies Bloom
by Vera and Bill Cleaver

Vera and Bill Cleaver's YA novella *Where the Lilies Bloom* recounts the plight of the nearly destitute Luther family living in the mountains of North Carolina during the early 1900s. It also highlights the resilience and ingenuity of children who are forced to become adults long before they leave their childhood years.

One evening, as the patriarch Roy Luther rises from his chair to take a step, he stops suddenly and grabs the back of his neck, while an exploding and rigid agony sweeps across his face. He screams, "profaning the stillness" (Cleaver 14) and pitches forward across the porch. His wife dead from an earlier botched surgical procedure, Roy neither wants nor can afford a doctor's treatment. His children must tend to his needs, cleaning up his vomit, attempting to get food down his throat, and bathing his body. The stroke leaves him unable to speak although his children sit bedside and beg him to try.

His daughter, fourteen-year-old Mary Call, is angry that her father "has allowed himself to be beaten down by the hospitable land, a greedy landlord, and poverty" (Kroman-Kelly 2). His death places an unfortunate burden on Mary Call, who becomes provider and protector of her siblings. Her older sister Devola rarely speaks, and she is so "cloudy headed" that things must be explained to her repeatedly; the two youngest still need motherly nurturing. Because she is underage, Mary Call makes the children pledge to keep their father's death a secret as long as they are able, for she fears the county service agents will divide them among different families. In order to keep this secret, they must sever all former friendships, yet their self-imposed isolation only garners them more hardship.

During the worst times of their distress, especially harsh winters when they need assistance, the Luther children, who have agreed to a pact of silence, steel themselves in stubborn independence and refuse all offers of succor from outsiders.

Even at the tender age of fourteen, Mary Call never complains. She wears the adult role that has befallen her with a determined spirit. In a clever move on her part, for she has no education or skill to earn a substantial income, she and Romey learn wild crafting from a borrowed book, but the elements of nature sabotage their efforts. Nevertheless, Mary Call made promises before her father's death that she intends to honor, mainly keeping her family together, no matter the cost.

The situation of the Luther family was not uncommon in the early 1900s when the leading causes of death were tuberculosis, influenza, and pneumonia; this time period was before advancements in medical treatment and easy access to doctors and hospitals. Folk medicines such as alcohol-based elixirs and poultices were primitive and largely ineffective. Prior to diseases being eradicated in the United States, families often lost children at birth or during childhood. Occasionally they also lost adults who literally worked themselves to death because they could not afford the time to rest or heal, so the oldest child was forced to usurp the role previously held by a parent. This sometimes required the child, without the necessary maturity or ability, to drop out of school and become caretaker of the home and the younger children. As is the case of the Luther family, one hardship after another was most often their lot.

Works Cited

Cleaver, Vera, and Bill. *Where the Lilies Bloom*. New York: HarperCollins, 1969. Print.
Kroman-Kelly, Inga. "Where the Lilies Bloom." *Masterplots II: Juvenile & Young Adult Fiction*, 1993: 1–3. Literary Reference Center. Web.

Granny Took
On Agate Hill by Lee Smith

In Lee Smith's novel *On Agate Hill*, narrator Molly Petrie finishes her education and is offered a teaching position at the Bobcat School in the remote mountain town of Jefferson. She boards with fellow teacher Martha Fickling, whose Granny Took suffers a stroke and must leave her mountain cabin to move in with Martha, leaving Molly to sleep on a cot in a cold lean-to.

When Molly agrees to watch Granny Took while Martha runs errands, Molly's beau, musician Jacky Jarvis, drops by and begins to sing for the two women. Granny Took, who has not spoken in months, is charmed by the rogue mountain man. When he sings "I'll Fly Away," tears run down her knotty face, and although she has no voice to sing along, she beats time on the side of the bed. After playing "Amazing Grace" on his harmonica, Jacky whisks Molly away for a daylong tryst. Their indifference toward the old woman is met with Granny's accusatory and fearful glares in her dark eyes, but she cannot speak words of protest at being left alone all day.

Later that evening, when Martha questions Molly's whereabouts all day, Granny Took snorts and makes strange choking sounds as her mouth works furiously to express her outrage, but no words come. Molly is too entranced by love to feel remorse about leaving the helpless woman alone—she has no obligation to be Granny's caretaker. After all, she is Martha Fickling's kin and responsibility, not Molly's.

Works Cited

Smith, Lee. *On Agate Hill*. Chapel Hill: Algonquin Books, 2007. Print.

Louisa Mae Cardinal
Wish You Well by David Baldacci

In *Wish You Well*, popular suspense writer David Baldacci pens a historical novel set in Appalachia in the 1940's. A "clean, clear prose ... mark[s] his stories, often told through voices of innocents" as is the case in *Wish You Well*, as Lou "unintentionally witnesses dangerous circumstances (Inge 178) on her rite of passage journey from life in the city to one on a working farm. The author delivers "bone-deep emotional truth" ("Forecasts: Fiction 171) as the characters struggle with both inner and external conflict.

Matriarch Louisa Mae Cardinal lives atop a Virginia mountain where she farms over 200 acres. Her character is based on the life of Baldacci's maternal grandmother Cora Rose, who called "the high rock home" (Baldacci ix) for many years. His mother, who was the youngest of ten children, also spent her youth there. The oral history he gleaned from these two women was fertile soil for storytelling, important to Baldacci who believes a personal interview gives the writer minute details and the "nuances that make a story fascinating, interesting to read, and appear more realistic"

(Hamilton and Jones 2). Thus the novel came to life through familial experiences in southwestern Virginia.

After their father is killed in a car accident in New York, Lou and Oz travel by train with their comatose mother to the Appalachian Mountains. Even though she is approaching eighty years old, Louisa Mae, a physically strong woman, is determined to teach Lou and Oz how to survive on a farm without the luxuries of modern conveniences, hoping they will love and respect the land as much as she does, but she teaches them much more, especially how to define the concept of family. A proud, independent woman, she instructs the children how to chop wood, build a fire, cook on a woodstove, plant crops, and care for the animals, and even if the weather does not cooperate with a fruitful bounty, how to manage just fine and be thankful for the bare exigencies. Her resilient pioneer spirit is her greatest asset.

When Louisa Mae is pressured by a coal company to sell her farmland, she fights their cupidity tooth and nail. However, "Louisa's refusal to sell her land pits her against her impoverished neighbors as well as a powerful company" (Piehl 248). Her neighbors cannot reap the financial benefits unless there is a unified, mass sell-out, so George Davis, the novel's villain, offers a warning threat when he burns down her barn.

The literary archetype of the barn burner is highlighted in William Faulkner's short story "Barn Burning." The antagonist is Abner Snopes, an uneducated sharecropper who resorts to cowardly barn burning to seek revenge on neighbors, his perceived enemies, just as Davis does in this novel. It is a typical situation of the "haves and have-nots," so for both George Davis and Abner Snopes, the ultimate motivations are greed and resentment toward those who have prospered. This same plot from Faulkner's "Barn Burner" is extended in the 1958 film *The Long Hot Summer* starring Paul Newman and Joanne Woodward. The protagonist cannot dispel his reputation as a barn burner no matter how many years lapse or how many miles away he travels.

Unable to stop the fire, Louisa Mae "dropped to the porch without a word" (Baldacci 278) and suffers a stroke from which she does not regain consciousness. An attorney, who is also a long-standing friend, tries to thwart infringement of her land by the corporate aggressors, but he speaks to an unsupportive jury backed by angry townspeople who have forgotten the respect they once held for Louisa Mae. It is a tell-tale sign that friendships are sometimes forged by and then lost because of money. Now they have a mob mentality with only greed on their minds. In a simply contrived turn of events, the children's mother, who for the entire time they have resided in the mountains has been in a coma, miraculously awakens and appears in the courtroom where she proves her children do indeed have a capable parent. It is highly unlikely that she could rise from her sick bed and be able to speak eloquently to a jury. However, this is the only perceived weakness in an otherwise beautifully written novel.

As a side note, Baldacci's *Wish You Well* was the first book selected in the All America Reads program. This choice is most likely due to Baldacci's portrayal of the protagonist Lou Cardinal as both an avid reader and writer. She follows in the footsteps of her deceased father, a well-known author. Additionally, Baldacci and his wife established the Wish You Well Foundation, which encourages literacy in the U.S.

Works Cited

Baldacci, David. *Wish You Well*. New York: Warner Books, 2000. Print.

"Forecasts: Fiction." *Publisher's Weekly* 247.29 (2000): 171. Literary Reference Center. Web.

Hamilton, Geoff, and Brian Jones. "Baldacci, David." *Encyclopedia of American Popular Fiction*. New York: Facts on File, 2009. Bloom's Literature. Web.

Inge, M. Thomas. "David Baldacci." *Literature: The New Encyclopedia of Southern Culture*. Chapel Hill: University of North Carolina Press, 2008. Print.

Piehl, Kathy. "Wish You Well." *Library Journal* 125.14 (2000): 248. Literary Reference Center. Web.

Esther Walton
The Waltons directed by Earl Hamner

Earl Hamner's heart-warming television series *The Waltons* spans several generations. He recounts the wonderful moments of mountain life even during the Great Depression. However, in the sometimes harsh environment of the Blue Ridge Mountains of Appalachia, tragedy also strikes families. Season 6 of the series titled "Grandma Comes Home" validates that circumstance.

Before her stroke, Esther Walton is a loving but stern disciplinarian of both her grown son John and her grandchildren; she is also a feisty wife to her husband Zebulon. The actress Ellen Corby, who plays Grandma Walton, suffered a stroke in real life, so her personal story line was seamlessly worked into the show's script. After a year's absence for rehabilitation, Grandma Walton returns to her Virginia home.

Welcomed by a joyous family, Grandma is not the only person who must adjust to her loss of speech. In their excitement as they gather around

Grandma, the children forget this fact and Jim Bob blurts out, "Grandma can't get a word in edgewise." She sees her great-grandchild for the first time as she receives kisses all around. Grandma nods, mouths "Hello," points, and uses other gestures to communicate. Additional signs of her condition are apparent—the stroke has paralyzed the right side of her body. In her halted gait, she first her lifts and then drags her leg forward. Her right hand curls inward and is more or less useless.

On a moonlit evening, tender and poignant words are spoken by John Walton as he stands on the porch with his mother. "I'm going to miss hearing the sound of your voice. In the meantime, we'll find out that there's nothing to be afraid of in the silence." He adds that just being near each other matters the most.

Although Grandma is determined to settle into life again on Walton Mountain, she discovers new limitations due to her stroke and muteness. While all other family members are outside, this former family storyteller tries to answer the telephone but can only gurgle unintelligible sounds. Sweeping the porch is difficult with only one hand; so is trying to securely hold her great-grandchild. Rather than allow her to be useful around the house, her family mollycoddles her to the point that she is resentful of their protective attitudes. She struggles to mutter protests, but they do not "hear" her.

Zeb is concerned that Esther's personality is quite different since her return. He cannot get a "rise" out of her now, no matter how ornery he is. Trying to find the cause of this change, he stays up all night to read her journal and is saddened to discover that she believes her loss of speech is punishment for being so sharp-tongued in the past, so although she cannot speak kind words, she has promised God that in the future, she will extend only love and affection to her family.

Works Cited

The Waltons. Dir. Earl Hamner. Perf. Michael Learned, Ralph Waite, and Will Geer. Warner Bros. Entertainment, 1977. DVD.

Vine's Cherokee Father
A Parchment of Leaves by Silas House

Silas House's novel *A Parchment of Leaves* relates the tale of Vine, a Cherokee woman who marries Saul Sullivan, a white man. Vine is her father's favorite child, so he is devastated when Saul takes her off the Buffalo Mountain settlement of Redbud to live in the flatland region of God's

Creek. Although not reared in the traditional Cherokee culture, Vine makes the trip on foot back up the mountain to visit family as often as possible and to stay connected to her Native American heritage.

When her father suffers a stroke, Vine rushes to his side to attend to both his physical and emotional necessities. His entire left side is paralyzed, but he reaches out his right hand to touch Vine's cheek. His face is drawn on one side, his brow is wet with cold sweat, and his shoulder and arm seem like wood. Vine, who hides her tears, is shocked to see him so still because he has always been a man of motion, always busy with work to do; now he looks like a corpse.

Vine's father has lost "ayeli," his center, an important Cherokee spiritual tradition. Common among many Native American tribes is "honoring the four directions ... creating and maintaining harmony and balance in the personal, social, environmental, and spiritual realms" (Garrett and Garrett 149). Of importance is stepping into the Native Circle to become aware of the energy available and how to use it for power in order to discover one's purpose. Some of the rituals used for healing "include sweat lodge, vision quest ... pipe ceremony, sunrise ceremony, sundance, and powwow" (150). Without knowledge and experience in these traditions, Vine is unable to help her father find his center.

Bedridden, her father can only whisper occasional prayers in Cherokee, a language Vine does not understand. She recalls how powerful and decisive he was when she was bitten by a copperhead. He immediately went to work on her without saying a word, even though she could see fear on his face. He prayed in a loud and strong voice the beautiful words of his native tongue until she felt comforted.

Now, in lieu of speech, he relies on "a slate and a stub of chalk" (House 136) lying across the blanket covering his legs to communicate his needs and wishes. The slate and chalk, normally used in classrooms during the early years of education, symbolize that Vine's father, once a proud and imposing figure, must now depend on these rudimentary items. He has become as helpless as a child; in a reversal of roles, she has become a parental figure and teacher, as well as her father's voice.

Works Cited

Garrett, Michael Tlanusta, and J.T. Garrett. "Ayeli: Centering Technique Based on Cherokee Spiritual Traditions." *Counseling and Values* 46.2 (2002): 149–50. Academic Search Premier. Web.
House, Silas. *A Parchment of Leaves*. New York: Ballantine, 2002. Print

PART II

Emotional Factors

6

Characters Who
Display Idioglossia
and/or Cryptophasia

Nell
Nell directed
by Michael Apted

The movie *Nell*, directed by Michael Apted, was filmed in North Carolina near the Eastern Cherokee Indian Reservation. The story was initially performed publicly on stage as playwright Mark Handley's *Idioglossia*. The screen version was later produced by 20th Century Fox in 1994. Nell's speech can be considered a combination of idioglossia and cryptophasia—her language is skewed by her mother's speech patterns due to a paralyzing stroke, and her twin speak is apparent as she continues to talk to her deceased sister May in the cabin mirror. When the film opens, Nell's childish voice is heard, but the audience cannot understand her speech. A sheriff's investigation uncovers the primitive existence that Nell and her mother have been living for years. Nell, a so-called "wild child" lacks both social skills and luculent language, for she has no knowledge of contemporary civilization.

Two doctors agree to unlock the mystery of Nell's unintelligible speech and feral lifestyle. She screams when Jerry tries to reach for her, but he finally gains her trust as her "gianga" or guardian angel. Incidents with a family Bible and Nell's communication in the mirror with May help the doctors slowly unfold the multiple layers of the enigmatic girl's life: her fear about the "evidors" or the evildoers, who raped her mother, triggered her stroke, and caused her pregnancy with twins Nell and May. The distorted language the girls learned was caused by partial paralysis affecting their mother's speech. Because it is the only language Nell has heard and spoken, she is unaware that outsiders cannot decipher her unique attempts at communication. Conversely, she does not understand them.

When unscrupulous teenagers in town discover her undeveloped sense of propriety, they have fun watching her imitate their movements and words. In her innocence, she pulls her dress up over her sylphlike body to reveal her "titties" while she mimics the boys' actions and words. Displaced from her beloved mountains in a mental hospital, Nell withdraws emotionally, refuses to acknowledge others around her, ceases verbalization entirely, and begins to exhibit autistic mannerisms such as glazed stares into space and rocking her body back and forth. In short, she has turned inward and moves through the hospital hallways in a zombie-like trance.

During the court scene, Nell uses Jerry as an interpreter to speak in her own defense and her own language: "You know big things but you don't look into each other's eyes," she says to the people gathered in the crowded courtroom. In a double entendre, Nell puts them in their *place* and also teaches them the importance of *place*—that her remote lifestyle in the mountains, her world of virtual silence except for the sounds of nature, has much more to offer than the noisy, rushed lives they live, often personally disconnected to others.

After Nell tells the doctors that they too are hungry for silence, Jerry and Paula understand what their intrusion in Nell's life has done to her. Living back in the mountains, why would she need to change or improve her speech patterns? The wildlife that surrounds her certainly will not question her manner or clarity of communication. She has no difficulty expressing herself with vocal tone and body language.

Clearly, there are numerous gaps or indeterminacies in the plot of the story about Nell. For example, how does her mother have the money to pay for the continual delivery of groceries? What has happened between the time of her mother's death and burial until the film opens? Jerry discovers an old newspaper article about Nell's mother, so why only now are townspeople and reporters interested in Nell and insist on sensationalizing her story? It is also unlikely that Nell, who has just come from a hospital's mental ward where she was virtually in a catatonic state, is ready to stand and address a courtroom full of strangers.

On the cusp of being a woman, as evidenced by the scenes of her naked in the lake, Nell is quite capable of surviving in her sylvan existence. She is uneducated, so it is improbable that she could ever easily transition to a place in modern society. Nell is perfectly content with her life in the mountains; it is not unreasonable, merely different. However, as soon as outliers step in, they label her a depraved waif and troubles begin. All the "do-gooders" in town, who are determined to save Nell, whether their intentions are misguided or based on personal or professional gain, are the real evildoers from whom she must be protected.

Works Cited

Nell. Dir. Michael Apted. Perf. Jody Foster, Liam Neeson, and Natasha Richardson. 20th Century Fox, 1994. DVD.

Twins Frank and Delores
Nightwoods by Charles Frazier

Charles Frazier's Southern Gothic tale *Nightwoods* is set deep in the Appalachian Mountains of North Carolina during the early 1960s. Packed with an "almost Shakespearian formula for violence, love and mayhem" (Caldwell 91), the novel's overriding themes include isolation, loss, identity, and the darkness of humanity. Nonverbal twins, Frank and Delores, whose names mean "truth" and "sorrow" respectively, indicative of their past, are inherited by their Aunt Luce whose name means "light," indicative of the future. After their mother Lily is murdered by her husband Bud, the children's step-father, the twins arrive at the abandoned mountain lodge where Luce lives as the caretaker; however, she is perplexed by their unusual feral behavior and glaring, distrustful eyes.

The delayed speech patterns of twins, who are often premature, are most likely caused by environmental factors, not genetics. Twins have the "worst language teachers" (Epstein 7): each other. The private language they share, which might seem like telepathy, often blocks communication with others. Researchers have studied two forms of secret language:

> (1) shared understanding—speech directed generally but unintelligibly to the parent, although apparently clearly understood within the child pair, and (2) private language directed exclusively to the other twin/sibling—not intelligible to the parent, but apparently clearly understood and used only within the child pair ... characterized by highly dependent relationships ... their high level of contact and shared experiences predisposes them better to understand each other [Thorpe et al. 43].

Frank and Delores have agreed to a pact of silence. Because they do not speak, stiffen their bodies at affection, remain stoic and silent against pain, and are quick to slip away from her watch, Luce is unsure of how to mother them. She slowly begins to deduce the reasons behind the children's immovable posture toward her. Most telling are their "bleak, silent tears" (Frazier 44) the first time she tries to unclothe and bathe them. Her suspicions of abuse at the hands of their rumored pedophile step-father are confirmed when she encounters Bud, who is determined to permanently silence the twins by entombing them in a dark, bottomless mountain pit.

An expert on the effects of psychological trauma, Dr. Judith Herman explains her stance on the relationship between atrocity and silence: "atrocities are acts so horrifying that they go beyond words" for people who experience them. This silence of victims plays into the hands of perpetrators like Bud who want to hide their crimes. In fact, "in order to escape accountability, the perpetrator does everything in his power to promote forgetting" (qtd. in Jensen 347), most often threatening to kill victims or their loved ones if they tell and then acting in indignant denial that the crimes were ever committed. Bud, as an imposing adult authority over the children, has used coercive control on the twins to break down their "resistance and spirit" by forcing them to engage in acts that are morally repugnant. Violence in isolation "creates disturbances in intimacy … no room for relationships of mutuality or cooperation" (354) as evidenced by the twins' detached attitude and withdrawal from Luce's attempts to care for them. Obstacles to justice are the mental walls that victims often construct; these walls do not come down until the danger has been removed and individuals feel safe once more. Only then can they break the silence, re-form connections, and begin to recover (357).

One of the most frightening attributes Frank and Delores display is a violent, predatory tendency. When they matter-of-factly kill a hen and then splatter its eggs all over each other's faces, one could surmise that they have an undeveloped appreciation for living things, and they do not understand the consequences of their actions. However, cruelty to animals by children is often a precursor to violence and criminal behavior later in life. It is also an indication that the children have been abused, perhaps by an adult who performed acts of animal cruelty in their presence to emotionally disturb them or to destroy their sense of safety by threatening that they could be the next victims of such treatment. Their subsequent animal cruelty could be in imitation of what they have observed, especially in an attempt to display power and control over a living entity smaller and more vulnerable than they (Johnston 1).

Obviously, there is a direct correlation between what they have witnessed in the past and what they now do. When it is revealed that Bud killed their mother in front of them after she found him with the children behind closed doors, and he has not been held accountable for his actions, their strange behavior is better understood. Dr. Herman notes that once people see "up close the evil human beings are capable of" they will never see the world, other people, or themselves in the same way (qtd. in Jensen 358).

Even more bone-chilling for Luce is the twins' obsession with fire. As soon as Luce turns her attention away from them, they look for something to torch. Their favorite pastime of playing the kindling game, in which they competitively arrange and re-arrange twigs for an imaginary fire, is most worrisome. Oddly, without provocation or reason, they seem to delight in destroying the possessions and property of others.

From pre-historic days, humans have always been fascinated with fire for a plethora of reasons including warmth, protection, cooking, communication, purification—the list is endless. Nevertheless, pyromania of children, an "impulse control disorder," allows them to reduce tension and stress or to receive instant gratification leading to euphoria. Some of its causes are parental psychopathology, lack of a positive father figure in the household, attention seeking, and revenge for past incidences, all factors in the twins' past which can be attributed to their relationship with their step-father. Specific indicators include setting fires purposely, feeling stress before setting the fire, having a heightened curiosity about fire, and experiencing satisfaction and relief after setting the fire ("Pyromania"). It appears that their behavior mirrors that of Bud, who was "early traumatized by fundamentalists raving about the blood of Jesus ... the sacred shedding of it" (Caldwell 91), for he burns Luce's personal items in the lodge fireplace as a warning threat to her and as evidence that he is in the vicinity.

Both of these aberrant behaviors, as well as their overt pleasure in destruction, retaliation against adults (especially after being victimized by neglect or sexual abuse), and running away from Luce are suggestive of anti-social personality disorder (APSD). Sadly, they may also be cries for help that Frank and Delores cannot verbalize.

Rather than vocal whining or whimpering, the twins growl, holler, hoot, or screech. Certainly this type of communication is difficult for Luce to interpret. Yet, the intensity of their angry body language indicates fear and self-preservation, understandable reactions to their past interaction with Bud. In a surprising scene in the novel, the children, who have been monosyllabic at best in their twin speak, by uttering only holophrases, say clearly, one-by-one, as they repeat to Bud their mother's final invective when she caught him sexually abusing the children, "I'll fucking kill you if it's the last fucking thing I do" (Frazier 205).

A seemingly unusual manifestation is the twins' lack of regret, sorrow, and guilt, but perhaps not so abnormal in their internal world where in their geminate minds only the two of them now exist. With their mother gone and Bud still a murderous menace, "they strive to learn, albeit bizarrely, how to be human in the face of great evil" (Caldwell 92). They physically band together and use their private language to become one against a society they do not trust.

Works Cited

Caldwell, Wayne. "Nightwoods." *Appalachian Heritage* 40.1 (2012): 90–92. Print.

Epstein, Randi Hutter. "Fix Speech Problems Early, Experts Now Say." *New York Times*, 30 November 1999, F7. Lexis Nexis. Web.

Frazier, Charles. *Nightwoods.* New York: Random House Trade Paperbacks, 2011. Print.

Jensen, Derrick. *A Language Older Than Words.* New York: Context Books, 2000. Print.

Johnston, Joni E. "Children Who Are Cruel to Animals." *Psychology Today*, April 2011. Previously in *The Human Equation.* Web.

"Pyromania." Encyclopedia of Mental Disorders. Web.

Thorpe, Karen, et al. "Prevalence and Developmental Course of 'Secret Language.'" *International Journal of Language & Communication Disorders* 36.1 (2001): 43–62. Academic Search Premier. Web.

7

The Voice of Glossolalia

Ginny Powell
The Truest Pleasure
by Robert Morgan

The Truest Pleasure, a narrative of love set in the early years of the 20th century, was named the *Publishers Weekly* Best Book of the Year in 1995. In this novel, "poverty dictates practicality" while the characters wrestle with "courtship, family, hard work, and matters of the spirit" (Conway 315). Ginny Powell, the narrator and protagonist of Robert Morgan's novel, finds spiritual fulfillment attending Pentecostal holiness services. The opening scene is of a brush arbor evening service attended by Ginny, her father Ben, and her stammering brother Joe.

When the preacher invites people to accept the baptism of fire, Joe jumps up and begins to shout, but the sounds he emits seem like babbling or gurgling. At first, Ginny thinks he is stuttering, but he is actually speaking in tongues. Her father waves a handkerchief while tears run down his face, but no sounds come from his mouth. When a sweating and emotionally wrought Preacher McKinney locks eyes with Ginny, she does not know what she is saying, even though she is aware that her tongue is moving. She hears a voice speak in tongues, but cannot discern the speaker, for the voice is unfamiliar. While issuing several strange sounds, she finally realizes that it is she who has been speaking in tongues. The preacher claims that in her "mouth is the light of stars" (Morgan 8) and she senses that time has been enhanced and intensified by the music.

"According to holiness Pentecostal beliefs, speaking in tongues represents the voice of the Holy Ghost, one aspect of the Trinity, actually inhabiting a person's physical body" (Puckett 156). Those who speak in tongues often describe it as an out-of-body experience over which they have no control. They are unaware of what they are actually saying, or what the Holy Spirit is saying through them, so other individuals are often designated as interpreters. After the service and while the family rides home in the wagon, Ginny does not want to speak about what happened in the arbor, for the experience of being filled with the Holy Spirit's voice seems too sacred to taint with the human voice.

Unfortunately, Ginny's inclination toward holy fervor is not shared by her husband Tom who refuses to accompany her to the brush arbor. Their difference of opinions regarding worship causes a major rift in their marriage. The division between this man and woman reflects the real life clash between the "Protestant work ethic" and "born again evangelicalism" (Conway 315). Tom, a faithful attender of weekly services at a local church, believes worshipers should be reverent as they reflect on the Sunday sermons. He eschews the incomprehensible babbling and wild, jerking bodies that are "slain in the spirit," earmarks of the Pentecostal experience. Thinking about Julie rolling around on the floor of the arbor in front of their neighbors causes him embarrassment. He suspects that she is being foolishly led toward some type of satanic worship and logically questions why the services occur only at night and in the woods. Julie has no answer for him except that she feels closer to God, although one night in a close encounter at the altar with other worshippers, the only thing she feels is a hand that reaches out to squeeze her breast.

Traditionally, in the mid-to-late 1800s, the man of the house made all decisions for the family, and his wife and children were expected to comply. The man was also considered the family spiritual leader, determining where, in what manner, and how often the family would worship, as well as leading nightly devotions in the home. Joe is understandably hurt and angered by Julie's rejection of his spousal spiritual authority. This couple has reversed customary roles; unlike most of the married women in Appalachian literature, Julie is outspoken and rebellious toward her quiet, reserved husband. The only times they are in harmony are when they toil together on the farm and when they become one flesh in their bed. Ginny's eventual epiphany occurs toward the end of the novel when she tends to her husband as he is dying; she realizes that both service and love making can be forms of praise. Most importantly, she understands that "silence is the language of God" (334), and to hear His voice she must be still and quieten her own thoughts.

Even though Ginny has brief moments of silence, she is eloquent and well-read, and is neither naturally quiet nor submissive. Giving an Appalachian woman from that era such a strong voice and allowing her to tell the story was an unusual choice on Robert Morgan's part. Readers must view Ginny through a trifocal lens. Her character is revealed by three important aspects of her life: spirituality, intimacy with her husband Tom, and an appreciation of the mountain landscape. Detecting which is of these is her "truest pleasure" is not an easy task, for their edges blur and overlap.

Works Cited

Conway, Cecilia. "The Truest Pleasure." *Appalachian Journal* 27.3 (2000): 314–17. Print.
Morgan, Robert. *The Truest Pleasure*. Chapel Hill: Algonquin Books, 1998. Print.

The Primitive Baptist "Dunkers" *Wish You Well* by David Baldacci

The setting of David Baldacci's novel *Wish You Well* is in 1940 atop a mountain in southwestern Virginia where twelve-year-old Lou and seven-year-old Oz have moved from New York to live with their great-grandmother Louisa Mae Cardinal. The acculturation of the children entails rising at 5:00am to milk cows, chop wood, and spend the rest of the day working in the expansive fields. Riding up and down the mountain on horseback or in a wagon driven by Eugene allows them to witness the lives of Appalachian people. One particular tradition they observe is baptism.

Eugene and the children espy a large gathering of people beyond several schooner wagons and automobiles. They watch a man with rolled-up sleeves submerge people into the muddy water of the McCloud River. Eugene informs them that the ritual being performed is a "dunking." One woman, whose baptismal attire is pinned-together bed sheets, moves in "small, deliberate circles, unintelligible chants drifting from her, her speech that of the drunk, insane or fanatically religious in full, flowering tongues" (Baldacci 228). Nearby, a man lifts up serpents in both hands.

Lou and Oz, who were christened in a formal ceremony in a New York Catholic church, are understandably fearful of the unusual sight. When they ask Diamond about the function of the poisonous snakes, he explains they are used to drive away evil spirits, and the preacher is not trying to drown the people being dunked. He elucidates, "them folk Primitive Baptists" (229) who have unusual beliefs such as women should not cut their hair or wear make-up. They also abide by particular tenets about heaven and hell, therefore strongly discouraging sinful acts.

They "live and die by the Scriptures," he adds. Lou is fascinated by the doctrinal wisdom coming from the lips of an uneducated boy who says that church is wherever he happens to be and he and God regularly "jaw fer a bit" (229).

According to Howard Dorgan, Primitive Baptists theologically have "no parallel in Appalachia" (8) except for a few similarities with the German Baptist Brethren who are also dunkers. They normally wait until adulthood to join the church and "go down to the water" (20), a practice also adhered to by the Anabaptists. Because the river baptisms do not occur frequently throughout the year (148) a large number of people are sometimes baptized when the rituals are scheduled.

The children are surprised when they see Eugene walking toward the river to speak to the preacher. While being dunked, Eugene is held under so long they begin to worry. Then Diamond pulls at his cowlick and follows Eugene, telling Lou this is his ninth time to be dunked, as he works on getting closer to heaven. He claims that the Bible promises an angel is sent to look over an individual each time he or she is dunked.

Works Cited

Baldacci, David. *Wish You Well.* New York: Warner Books, 2000. Print.
Dorgan Howard. *In the Hands of a Happy God.* Knoxville: University of Tennessee Press, 1997. Print.

Adam, Blue and the Professor
Sunday's Silence by Gina B. Nahai

Sunday's Silence opens in the Summer of 1975 in Knoxville, Tennessee, where journalist Adam Watkins has left his assignment in Lebanon and returned to investigate the death of his father Little Sam Jenkins, a legendary Holy Roller known throughout Appalachia, but a man Adam barely knew. His mother Clare had seduced Little Sam, who gave in to her "temptation with all the force and fury aroused in him by the snakes" in the church (Nahai 41), but she failed in her attempts to prove the paternity of her illegitimate son. The contrast between what Little Sam professed and how he lived is the epitome of hypocrisy found in manipulative preachers who "feel called" to the ministry. Married four times, Sam preached that divorce is a sin; he fathered multiple children but refused to care for them, all the while telling congregations how precious God's children are; he planted his seeds in any woman who would lie down with him, yet he did not hold back his scathing words of judgement: the "seeds of the mother will be reaped by her children" (43).

Two places of horrific living conditions haunt Adam's memory: a derailed, rusted-out freight car, where he lived isolated in filth and with constant hunger; and The Tennessee State Home for Children, where his mother abandoned him to suffer severe beatings from the superintendent for his defiance and silence, yet "he did not move or make a sound" (123) during the brutal punishments. Like other Appalachian fiction, Nahai's novel is about a character who runs from his or her past but eventually returns home, searching for truths.

The alleged murderess of Little Sam Jenkins is Blue Kerdi, who moves in silence like a mythical apparition and figuratively seduces every man who looks upon her; with Adam, the seduction is literal. He describes Blue as "water … clear, transparent, and strong" (Nahai 13) and likens her voice to smoke with its "seductive power of a Scheherazade" (Zaleski 50). A newspaper account about the murder, allegedly caused by Blue handing a poisonous snake to Little Sam, identifies her as a "snake-handling, strychnine–drinking, fire-breathing" (Nahai 16) temptress, but she is different from the Holy Roller women who consider her a Jezebel. Blue fears neither a Holiness code, nor God, nor her husband. She is judged for her silence in the church for never testifying, speaking in tongues, or showing interest in the sermons, yet she handles snakes at every service.

The Pentecostal Holiness Church has set certain tenets for true believers:

> Faith in three stages: Regeneration … salvation from sin; Sanctification … set apart on the course of a strictly moral, self-denying, ascetic lifestyle to prepare believers for the final stage similar to that of the followers of Christ as recorded in Acts of the Apostles 2:4; and Baptism of the Holy Ghost … filled with the spirit … to speak with other tongues, as the Spirit gave them utterance [66].

Concerning her novel with an intensely complex plot, the author "claims that she wanted to compare the fundamentalist regions of Appalachia with those of her native Iran," but Lieding avers that objectivity is missing, and rather than a focus on the "fabric of Appalachia," the book displays only its "fascinating anomalies" (109). Nahai certainly did her homework to include accurate geographic details about the region, but all the mountain people are characterized as poor, ignorant, and gullible. In the middle of the novel, the reader is abruptly whisked away from Appalachia and taken to Kurdistan, an awkward but necessary journey to explain Blue's origins and why she marries the odd, small professor, as well as the back story about her fearlessness of snakes.

Many characters experience times of silence and/or speaking in tongues. Little Sam Jenkins, who survived 446 snakebites and always refused medical care, was once bitten on the tongue by a copperhead. He continued to preach until his tongue turned black "as shoe polish" and swelled until he could no longer speak. Adam's grandmother Rose is one of Little Sam's most fervent followers, "handling snakes and talking in tongues and moving with the spirit, [falling] unconscious to the floor in every church gathering" (39). From fear of punishment, the boys at the state home move noiselessly and whisper to each other. A mute woman's voice is restored by Sam during a healing service. In Europe, the professor remains silent to guard his identity as an Arab Jew. Blue calls to Adam in silence, enters and withdraws in silence, and together they are silent, spoken words unnecessary between them.

Adam's disillusionment in humanity teaches him that yearning "for safety is man's greatest weakness" (126) and his inclination to stay connected renders him powerless. After he leaves Appalachia, he relies only on his own resources, until he returns and meets beautiful Blue.

Works Cited

Nahai, Gina B. *Sunday's Silence*. New York: Washington Square Press, 2001. Print.

Leiding, Reba. "Sunday's Silence." *Library Journal* 126.17 (2001): 109. Literary Reference Center. Web.

Zaleski, Jeff. "Sunday's Silence." *Publisher's Weekly* 248.38 (2001): 50. Literary Reference Center. Web.

Janet Hollar
Tear Down the Mountain:
An Appalachian Love Story
by Roger Alan Skipper

"Blessed are they who hunger and thirst after righteousness, for they shall be filled" (Matthew 5:6). This verse begins Roger Alan Skipper's debut novel *Tear Down the Mountain,* set in a church under construction in rural West Virginia. In the initial chapters concerning the Holy Ghost Fire Revival meeting at Knobby Creek Church, Skipper endues his work with various colloquial references to the speech patterns of those speaking in tongues. He writes that church members' "blaze of voices had burned to a bed of hot coals" and they "welled like a thunderhead, slopped out, receded and surged again" (5); their "voices like dogs,' give it up, turn it loose" (20). Samarin defines the voice of glossolalia as a "meaningless but phonologically structured human utterance believed by the speaker to be a real language but bearing no systematic resemblance to any natural language, living or dead" (qtd. in Poloma 421); however, believers attest that the Holy Spirit is speaking through them, so if there is no interpreter present, only God needs to understand.

Once again Janet Hollar yearns to be blessed with the gift of tongues. For sixteen years, God has been silent, but now the Holy Spirit has taken hold of her, illustrated by uncontrollable muscles wrenching in her limbs. Gathered around her, church members chant and praise the Lord. Some tell her to let go and others to hang on, but while they "spouted out tongues" (Skipper 3), Janet's mouth remains frozen and "stoppered up" (4–5). The words will not take root in her mouth. She understands that she does not fit in—that until she becomes a Holy Ghost "growed-up" (10) who speaks in tongues, the church will not allow her to teach Sunday school or even collect fundraising money. Sadly, the one institution that should welcome and accept all believers narrow-mindedly rejects one of its own, merely because it is believed her faith is not strong enough to be wholly sanctified with this spiritual gift.

The evangelist encourages congregants to continue their emotional frenzy and physical flailing, common during a special week set aside for a Southern revival when the weather is hot as Hell. Hoping to whip up more people for the next night's service, he shouts above the noisy crowd while he gulps for air between each plea. "Bring your friends-a ... loved ones-a ... strangers you meet on the highways and byways-a" (6).

In Appalachia, one can find "a variety of denominations that differ fiercely in doctrinal principles" (Nunnally and Reid 182), but many in remote areas agree on an "inspired-impromptu" style of preaching that in some Southern churches is a precursor to the worshipers speaking in tongues. Sermons are delivered in extemporaneous-rant style in a "loud, physically altered voice, punctuated by panting, thought-marking ejaculations (haah), holy catchwords such as *glory* and *hallelujah,* and glossalalic outbursts" (183).

In his book *In the Hands of a Happy God,* Howard Dorgan discusses the results of his research on five particular aspects of old-time hermeneutics:

> Extemporization, the total yielding of oneself to a spur of the moment speaking process to allow God's thoughts to be processed.... Distinctive delivery modes featuring dramatic and exaggerated cadence, chant, song, and inflection.... Emotionality that demands that the speaker yield to tears, shouts, wails of laughter, or other forms of deeply felt personal responses.... Physicality, the delivery being enhanced by dynamic gestures, pronounced strides and leapsconstant movement.... Transcendence, the claim being that the "blessed" preacher is 'carried out,' lifted above the natural state to a very special status of communication, with the understanding that at these moments God takes control of a message [128].

If these expectations are not met, the preacher may be perceived as cold, dead, and unblessed rather than alive, quickened by the touch of God. Normally, during the inspired meetings, the preacher and elders begin the emotional mannerisms. Then the women join in with shouts, cries, arm waving, and spirited movements up and down the aisles (137–38), often ending at the altar with being slain in the spirit by holy fire. Poloma describes the experience as "going under the power or resting in the spirit … so filling a person with a heightened inner awareness that the body's energy fades away" and the individual usually drops to the floor (421). Janet aches to be an active participant with manifestations of the Holy Spirit upon her, but God remains elusive.

After a long time in the church waiting for God to answer her prayer, Janet needs respite and cooler air, so she slips out the back door of the sanctuary and follows a stream of cigarette smoke to find out who is at the other end. Sid Lore, a transplant from Tennessee who has been watching her from outside the doorway, looks and talks like the devil himself. Even though Sid mocks, and in her opinion blasphemes the Holy Ghost, Janet is drawn to him, as "poverty and pipe dreams mark the lives of … the outsider couple" ("Tear Down" 36). Each acknowledges and feels the repercussions of being labeled a misfit, for while Janet attempts to draw Sid into the church, he tries his best to draw her out.

Works Cited

Dorgan, Howard. *In the Hands of a Happy God: The No-Hellers of Central Appalachia.* Knoxville: University of Tennessee Press, 1997. Print.

Nunnaly, Thomas E., and Jennifer Reid. "Preaching Style, White." *Language. The New Encyclopedia of Southern Culture.* Volume 5. Chapel Hill: University of North Carolina Press, 1989. Print.

Poloma, Margaret M., and Brian Pendleton. "Religious Experiences, Evangelism, and Institutional Growth within the Assemblies of God." *Journal for the Scientific Study of Religion* 28.4 (1989): 415–31. JSTOR. Web.

Skipper, Roger Alan. *Tear Down the Mountain: An Appalachian Love Story.* Brooklyn: Soft Skull Press, 2006. Print.

"Tear Down the Mountain: An Appalachian Love Story." *Publishers Weekly* 253.29 (2006): 36. Literary Reference Center. Web.

Preacher Clyde Freeman
The Evening Hour by Carter Sickels

Cole Freeman walks through the dilapidated building which had once been the Pentecostal church, an unadorned "room with aisles big enough for the ladies to fall down in fits of passion" (Sickels 46), that his grandfather Clyde Freeman pastored. Cole stands behind the battered pulpit as if looking out on a congregation, an ironic image for one afraid to speak and whose peers shunned the boy who belonged to a church full of crazy snake handlers. He recalls his grandfather's delivery, a blend of Holiness and Baptist, as he preached hell fire damnation for hours in an "old-timey gasp … sucking in and spouting out air" (47) ending each phrase with an "ah" modulation. His warnings of fiery punishment were unlike the words of other preachers who spoke of blessings, grace, and joy.

On special days, the pulpit was bookended by crates of snakes, silent for a while; then they began to rattle. The church followed the New Testament verse, "They shall take up serpents" (Mark 16:18). His grandfather, who touched the snakes only if he felt God had anointed him, was then afraid of nothing:

> He would reach into the hissing, slithering pile as if in a trance and hold a snake above his head and shout. At first the congregation would hush, a quivering silence falling over them, and then a collective rush of sound would follow— gasps, praises to God. Some would go forward and pass the serpents … people shouted, wept, danced. Once he watched an old man drink strychnine [48].

Timothy Yeung's research reveals that Pentecostal beliefs have come under attack for being grounded in emotionalism as well as anti-intellectualism. However, he gives credence to the sincerity of believers in their worship practices. They have "protested against 'hollowness,' the use of religious words without religious experiences to back them up" (58). Vondey reports in Todd Breneman's book the claim that Evangelicalism promotes "affections, feelings and emotions" to validate their tenets, but Pentecostals explain that this theology stems from their "native environment" (Vondey 201). Sickels tactfully paints a picture of the sincere pulse of the "Pentecostal faith [and] guilt that so often plagues societies where the fundamentalists are the majority" (House 96).

When Cole took his boyhood friend Terry Rose to hear his grandfather preach, at first Terry sang the gospel songs, praised God along with other worshippers, and even dropped to his knees. Cole was disappointed when Terry later said that speaking in tongues was not real. Then he made fun of the women whose bodies had been shaking in holy fervor. Terry rolled around on the ground and mimicked their movements and words, "breathing heavily and crying, 'Oh, Jesus, oh,' grabbing himself and writhing around" (122).

Preacher Freeman had looked forward to the day when his grandson would lift a serpent, testify, and preach like Cole's mother Ruby did when she was only eleven years old. That was before she turned her back on God and became a harlot, according to her judgmental father, but she had no problem speaking, her voice clear and sure; however, no one wanted to hear Cole's stammering, stuttering speech. Cole had heard rumors about his mother, minimal information gleaned "from the family silence, the quiet that was wrapped around her name" (48). He had been told that she abandoned him, but the truth is revealed after his grandfather's death— her father had run her off after she gave birth to her illegitimate son. Apparently, this man of God judged and exiled his daughter either to punish her or to save his own reputation in the community.

Clyde met his wife Dorothy while he was preaching throughout the coal camps in West Virginia. During a tent revival in Wolf Run, Dorothy's sisters were only curious to witness "all that tongue speaking … and hollering" (97), but Dorothy was smitten. Clyde baptized her, but she did not receive the Holy Ghost until after they were married. While working in her vegetable garden one day, she sensed an unusual feeling before she knelt down in the dirt and began to pray. "Next thing I knowed I was speaking another language" (97). Unfortunately, after the "holy-roller revival," Clyde changed from a hardworking man to one who did not "lift nary a finger on the farm" (98) because he had been called to preach.

Works Cited

House, Silas. "Carter Sickels. The Evening Hour." *Appalachian Heritage* 40.4 (2012): 94–97. Print.

Sickels, Carter. *The Evening Hour*. New York: Bloomsbury, 2012. Print.

Vondey, Wolfgang. "Homespun Gospel: The Triumph of Sentimentality in Contemporary American Evangelicalism." Todd M. Breneman. *Religious Studies Review* 40.4 (2014): 201. Web.

Yeung, Timothy. "The Characteristics of William Seymour's Sermons: A Reflection on Pentecostal Ethos." *Asian Journal of Pentecostal Studies* 14.1 (3011): 58. Web.

Sarah Beth Childers
Shake Terribly the Earth
by Sarah Beth Childers

Shake Terribly the Earth, Sarah Beth Childers' memoir collection published in 2013, is replete with tales of her childhood in Huntington, West Virginia. The book "announces a new clear voice in Appalachian nonfiction, free of cant, free of even the rumor of a stereotype" (Oderman back cover) and contains authentic narratives with universal themes about

Childers' family, school events, religious rituals, and social activities in Appalachia. The title alludes to Isaiah 2:21, the verse with which she prefaces her book: "To go into the clefts of the rocks, and into the tops of the ragged rocks, for fear of the Lord, and for the glory of His majesty, when he ariseth to shake terribly the earth." Nicole Del Cogliano commented that the "strength of this book is in its ability to evoke our own personal responses" (376).

In the chapter titled "At His Feet as Dead," another Biblical allusion in Revelation, Childers relates her Holy Spirit baptism at the New Life Victory Center when she was only ten years old. Eager to sit at the feet of Jesus in the "throne room of Heaven" (Childers 73), Sarah Beth stepped forward to receive the Spirit. Her Sunday school teacher placed her hand on Sarah Beth's forehead and prayed fervently "in tongues, a cacophony of syllables," and waited for Sarah Beth to discern the winds of Pentecost and be blessed with the spiritual gift. Emotionally crushed, Sarah Beth cried because her ability to speak this "foreign" language did not materialize. She began to whisper the familiar phrase she had heard from her mother's lips, "Shenkavadonka" but it was not from her own soul. Expected to fall to the floor when slain in the Spirit as other children around her had already done, Sarah Beth remained upright, outside the "throne room." Eventually she grew weak from standing so long, so she decided to lie on the floor beside the other children who had actually felt the move of the Holy Ghost. Uncertain of the anticipated mode of conduct, Sarah Beth had a spurious spiritual awakening.

Childers' pretense of being overwhelmed by the Holy Spirit is similar to writer Langston Hughes' painful childhood experience. In his essay "Salvation," Hughes recalls summer revival meetings at his aunt's church. Before one particular service, the church members were determined that all the little "lambs" were to be saved that night. The adults sang, prayed, shouted, groaned in the spirit, and lay hands on the children. While most of the lambs went forward to the altar to be saved, twelve-year-old Langston kept waiting to see the light right before Jesus would come to him, just as his aunt had described. Langston was unfamiliar with religious jargon, so he believed her words were literal; he was disappointed that he did not see a light, and Jesus did not show up to save him. Fearing the church service would not end until all children were seated on the mourner's bench and realizing he was the dilatory lamb, Langston rose to his feet. As he walked to the front of the church, the entire congregation broke into "waves of rejoicing" (Hughes 153) because of his lie, his false salvation experience, his innocent hypocrisy. That night he cried in bed, no longer believing that there was a Jesus. Although the pressure from the adults was well meaning, unfortunately they forgot that salvation is a personal experience, not an event that can be scheduled ahead of time and marked on a calendar. Childers eventually realized this truth when she had a genuine holy baptism at age thirteen.

During the worship service of praise at New Life Victory Center, Sarah Beth observed church members who raised their hands, "stamped their feet, clapped wildly … sobbed, shouted, and twirled as they ran laps around the sanctuary." Shouts of "Amen" and "Praise the Lord" rang out from those who were "drunk on Jesus" (78). People prophesied in tongues and on occasion, worshippers would be caught up in holy laughter, which spread from one individual to another, no logical explanation for its origin.

Beth Newberry noted that throughout the memoir, Childers was successful with "well- crafted scenes, balanced with dialogue and appropriate amount of descriptive detail" (124). An interesting point that Childers shares is that because she was reared on the hallowed King James Version of the Bible, she heard the "vocabulary and verb forms of 1611 mixed freely into Appalachian speech" (80). The language seemed quite natural to Childers due to her background, a tug-of-war between her mother's Pentecostal religion and her father's Fundamental Baptist doctrine.

Works Cited

Childers, Sarah Beth. "At His Feet as Dead." *Shake Terribly the Earth: Stories from An Appalachian Family*. Athens: Ohio University Press, 2013. Print.

DelCogliano, Nicole. "Shake Terribly the Earth: Stories from an Appalachian Family." *Appalachian Journal* 41.3/4 (2014): 375–77. Print.

Holy Bible King James Version. Nashville: Thomas Nelson, 1981. Print.

Hughes, Langston. "Salvation." *The Short Prose Reader*. Ed. Gilbert H. Muller and Harvey S. Weiner. Boston: McGraw Hill, 2009. Print.

Newberry, Beth. "Shake Terribly the Earth: Stories from an Appalachian Family." *Appalachian Heritage* 42.2 (2014): 123–26. Print.

Oderman, Kevin. Back cover of *Shake Terribly the Earth*.

A Stuttering Silence

Cole Freeman
The Evening Hour by Carter Sickels

The setting of most well-known Appalachian literature is in the past, so readers not from the region might envision women still washing clothes on a scrub board, children bathing in a tin washtub on Saturday nights, and shotgun-toting men distilling moonshine in remote areas of the mountains, all stereotypes still portrayed by the media. Carter Sickel's debut novel *The Evening Hour* is set in present day Appalachia in Dove Creek, West Virginia. It examines "the dark, wonderful heart of Appalachia … its complex beauty, ugliness, joy and sorrow" (House 94) and addresses "the more troubling aspects of contemporary Appalachian culture, including mountaintop removal coalmining, and prescription drug abuse" (Morton 362), but the author also draws attention to gender issues.

The protagonist, twenty-seven-year-old Cole Freeman, struggles to come to terms with his traditionally perceived feminine position as an aide in a nursing home, but the types of patients and their conditions are a perfect combination for his masculine side business of buying and selling prescription drugs, such as OxyContin, Xanax, and Valium, with much of the extra income used to support his grandparents.

Cole's stuttering issues began in boyhood. He always felt like an outsider, the weird preacher's kid who could quote scripture but was not interested in sports or the other hobbies of his peers. His grandfather, a hardcore Pentecostal preacher, had prayed in earnest for God to remove his stutter. When the prayers were not answered, his grandfather, who sergeant-drilled him with scripture memory, ordered Cole to speak through his stuttering. He "has been scarred by the fanatical Pentecostal religiosity of his sanctimonious grandfather" (House 95) who deemed his grandson's speech as God's punishment and that he has reaped the sins of his mother, but Cole always took comfort in the words of Moses, "I am slow of speech and of a slow tongue" (Exodus 4:10), for he knew God had tapped Moses, who lacked eloquence, as his servant and used him in a mighty way.

Sitting many nights at the kitchen table with an open Bible, Cole tried to read the scripture clearly. Memorizing verses was easy for him, and his grandfather was pleased that he learned quickly, but "it was the speaking that gave him trouble" (40) because the words "were bunching up in his mouth" (52). A well-known and revered preacher for most of Cole's life, his grandfather is now in the early stages of dementia, and his speech has been altered by a stroke. This godly man, who had delivered fiery sermons from the pulpit for many years, says "fewer words" (5) each day. Cole transfers him to the nursing home so that he can care for him, but his condition worsens. Attempting to speak to Cole, he wheezes in loud, hoarse gasps. His mouth begins to move in a "strange, ugly way … gumming and spitting, his tongue pushed out over his bottom lip like a worm" (90).

Cole has always been a shy, quiet soul around other people. "All his years of stuttering had taught him something about silence. He spent most of his childhood too terrified to speak" (Sickels 16). Classmates laughed at him and teachers pitied him. Cole ignored the taunts until students gave up and walked away. When he was called on in class, he would mumble his words to mask their halting delivery. He was told repeatedly by classmates to "Spit it out, retard" (59), a hurtful comment he has not forgotten.

His stutter slowly began to disappear, but even now in certain situations, when he is tired or nervous, especially around women, he reverts to old habits with his "twisted … tongue in rippled knots" (9). Although his mouth seems ready and his mind knows the words he wants to utter, he still cannot control his tongue-tied speech. Unintentionally caught in a drug fracas, Cole has a gun pointed at this face. Trying to diffuse the volatile situation, Cole takes a deep breath, "trying to gain control over his tongue, his mouth, his words" (193). His best boyhood friend Terry Rose returns to Dove Creek, yet Cole initially avoids him; when he is confronted by Terry, his voice stammers and then stops, but Terry had never minded Cole's stutter. He has had few friends over his lifetime, for as soon as Cole would open his mouth, he was treated as an outcast. His mind could formulate coherent thoughts, but no matter how much he yearned to speak, his "words came out mangled" (59).

After Cole's mother Ruby, whom he saw only once when he was ten years old, returns for just one day, Cole yearns to go with her, but when he tries to ask her permission, "his tongue felt heavy and flat" (110). After several unsuccessful attempts, he begins to stutter uncontrollably. When she comes home for her father's funeral, Cole agrees with his grandfather that she is a whore. Ruby tries to reach out to her son, but he pulls back to avoid her touch, his "tongue thick and hurting with words never spoken" (101).

Before a huge sludge spill wreaks havoc on the sides of the mountain and valley below, the author describes the effects of the mountain top removal on both the residents, startled by the thunderous blasting "which ripped through the silence" (41), and the land, once forested hills now barren and covered in dust. Sickels, "by juxtaposing decay with natural beauty, captures the darkness and hope of the environmental justice movement" (Morton 363). Although devastated by the unspeakable loss, Cole helps to search for bodies swallowed up and swept away by the dark, smelly floodwater. Even when his mouth does not work, Cole recognizes he can be useful to the community by work the rest of his body accomplishes.

Attending a town hall meeting with a girlfriend who has helped to build his self-esteem, Cole surprises himself, as well as those who know him well, when he steps out in the aisle and speaks eloquently in rebuttal to the coal company's representatives who dodge answering questions about their culpability, repeat false concerns, and make promises they do not intend to keep. Seeking to establish a respectable place and purpose in Dove Creek, when he stops dealing drugs, Cole begins to mature "naturally through his interactions with other activists" (Sickels 362) and finds his voice to speak about issues important to his entire community.

Works Cited

House, Silas. "Carter Sickels. The Evening Hour." *Appalachian Heritage* 40.4 (2012): 94–97. Print.

Morton, Jessica. "The Evening Hour." *Appalachian Journal*. 41.3–4 (2014): 362–63. Print.

Sickels, Carter. *The Evening Hour*. New York: Bloomsbury, 2012. Print.

9

Silenced by Trauma or Grief

The characters in this chapter are silenced by a variety of traumatic experiences, either physical or emotional and sometimes both, especially the death of loved ones, rape and post-traumatic stress disorder (PTSD).

Jane Woodrow (Woody) Carmody
Tomorrow River by Lesley Kagen

Similar to Frank and Dolores, the traumatized, mute twins in Charles Frazier's *Nightwoods* who communicate in cryptophasia when they do speak, Lesley Kagen's *Tomorrow River* centers on Shenny and Woody, who also engage in twin speak, but only Woody is mute. Both Frank and Dolores witness their mother's murder at the hands of their stepfather, but Woody, who utters her last words "Mama ... gone" (Kagen 105), believes her mother has been strangled to death by the twins' paternal grandmother.

Set during the summer of 1969 in Rockbridge County, Virginia, *Tomorrow River* introduces the reader to Shenandoah (Shenny) Wilson Carmody and her twin Jane Woodrow (Woody) who live at Lilyfield, the prestigious estate of the wealthy Carmody family. Identical in physical appearance, these sisters could not be more dissimilar. Shenny is a bold eleven-year-old who cannot corral her sassy tongue while Woody "will not say one word ... she's gone mute" (10) since her mother's disappearance. Shenny, the narrator and most well-developed character, is "optimistic, determined, devious, precocious to the point of implausibility, and wrong about practically everything" (Hiett 45). In hopes that Woody will find her voice again, Shenny is tenacious in her sleuthing to find their mother, but she must keep it a secret from their father, a renowned judge whom Shenny addresses as His Honor, a sign of the emotional detachment and dysfunctionality of their paternal relationship.

Shenny assumes her mother's role to love and care for the fragile Woody who seems unable to do much for herself, but her greatest challenge is to protect her sister from their cruel father. A "raving drunk who locks the girls in the root cellar overnight when they disobey his orders to stay home" ("Tomorrow River" *Kirkus*, 104), he forces them to spend the entire time on their knees.

This inhumane act is similar to the punishment Myra receives from her husband John in Amy Greene's *Bloodroot* when he locks her in the narrow crawl space under their house where she must lie face down all night. In Sue Monk Kidd's novel *The Secret Life of Bees*, fourteen-year-old Lily Owens kneels on grains of uncooked rice, punishment for disobeying her father, T. Ray. The positions these females are commanded to assume indicate, of course, submissive postures to their authoritative male abusers.

Walter Carmody also threatens to send Woody away if she does not speak soon, but she is unable to do so even with Shenny's urgent coaxing. Interestingly, although there is no mention that Woody is autistic, she displays several signs of the syndrome—at intervals "standing stone cold still" (Kagen 154), perhaps in a seizure, with a faraway look as if sensing danger, rocking her body back and forth, wagging or flapping her arms while spinning around, repeatedly blinking her eyes, sucking her thumb, emitting strange noises, and abruptly running away. When Shenny observes Woody's body go rigid "as stiff as her name" (61), and locks her eyes, she knows her sister is ready to take flight.

The major symptom of autism that Woody lacks is a strong aversion to touch, although she is selective in who can come near her. Woody does allow Shenny and occasionally E.J., a playmate, to touch her. When Woody is particularly stubborn and refuses to follow her sister, Shenny resorts to two words: "root cellar," and Woody immediately complies. Shenny fears her sister has "turned completely inside out" (25), but often after a violent crime, the brain of the traumatized individual has difficulties sorting and filing information, thus the resulting systems seem to be out of order, as if the synapses are not connecting. A doctor has examined Woody and pronounces her vocal chords to be healthy; his diagnosis is "hysterical muteness" (52).

Before Evelyn Carmody's disappearance, the girls engage in twin speak, terms which Shenny continues to use in secret to Woody. Some of their code words and meanings are: grimmery—worried; hushacat—everything will be all right; *bellow-bellow*—do not be afraid; *meetone*—I'm hungry; *rabadee*—I'm sorry; *cantaboo*—run; and their favorite, *boomba*—love. When Shenny places Band-Aids on Woody's raw knees, she wants to express her appreciation to her sister, so "slowly, she opens her mouth ... parts her lips" (166) but merely sticks out her tongue to lick the side of her twin's face, so Shenny replies in the same manner.

Shenny informs the reader, "The Carmody girls are good at keeping our mouths buttoned up. Practice make perfect" (119), a statement that is possibly ambiguous. The obvious reference is to Woody's muteness, but also to Shenny's ability to keep secrets about the girls' clandestine adventures as they search for their mother. They eavesdrop on conversations, question and spy on townspeople, and remain silent about the potential clues they find.

Another theme throughout the book is the Southern mores and unwritten rules of "Thou shalt" and "Thou shalt not," which dictate how women should appear and behave in the presence of men, especially their fathers and husbands, and the unpleasant consequences of ignoring those guidelines. Intelligent and independent Evie Carmody discovers how serious the powerful Carmody men are and remarks to Walter, "You're trying to snuff out my spirit" (88). Refusing to allow his wife to work, he is angry at her disinterest in joining The Ladies Auxiliary. She is also appalled by how the men belittle the black people in their town and is saddened by the jokes the men make about individuals who are physically or mentally different. Her mother-in-law, who panders to her own husband, tries to rein in Evie's rebellion against the way things are done in the South, but to no avail.

Her journey for the truth teaches Shenny about the fallacy of first impressions. A rite of passage occurs when Shenny discovers that people and appearances can be deceiving. Perhaps the worst realization is that the Carmody males—her grandfather, her uncle, and her father—are at their core, evil men who use their power and wealth to remove any obstacle or individual who deters them from getting their way. Nevertheless, reuniting with their mother restores peace and safety to the twins' lives. A second physician who examines Woody explains that her artistic mind cannot process the horror she has witnessed and experienced, so as protection it caused her to stop talking, for out of sound, out of mind. Even though her initial attempts to speak again are "gobbled-gook" (Kagen 334), Shenny cherishes the sound of her sister's voice.

Works Cited

Hiett, John. "Tomorrow River." *Library Journal* 137.12: 45–46. Literary Reference Center. Web.

Kagen, Lesley. *Tomorrow River*. New York: New American Library, 2010. Print.

"Tomorrow River." *Publishers Weekly* 257.11 (2010): 37. Literary Reference Center. Web.

Mark and Maggie Underhill
The Hangman's Beautiful Daughter
by Sharyn McCrumb

Sharyn McCrumb, who has established a solid literary career among contemporary Appalachian writers, "considers herself primarily a story-teller" (Mosby 3). She is best known for her Ballad novels, which focus on "the culture of Appalachia, a depiction of the region, its society," (Silet 1) and the individuals who feel a strong affinity to the past. McCrumb's novel, *The Hangman's Beautiful Daughter*, which won The Best Appalachian Novel Award in 1992, is framed by a cast of characters, all loners who live in Dark Hollow, Tennessee. McCrumb comments that the theme of her novel was "being 'betwixt and between,' to be caught in a liminal state between life and death ... the polluted river, the stillborn child ... the old woman with the sight who talks to the dead ... the young suicide who still contacts his grieving sister—involved someone or something lingering on the threshold ... reaching both ways" ("Keepers 185).

Although McCrumb thoroughly develops all her characters, the most endearing and intriguing is Nora Bonesteel, first introduced in this novel and a woman who has become her recurring signature character. The author says that "through Nora Bonesteel, I channel the Cherokee folk tales, the mountain legends, and the family ghost stories—changed, perhaps to fit the narrative, but not invented, because I don't have to. In Appalachia, the magic is already here" (McCrumb *Appalachia* 51). Nora "learned early to live with solitude, and finally, to like it" (McCrumb 107). Like a lofty fortress on Mount Olympus, Nora's house sits atop Ashe Mountain. Guided by premonitions, she possesses the wisdom of Solomon and shares it with others when it concerns them, yet the locals are fearful of her gift of the Sight, so they keep their distance.

Regarding the brutal murder/suicide at the Underhill farm, the dead rabbit with no blood on it is an enigmatic clue to the crime, but readers might think it only an odd detail and discount it ... until the truth is revealed later in the narrative. Obviously suffering from shock, Mark and Maggie sit together in silence on the sofa staring mindlessly at the television screen, but still, their behavior seems unusual in this situation. "Alone, alone, all all alone" (McCrumb 48), Maggie says dramatically, as if her portrayal of Ophelia in the school play has transcended her present life. In fact, astute readers will notice elements of the Shakespearian tragedy that the author weaves throughout the plot of the novel.

Reserved and "courteous but wooden in their replies" (58), Mark and Maggie offer minimal information about their family dynamics to the sheriff. During the graveside service, they stand close together but separate from the rest of the mourners and remain unemotional, "their impassive faces studied the ground in front of them, never once straying to take in the sight of the four coffins" (65). Not a tear is shed by either one.

While together, they do not speak to each other. Although teachers and classmates attempt to offer condolences, Maggie remains stoic. Believing them only curious, she refuses to respond to their genuine concern. However, she does retreat to the restroom to cry quietly over some unkind comments. Mark is impervious to everyone at school who extends sympathy or advice to him. When the sheriff suggests grief counseling, Mark declines for both of them without consulting Maggie, even though the siblings are not coping well with the patricide, fratricide, and suicide that have shattered their world. Clearly, they have adopted their parents' vehement mistrust and lack of acceptance of outsiders.

They grow more aloof and never speak to each other about their loss. Mark sleeps for hours on end, a symptom of his depression, but Maggie seems to be more affected by the tragedy. While studying a family portrait hanging above the living room sofa, she tries to discern the turning point when the Underhills' lives went terribly wrong.

Maggie maintains her indifferent attitude at school but loathes living in the cold stillness of the house with shadows of bloodstains on the walls, visual reminders of Josh's handiwork. The siblings continue to move throughout the house like zombies, seemingly uncaring about their future. Maggie refrains from revealing the recurring nightmares she suffers and Mark does "not break his silence" (130). It occurs to Maggie that they might as well live alone since "their paths seldom crossed" (224) and Mark, who maintains an inward focus, apparently does not "mind her silence" (224).

Under normal circumstances, one might expect the teenagers, even if they were not close before the tragedy, would lean on each other for comfort. However, Mark seems oblivious to Maggie's prolonged grief over Josh and the depression she suffers. He, on the other hand, becomes obsessive about finding a clue to the location of the treasure. Both of them seem headed toward a black hole of despair which will necessitate a long ladder from which to climb. Perhaps they treat each other in such an icy manner because they *are* close in age, and their family proclivity for silence has hindered an emotional bond between the siblings.

In her article about trauma caused by the murder of loved ones, Dr. Sarah Goodrum would categorize individuals in this type of situation as bereaved "victims" who through shock or disbelief are able to contain or "control their physical expressions of emotional upset" (143). Dr. Elaine G. Caruth reports that the contemporary study of trauma focuses on the derivation of "history and memory" (8), but she also refers to the factors at the core of Sigmund Freud's research on trauma. One principle centers on disturbing dreams, such as Maggie's, replaying for victims the "horrifying scenes of death they have witnessed" (7), especially if they are totally unprepared to deal with death and its aftermath. On the other side of town, nightmare sequences of war also disturb both the sleeping and waking of Deputy Le Donne. Teenagers, like Mark and Maggie, are at the stage of their lives when they begin to ponder their own mortality, but they have not reached a maturity level or developed the emotional skills needed to contend with the reality of death.

Maggie eventually reveals to the reader the years of brutal beatings from their father who relished dispensing pain with his wooden paddle "Sergeant Rob," while their mother, no "maternal refuge" (250), was complicit. Besides having a cruel side to his personality, their father did not transition well from military to civilian life after his retirement but continued to demand a rigid, controlling environment for his family. The children remained fearfully silent due to his outbursts of rage, and they learned not to speak of the beatings, or they would be more severe the next time. Sadly, young Simon learned to imitate his father's irrational and despicable behavior.

Only mountain people can fully understand and appreciate the sentiments of home that are well described in the scene of "The Santa Claus Train." Sheriff Spencer Arrowood arrives to monitor the custom of presents being thrown to waiting children when he muses about the various people he observes:

> Living in the mountains cost most of these people on the hillside ten years of their lives. And maybe a future for their children. But they wouldn't leave—not for jobs or love. Those that did leave sickened in exile in the ugly cities of the Midwest, pining for the hills of home. Even people who weren't poor … could make more money and advance in their careers by moving elsewhere, but they continued to stay in the shadows of the mountains. Why can't we just get out of these hills? he wondered for the thousandth time. Why are we so willing to sacrifice so much to live in this beautiful place? If this were the Garden of Eden, God couldn't drive us

out of here with a flaming sword. We'd sneak back when the angel wasn't looking [177–78].

An unusual telephone call is a hint to the reader of the possibility that two of the Underhill children might have the Sight or at least experience excursions as does Nora Bonesteel, the character for whom the Celtic notion of liminality resides in the novel. Scottish writer Elizabeth Sutherland notes that this "philosophy is the merging of dark and light, natural, and supernatural, conscious and unconscious" (qtd. in "Keepers" 185). When Nora senses Josh's spirit approaching her on the mountain, she withholds judgment of his violent deeds and advises him to let go of his past. Her gift manifests itself in patience, wisdom, and pensiveness long before she acts.

Le Donne wonders what emotions Maggie and her brother are holding back as he watches her sing "like a plaster angel" and then acknowledges, as in his own life, the difficulty in pinpointing emotions one is restricting, "love or hate, fear or rage" (196). Like Shakespeare's tragic Ophelia, Maggie almost loses her life in the water until Josh's beckoning spirit saves her.

Works Cited

Caruth, Cathy. "Parting Words: Trauma, Silence, and Survival." *Cultural Values*. 5.1 (2001): 7. Academic Search Premier. Web.

Goodrum, Sarah. "The Interactions between Thoughts and Emotions Following the News of a Loved One's Murder." *OMEGA* 51.2 (2005): 143–60. Academic Search Premier. Web.

Hilyard, Nann Blaine. "The Hangman's Beautiful Daughter." *Library Journal* 118.5 (1993): 126. Academic Search Premier. Web.

McCrumb, Sharyn. *The Hangman's Beautiful Daughter*. New York: Onyx, 1992. Print.

McCrumb, Sharyn. "Keepers of the Legend." *Bloodroot: Reflections on Place by Appalachian Women Writers*. Ed. Joyce Dyer. Lexington: University Press of Kentucky, 1998, Print.

McCrumb, Sharyn. *Sharyn McCrumb's Appalachia*. Oconee Spirit Press, 2011. Print.

Mosby, Charmaine Allmon. "Sharyn McCrumb." *Critical Survey of Mystery & Detective Fiction*, 2008. Literary Reference Center. Web.

Silet, Charles L.P. "Sharyn McCrumb." *Guide to Literary Masters and Their Works*, 2007. Academic Search Premier. Web.

Sally Swanger
Cold Mountain directed by Anthony Minghella

The historical novel *Cold Mountain* by Charles Frazier (1997) offers a rich "rhetorical, ornate, 'modernist prose' that emphasizes voice rather than image and action" (Hovis 493) instead of the minimalist approach that became popular during the late 20th century. An example of Southern literature in which the past is unfolded through dialogue (Jones 620), it rendered easily to its adaptation on the screen by Anthony Minghella in 2003. Set in North Carolina's Haywood County in the Pisgah National Forest during the Civil War, *Cold Mountain* is based on the experiences of Frazier's own great-great uncle.

The story of W.P. Inman's journey home to his love Ada Monroe, is a "gripping tale of female survival and solidarity as well as a hymn to the stark, unforgiving beauty of the southern Appalachians" (Boswell). The main focus of the narrative is the impact of war on those left behind, especially women. With few men to help manage the farms, austere weather, and a short supply of money and food, Cold Mountain is indeed a cruel place to exist. Frazier's work is appropriately titled—the women's beds are cold for lack of menfolk, the unforgiving land does not yield to the plow, and the brutalities and trauma of war leave empty places at the table as well as painful voids in the heart.

After Ada's father, the Reverend Monroe, dies and she is left entirely alone at Black Cove, her pride keeps her from revealing the hardships and destitute circumstances in which she finds herself. Depicting a common reaction by mountain people when charity is offered, Ada hides and pretends to be away when Esco and Sally Swanger come to check on her. Although from a bustling city, it seems she has adopted the mindset of proud Appalachians. Ada, the protagonist of the novel, is out of her natural environment. No pioneer, she is a dainty, former Charlestonian who reads classic literature, plays the piano, and knows how to offer Southern hospitality to guests, but she has no experience in planting crops, raising livestock, firing a rifle, fixing fences, or even cooking. The Swangers send stalwart Ruby Thewes, a most likeable and resilient character, to teach Ada the "language" of Cold Mountain, "the processes by which the mountain culture is perpetuated ... for Ada a form of initiation" (Bruccoli and Baughman).

Neither does Ada know the language of love. While she waits for his return, Ada reflects about Inman, "I count the number of words that passed between us, Inman and me—not very many." Not only geographically out of place, Ada journeys into unfamiliar emotional territory with her feelings for Inman. Rather than speak to him verbally, she carries trays to serve various beverages and plays her beloved piano, hoping the music will catch his attention and speak her convictions when words fail her. Inman too is painfully shy around Ada; in his awkward attempts to convey his feelings for her, he appears at social events, always remaining outside, and is able only to sputter, "If it were enough just to stand, without the words." In her letter to him, Ada writes about her "silent fear that in the years since we saw each other," the war would change everything that had transpired between them.

Of interest is the book Ada gives to Inman. Throughout his war experiences and journey home, he carries Ada's photograph inside William Bartram's *Travels Through North Carolina,* whose descriptions helped other writers "shape early impressions of the region's landscapes" (Watkins 35) and the inhabitants who called it home. Bartram, like Inman, traveled alone through the Blue Ridge Mountains and had to overcome seemingly unsurmountable obstacles to reach his goals and to survive (Bynum 97).

The sweethearts, who barely know each other, communicate much more with their eyes than the few words they manage to speak. Holding onto the memories of the impromptu, passionate kiss of departure, they exchange few words the night they are reunited, but bashful glances acknowledge that they will make love for the first time.

Inman's being gunned down the following morning in a shootout with the Home Guard is foreshadowed years earlier by the sight Ada sees when she looks down the Swangers' well and sees in the mirror crows surrounding a fallen figure, an obvious symbol of death. Ada's unrealistic hope clings only to the dark figure walking toward her in the watery vision. Inman manages to survive four years away from Cold Mountain, both as a Confederate soldier and a deserter in a long journey back to Ada. That he has only one night with her is bittersweet irony.

In Frazier's novel, Esco Swanger relates a troublesome tale about the Owens family in a neighboring town who are suspected supporters of the Federals and are threatened by the marauding Confederate Home Guard. They slap both the man and woman, trying to coax Mr. Owens to reveal where he has buried a hoard of gold and silver treasure. Even after the Guard shoots the family's pair of bird dogs, ties Mrs. Owens' thumbs together and hangs her over a tree limb, he refuses to speak. Apparently his lucre takes precedence over his wife.

However, in Minghella's film adaption, the Swangers are terrorized by the Cold Mountain Home Guard, character foils to the peaceful, God-fearing citizens. Esco and Sally's two sons abandon their military posts and conceal themselves in the shelter of the family barn, symbolic of their mother's womb where they are protected from the outside world. Mortified, Sally watches from the cabin window as the Home Guard hang Esco's body from the clothesline, freshly-laundered sheets representing the sanctity of home being soaked by blood, indicating the brutality of war that reaches far beyond the battlefield and the scars left behind.

When Sally screams, one of the guardsmen, hoping to bring her sons out of hiding, yells, "Come on out, Boys. Mama's calling!" As they burst from the barn, they leave the safety of the metaphorical womb and become vulnerable to the fate which awaits them on the outside, much like aborted babies. "No!" is the last audible word Sally screams. The boys, who have consciously exchanged their Confederate muskets for peaceful farm rakes and hoes, are defenseless against this band of sharp-shooting men.

While Ada and Ruby struggle to free Sally from the fence, she whispers the words, "Don't bother." The rope around her neck represents the umbilical cord which connected Sally to her sons, and removing it parallels the separation of the sons from their mother. Rather than live with an empty womb, Sally prefers to die with them, forever maintaining her maternal connection in silence. Additionally, the literal tightening of the rope around her neck is a symbolic severing of her vocal cords and foreshadows her inability to ever speak again.

The brutalization of witnessing the murders of her husband and sons is more than she can endure, and it has taken its worst toll on Sally—the loss of her voice. Trauma specialist and expert psychologist Judith Herman notes that "in the aftermath of trauma," victims are affected both biologically and psychologically. At times, individuals in extreme grief completely shut down to the point that they feel nothing, not even pain, and eventually lose their identities. They may become passive and uninterested in initiating mutual relationships, but the emotional breakdown makes them incapable of resistance to external forces (qtd. in Jensen 351–54).

This is certainly applicable to Sally, for throughout the remainder of the film, she is passively compliant but mute. She smiles occasionally and nods her head in acknowledgment when spoken to, but she does not initiate communication. She is most responsive to the Appalachian tunes played by Ruby's father and his musical sidekicks and fellow deserters. When one of them observes Sally's silence, he asks, "Don't she ever talk?" to which Ada and Ruby reply in unison, "Can't!"

Works Cited

Boswell, Marshall. "Frazier, Charles." *Encyclopedia of American Literature: The Contemporary World, 1946 to the Present.* Volume 4. New York: Facts on File, 2008. Bloom's Literature. Web.

Bruccoli, Matthew J., and Judith S. Baughman. "Ada Monroe." *Student's Encyclopedia of American Literary Characters.* New York: Facts on File, 2009. Bloom's Literature. Web.

Bynum, Dixon. "Nature Writing and Writers." *Literature: The New Encyclopedia of Southern Culture*. Chapel Hill: University of North Carolina Press, 2008. Print.

Cold Mountain. Dir. Anthony Minghella. Performers Jude Law, Nicole Kidman, Donald Sutherland, and Renee Zellwegger. Miramax, 2003. DVD.

Frazier, Charles. *Cold Mountain*. New York: Atlantic Monthly Press, 1997. Print.

Hovis, George. "Minimalism." *The Companion to Southern Literature*. Ed. Joseph M. Flora an Lucinda Hardwick MacKethan. Baton Rouge: Louisiana State University Press, 2002. Print.

Jensen, Derrick. *A Language Older than Words*. New York: Context Books, 2000. Print.

Jones, Diane Brown. "The Past." *The Companion to Southern Literature*. Ed. Joseph M. Flora an Lucinda Hardwick MacKethan. Baton Rouge: Louisiana State University Press, 2002. Print.

Watkins, James H. "Autobiography and Memoir." *Literature: The New Encyclopedia of Southern Culture*. Chapel Hill: University of North Carolina Press, 1998. Print.

Fia Forbes
The Last Sin Eater
by Francine Rivers

Francine Rivers' 1998 novel *The Last Sin Eater* is set in the Smoky Mountains during the mid–1850s. Adapted to film by Michael Landon, Jr., the book's subject, although considered by some critics as mythology because of its attempt to reconcile man's origin, purpose, and afterlife, is historically based on a religious tradition brought to Appalachia purportedly by immigrants from the British Isles, Wales, and Scotland who settled in the region. The text references numerous parallels to Biblical characters, events, and proverbs, so it can accurately be considered an allegory, specifically due to the characters' seeking atonement for sins, similar to the character Christian in John Bunyan's *Pilgrim's Progress*.

Ten-year-old protagonist Cadi Forbes is miserable "living in a house filled with sorrow and silence" (Rivers 77). She grieves from her mother Fia's rejection, believing it stems from her blaming Cadi for the drowning of her baby sister Elen. Fia turns her face and will not speak to her daughter. "No words passed between us. Not even a look. I was ... abiding under the shadow of death" (17). Fia is not the only silent one in the novel. Fear of reprisal causes some characters to hold their tongues, perpetuate lies, or withhold important truths. The author does not reveal the reasons for the many secrets until the novel's end, a true denouement.

Cadi's role is symbolic of humanity—impulsively speaking, reacting, or behaving in regrettable ways, then seeking forgiveness. Like St. Paul in Romans 7:19, she laments that she does not do that which she should, but does "the wrong I hated" (71). When her Granny Forbes dies and the sin eater comes to take away her sins, the entire assemblage turns its back except Cadi, who disregards stern warnings and makes eye contact with him. Seeing sadness in his eyes and hearing sorrow in his voice make her inherently curious about him and his function, so Cadi's primary goal is to find the sin eater, the detested outcast, and ask for absolution while she is living, hoping to regain her mother's love, break the wall of silence, and receive forgiveness.

A character similar to the Biblical John the Baptist, suddenly appears and begins to proclaim the ways of the Lord in a voice that carries throughout the valley. However, he likens himself to St. Paul, who formerly called Saul, was a sinful man of the world. The messenger tells Cadi that "the Lord spoke my name. In the midst of a storm, He struck me down so that I could not move or speak" (168). Similarly, when Saul, who persecutes Christians, is on the road to Damascus, he is struck by a flash of light from Heaven and rendered blind for three days (Acts 9:4–7). Another Biblical character with a similar story is Jonah, who disobeys God's mandate and boards a ship to flee his destiny. A literal storm arises and Jonah finds himself thrown overboard and in the belly of a great fish for his punishment. Like Cadi, these men are given warnings from God and are punished, yet eventually receive mercy after their repentance.

Kai, of the ruling family, seems to fear losing control of the community, so he commands people to stay away from the man of God because he will "set sons against fathers and fathers against sons" (106), an allusion to Exodus 34:7, in which the Lord tells Moses that he "will by no means clear the guilty; visiting the iniquity of the fathers upon the children."

Also noteworthy is that young Cadi and her friend Fagan are chosen to take the message of the man of God to the rest of the villagers. In Matthew 18:3–6, Jesus tells his disciples that unless they humble themselves like children, they will not enter the kingdom of Heaven. When they are charged to go together, as Jesus sent his disciples "two by two" (Mark 6:7), an obedient Cadi says to Fagan, "Wherever you go, I'll go" (279) the same sentiments spoken by Naomi to her mother-in-law Ruth, as a sign of her loyalty and commitment (Ruth 1:16).

To stop Brogan's attack on his own son Fagan, Cadi picks up a smooth stone and throws it at the back of Kai's head. Startled, he believes the rock comes from someone who has a "dead aim with that slingshot of his" (198). This scene parallels the Old Testament story of the young shepherd David who smites Goliath by hitting the Philistine giant with a rock from his slingshot (I Samuel 17:49). When an injured Fagan cannot go farther up the mountain, Cadi hides him "in the cleft of the rock," a symbolic place of safety where God also secures Moses (Exodus 33:22).

Of course, the sin eater is symbolic of Christ Jesus who, in Biblical accounts, takes upon himself the sins of the world. The bread and wine provided for the sin eater are the same items served to Jesus' disciples at The Last Supper. The history of the sin eater, in an apotropaic ritual, follows a fairly prescribed sequence of events with slight regional variations. The reviled individual kept his face covered beneath a hood, so that others could not see the ugly consequences of sin. Likewise, God turns away his face when his son takes the sins of the world upon himself while hanging on the cross. The sin eater, called when death was near, would be offered bread, and sometimes salt, on the chest or stomach of the moribund or deceased. A drink of wine, milk or beer was supped from a wooden mazer bowl. In some instances, the vessel was burned or the sin eater brought his own, and a pittance accompanied the beggar's feast. His purpose was to "eat" the sins, transferring them to himself and assuring the deceased's entry to Heaven. He also spoke an incantation to prevent the soul from roaming the Earth. Afterwards, he was shunned, sometimes driven away, like the Biblical scapegoat sent to the wilderness to die after receiving the people's sins at the temple altar. Interestingly, the Catholic Church, which ceased buying of indulgences during the Middle Ages, ex-communicated anyone claiming to be a sin eater, a usurper of the role of the priest during the last rites.

Patriarch Laochiland Kai, like a cult leader or false prophet who demands that his followers put complete trust in him, leads the Scottish clan to America and decides that the sect must designate a sin eater in the new world. The system used to single out the cursed individual is by drawing lots, the same way the priest Aaron chooses the scapegoat that will receive all the sins of the Israelites (Leviticus 16:8–10). Because Kai tells the people that the lot will fall to the one with the greatest sin among them, his ritual more closely resembles the one that Joshua performs (Joshua 7:14–18) to determine the Israelite who has kept the spoils of war, even though God had commanded that everything be burned. When Achan is discovered as the offender, he is stoned.

Shirley Jackson's short story "The Lottery" echoes the drawing of lots each year to decide which individual will be stoned to death. The purpose of the rite is unknown to the villagers, yet they accept and blindly follow the precepts of the past, seemingly without emotion as they pelt a neighbor or family member with the largest stones they can find. Brogan Kai expects his community to do the same, to follow him without question. Both the novel and the short story send a strong message about the foolishness of perpetuating a ritual which results in the death of an innocent person. The mythological tradition of sacrifice, usually of a virgin and often the daughter of a tribe's chief, to appease the gods and to insure good crops, is possibly the basis for these story lines.

The strength of Francine River's novel is its characterization. Cadi, her Granny Gorawen Forbes, healer Gervase Odara, elderly Miz Elda Kendric, and especially Bletsung Macleod, who has loved the sin eater for twenty years, are all fascinating female characters. They match strong and intriguing Biblical females, who are loved dearly by Jesus, which include Mary and Martha, as well as his mother Mary and Mary Magdalene, the first women to whom the risen Christ appeared. The reader can easily discern that one of the author's purposes for writing this novel is to present the plan of Christian salvation against the backdrop of a pagan ritual.

Works Cited

The King James Study Bible. Nashville: Thomas Nelson, 1975. Print.
Rivers, Francine. *The Last Sin Eater*. Carol Stream, IL: Tyndale House, 1998. Print.

Vine Sullivan
A Parchment of Leaves
by Silas House

Silas House's novel *A Parchment of Leaves* is set in Kentucky in the early 1900s. Vine, a beautiful Cherokee woman, leaves her native settlement of Redbud when she marries a white man named Saul Sullivan. Vine works diligently to gain acceptance from Saul's mother Esme and brother Aaron who are at first wary of Saul's choice of a Cherokee to be his wife. Unfortunate circumstances foreshadow an event that would be divisive for any family.

Vine cautiously approaches Saul one evening at dinner, but "as always, he ate silently, and I knowed that I would get no reply from him" (House 74). In some households, eating in silence is a common precept in order to enjoy a meal without digestive interruption and to give full attention to eating. Vine waits to reveal her fears about Aaron constantly watching, following, and suddenly appearing wherever she goes, yet Saul dismisses her apprehension and calls her foolish. Rather than respect his wife's plea, he ignores her and refuses to discuss it with her, even though others have also noticed Aaron's menacing behavior (75).

Of course, Saul would be reluctant to believe that his own brother is a threat to Vine, for in his mind, family does not violate family, and even though he loves Vine, he may believe that Aaron would not be interested in an Indian woman. Saul says nothing to Vine and refuses to meet her eyes. Thus Vine feels alienated from her husband, knowing he favors his brother over his wife. This is a setback to her initial acceptance into the Sullivan family and another reminder that she is an outsider, a Cherokee among white people.

While Saul works away from home, Vine is silenced from the violent rape of a drunken Aaron. Like a mama bear protecting her cub, she makes sure he does not repeat the act on Birdie. Only by a continuous surge of anger, adrenalin, and sheer grit is she able to bury his body, but she must never speak of the violation. Who would believe her story since no one believed her warnings? Disposing of Aaron's body is clever because he often leaves home without notice for long stretches of time. Although Aaron's disappearance does not raise suspicion, Vine's sleeping for almost a week does, for she is known for working from sunup to sunset.

After the tears between her legs begin to heal, Vine is determined not to speak of the rape or the murder, no matter how forcefully family and friends coax her to reveal the cause of her illness. The experience is not only too painful for Vine to recount, but she knows that its revelation could tear apart her family. Although she is a victim of Aaron's assault, she remembers the effort she made to be fully accepted by her white in-laws. As a result of her secret, she is victimized repeatedly, forced to remain silent when family members begin to surmise about Aaron's disappearance. Even though Vine's guilt and shame are overwhelming, she proves that she will be a survivor of this ineffable trauma—for her husband and her child—but first she must forgive herself.

Works Cited

House, Silas. *A Parchment of Leaves*. New York: Ballantine, 2002. Print.

Nola Barrett
In a Dark Season by Vicki Lane

Vicki Lane continues to receive acclaim for her series of chronicles about Elizabeth Goodweather (see *Signs in the Blood*, Chpt. IV), a likeable and recurring character in her novels, just as the fascinating Nora Bonesteel is in fellow Appalachian writer Sharyn McCrumb's canon. Both literary journalists and other writers such as McCrumb praise Lane's perspective of Appalachia. *In a Dark Season*, set in North Carolina, is no exception, for Lane's research of the history of Appalachia is evident by the book's structure with an antiphony of voices from the mid–1850s to the present, as well as her excellent use of diction.

Lane opens her novel with these lines: "The madwoman whispered … the old house spoke … no answer came, only the mocking echoes of memories" (1–2). She deftly weaves Gothic details such as "naked baby dolls twisted … dangling by nonexistent necks" (4) from beginning to end of her suspenseful narrative.

The silent character of *In a Dark Season* is Nola Barrett. Desperate to escape her past sins, she jumps from the porch of the old Gudger Stand house, a former drovers' inn. The author gives readers an interesting and informative history about the drovers' interactions with one another, both in camaraderie and competition, and how important the inns were for respite from their grueling work. Their story is the antecedent action and subplot of the novel.

Nola manages only to injure herself physically while remaining in an emotional hell, the causes intermittently hinted at throughout the book's pages. Elizabeth Goodweather is perplexed by the suddenly confused and voiceless Nola, former English literature professor at Mars Hill College and a ravenous reader and writer. Placed in the confinement of a nursing home, Nola is painfully aware of the "bewitchment of her tongue … she could think an action, but movement, it seemed, was restricted" (51). Her condition appears to be the result of a stroke, and the doctor, hired by one of her adversaries, confirms it. He also claims that she suffers from "lalorrhea" his mispronunciation (a red flag for readers) for the medical term "logorrhea," which means pathologically incoherent speech.

Nola's experience sheds light on elder abuse, a common problem in nursing homes with low standards for care. The most prevalent forms of maltreatment include "physical, psychological and sexual abuse, financial exploration, and neglect" (Natan and Lowenstein 20). Patients who have had strokes or are in advanced stages of dementia are easy targets—they cannot speak, therefore, they cannot report the abuse. Incidents of mistreatment are most often the result of the work environment: lack of nursing staff, unqualified or undertrained staff, frequent turnover, and a high number of patients to serve. A major underlying cause of this situation is to "maximize profits" (20).

Nola strains to overcome her torpor and form elusive words, yet they disappear before she can utter them. "Without speech, she was powerless

... where were the words?" (124). When trying to communicate during normal conversation, nothing but a "garble of nonsense syllables" (106) comes from her twisted lips. Conversely, she is able to recite lines of classic poetry to convey her situation in a secret "literary code" to Elizabeth, also an avid reader who recognizes the verses and deduces that an enemy is trying to keep Nola silent by sedation. Keeping patients medicated, and in some instances over-medicated to the point of oblivion is another unfortunate tactic used by untrustworthy elder care facilities. With patients in immobilized conditions, fewer staff are needed, and their work-load of tending to patients' needs decreases.

In the end, the combined critical thinking skills of Elizabeth, Nola, and Blake overcome the evil of unpolished miscreants in Marshall County. This fact illustrates the range of education among residents of the mountains, thereby helping to dispel the negative stereotype of all Appalachians portrayed as ignorant hillbillies.

Works Cited

Lane, Vicki. *In a Dark Season*. New York: Random House, 2008. Print.
Natan, Merav Ben, and Ariela Lowenstein. "Study of Factors That Affect Abuse of Older People in Nursing Homes." *Nursing Management* 17.8 (2010): 20–24. Academic Search Premier. Web.

Spence Hall
On Agate Hill by Lee Smith

Lee Smith's writing is known for its "emphasis on the folklore, myth, and landscape" of Appalachia (James 420). In her novel *On Agate Hill*, the character Junius Hall, the owner of Agate Hill, calls his plantation "a sad place of sorrow and death" (Smith 16). His thirty-five- year-old giant of a son Spence has returned from the Civil War, where he witnessed the death of his brother Lewis at the battle of Petersburg, and then disoriented, wandered around on foot until he was found. After the violence he endured during the war, Spence returns home with typical symptoms of post-traumatic stress disorder (PTSD), a diagnosis unheard of in the 1800s. Those who suffered from it at that time were commonly regarded as being crazy from the ravages of war.

Rarely speaking and labeled insane, Spence displays behavior that vacillates from gentleness to unexplainable aggression. For example, he carefully baits the little girls' fishing hooks but then grabs a huge catfish with his bare hands and smashes its body on the rocks. His clothing covered in blood, he merely grins in a huggermugger way when asked for an explanation. Spence simply cannot find the words to answer probing questions about his actions, for he is most content when left alone in his internal world.

Sorrow seems incapable of reaching his damaged soul. On the other hand, because of his war trauma, perhaps he cannot bear further sorrow, so he blocks it from his mind as a means of coping with unpleasant experiences. This point is supported by his reaction to his dying, almost comatose father, for whom Spence pulls out his harmonica and plays music unsuitable for the solemn moment. The reader, along with Molly, may wonder if he even realizes that Junius is his father. During the funeral procession, he continues in this manner, smiling and waving to passersby. Mourners are shocked when he says not a word but grabs a shovel to dig the grave while the rest of the family remain stoic. This particular response might be caused by natural stimuli, because since his return, he has worked daily with farm implements.

One thing Spence does remember is his military training. If a situation becomes threatening, he is ready for battle. Spence speaks no words of warning but immediately springs into action. When the homestead's ownership is contested, he throws a Yankee off the front porch and later jabs a pitchfork into a lecher who tries to rape Molly, all the while moaning and making unintelligible noises. Though family members are unable to interpret the meaning of his sounds, they can rest assured that no harm will befall them if Spence is nearby.

During the antebellum period, a black man who dared to approach a white woman was punished severely, often by a lynch mob. When Rom speaks to a married white woman inside a country store and several men follow him outside to beat him, a silent Spence wades into the foray until another man comes out of the store with a shotgun and shoots a seemingly invincible Spence in the back of his head. Spence cares not about skin color or understands societal biases, for when he sees his beloved friend in trouble, he does not hesitate to act.

Spence has, of course, lost his ability to function alone in society, yet for the people he knows and loves best, he is loyal to a fault. He recognizes that his size and strength are the ultimate gifts he can offer his family, so whenever they are in danger, his protective instincts surface naturally. In this way, he is similar to Michael Oher, about whom the film *The Blind Side* is dedicated. In the film, Michael, also a quiet man, uses his brawn to settle any altercation. His muscular strength proves advantageous to

S.J., who is protected during a vehicle accident; his high school team on Friday nights; and his advancement to the professional football arena.

Spence's demise occurs while he tries to rescue Rom; he is naively unaware that the group of men can overpower him, not in a fair fight, however, but with the unfair advantage of a weapon. How ironic that Spence survives years of fighting Civil War battles, yet after his return home, he is brought down by a prejudiced coward on the front porch of a country store.

Works Cited

Boggess, Carol. "On Agate Hill: A Novel." *Appalachian Journal* 35.4 (2008): 385–88. Literary Reference Center. Web.

James, Katherine H. "Smith, Lee." *Literature: The New Encyclopedia of Southern Culture.* Ed. Thomas Inge. Chapel Hill: University of North Carolina Press, 2008. Print.

"A Review of 'On Agate Hill.'" *Publishers Weekly* 253.30 (2006): 51–52. Contemporary Literary Criticism. Web.

Smith, Lee. *On Agate Hill*. Chapel Hill: Algonquin Books, 2006.

Evalina, Pan and Other "Guests"
Guests on Earth by Lee Smith

Well-researched history and fiction wed in Lee Smith's thirteenth novel, *Guests on Earth*. Appalachian fiction writers like Smith "draw from the rich linguistic traditions of their home regions" (Minnick 154). For Lee Smith, they are the states of Virginia and North Carolina:

> Lee Smith fills her southern tales with humorous encounters and narrative revelation. From the outrageous to the understated, from tales of supernatural encounters to the fervor of religious revival, Smith has marked out a distinctive southern territory in which to explore a variety of southern voices. In short stories and novels that resonate with the land, the people, the customs, and the language of the south, particularly the Appalachian area, Smith has earned a well-deserved place as a writer of strength and vision [Andrews 1001].

In an interview with Jason Howard, Smith explained that she included so many characters in her book *Guests on Earth* because each character makes a statement about "women and madness" (Howard 55). The title comes from a letter that F. Scott Fitzgerald wrote to his daughter Scottie in 1940 and is quoted by Smith on the introductory pages: "The insane are always mere guests on earth, eternal strangers carrying around broken decalogues that they cannot read," which Smith notes "implies that the mentally ill can never fit in, they're always 'guests on earth,' homeless" (57) yet "these people are not 'other.' They are us" (59). Locklear explains that characters, much like protagonist Evalina, can be in a "liminal space, what Lee Smith calls the state of an 'exile' which can allow for a negotiation between multiple discursive worlds" (3).

Spanning the decades of the 1930s and 1940s, the novel begins and ends in New Orleans, but the bulk of the narrative is set at Highland Hospital in Asheville, North Carolina. Susan Tekulve stated that Lee's book is a "parable about a quietly subversive girl" who while living in an "authoritarian society" (110) submits to the conventions of a limited environment.

Narrator Evalina Touisant's mother Louise, an exotic dancer and courtesan in a New Orleans brothel, falls in love with wealthy gentleman caller Arthur Graves, whose surname foreshadows Louise's death after he provides a home to enjoy Louise "at his beck and call." On moving day, their cat Madame runs out into the street. The cat's name and the fact that it never returns are symbolic of the lifestyle that Louise gives up to become monogamous with Arthur, even though he cannot reciprocate.

When Graves takes Evalina to his home where she is miserable and unwelcome, she can find no words of protest against the powerful man, but her despondency causes her to cease both eating and speaking (Smith 14–15). Although she is not mentally ill, Graves sends her to Highland Hospital in Asheville, "celebrated for its unorthodox treatments" (Haggas 45). She is, for the most part compliant, a natural tendency she learned from her complete obedience to the nuns' directives. Fearing judgment, Evalina is reticent to divulge details of her past (odd, since self-disclosure is not advised at Highland), so she is labeled resistant to therapy. In an ironic twist, the psychiatrist lacks communication skills—he struggles to find words, "letting a silence fall and extend" (217) during their sessions.

Evalina, who is prone to silence and long bouts of anorexia, encounters a variety of fellow guests including world-renowned Zelda Fitzgerald with her off-and-on psychosis. Other silent guests Evalina meets include Lily Ponder who quietly stares into space, totally mute after her entire family is killed in an automobile accident (Smith 26). Lily does eventually find a semblance of voice, but she uses it to speak single words of scorn or sarcasm, almost as if her voice manifests itself uncontrollably like those of individuals who suffer from Tourette's Syndrome. Two prisoners of anorexia, the extremely thin Gould sisters, speak only to each other in cryptophasia, a private language common between twins.

As a result of Robert's suicide, Evalina is distraught, unable to play the piano, eat, or speak. Being abandoned by her lover, learning that she is a product of incest between her mother and grandfather (130), and losing her daughter are experiences that occur in rapid succession. Evalina is attended during labor by crossdresser Madame (here's that symbolic reference again) Romanetsky. Evalina, devastated when the infant dies in her arms, names her daughter Pieta, meaning "pity," an allusion to artistic renditions of *La Pieta,* Christ lying across the Virgin Mary's lap after he is taken down from the cross, a symbolic reference of both sorrow and sacrifice, as well as a connection to the paintings and statues Evalina and her mother had viewed at the cathedral.

These circumstances, unfathomable to her fragile mind, send Evalina into a silent stupor, for her despair is profound. She is probably suffering from Post-Traumatic Stress Disorder (PTSD) which is caused by external stressors that trigger internal breakdowns. When a course of the most severe insulin shock treatment is ordered (131) and she gains consciousness, her eyes and mouth will not cooperate. She attempts to speak, but only "horrible sounds would issue forth from my mouth" (132). She is unable to utter a single intelligible word.

Marked silences also surround Zelda Fitzgerald, an Alabama Southern belle whose first breakdown occurred in 1930 when she was diagnosed with schizophrenia. She was admitted to several facilities before coming to Highland, where she received periodic treatment. In the novel, Zelda choreographs, with the other guests, "The Dance of the Hours," the same ballet she performed at a country club in Montgomery where Scott saw her for the first time and fell in love (Harmon 84). Although he was aware of the mental instability of several of Zelda's family members, he chose to ignore those warnings and marry the beautiful, blond flapper, whose world was one of "textured sensuality" ("Z" 37).

Creative to a fault (she was a painter, dancer, and writer), and like a chameleon in both physical appearance and personality, Zelda is at times congenial, kind, and nurturing. Her grace, as she dives into the hospital pool or dances in the gym, and her flamboyant stride into a room evoke perfect silence in those who stop to watch and admire her, yet her mood swings are quick and sometimes destructive, especially her public drunkenness with husband Scott. Zelda often stands apart from the other guests, "smoking and frowning and moving her mouth" (45), but she is merely carrying on an internal discourse.

During lunch at the Grove Park Inn, Zelda and Scott, who were "high-strung" and "deeply self-absorbed" (84), toy with their food and drink heavily, but neither speaks (56). Perhaps her frequent hospitalizations have driven a wedge between them and they can no longer find common ground. Her reputation tainted by mental lapses, and his from alcoholism and womanizing, the Fitzgeralds no longer enjoy the fanfare they once attracted from an adoring public. Candace Smith remarks that not only does the novel *Guests on Earth* shed light on the Fitzgeralds, but also "the plight of women and mental patients in the early twentieth century" (63). In an early letter to Zelda, Scott wrote that he wished "princesses could be locked up in towers" (85). Ironically, Zelda lost her life in the fire that engulfed the central tower section of Highland.

Lee Smith's most thorough and compelling characterization is the mysterious Pan Otto, whose name is indicative of his feral nature and woodland existence. His mythological counterpart, the Greek god Pan, is associated with natural settings such as caves and is known for his love of the hunt alongside the nymphs, whom he tries to seduce but is unsuccessful due to his goat-like appearance. The novel's Pan is dark, small, and handsome (166), a boy found nearly frozen to death in a chicken cage who "walked on all fours or maintained a crouching posture, ate with his hands, and did not speak or make eye contact" (170).

A similar literary parallel is Jean-Nicolas Bouilly's French play *L'Abbé de l'Epée* about a man who strives to prove the identity of, and return him to his "rightful social position" (McDonagh 655) an abandoned teenager who is deaf and mute. Simultaneous to the play's run in the early nineteenth century, a feral boy was found in the woods of Aveyron, sent to Paris, and examined by the intelligentsia. Much speculation ensued about the wild boy and the "place of the mute in society." Literary narratives about the boy and "disability characterization" occurred, thus suggesting that the disabled character "acts as a repository of symbolic and metaphorical possibilities" (656), for once muteness is revealed, audiences wonder at the cause, meaning, and oftentimes reasons for concealment (657). Additionally, the identity of the mute is often symbolic of those "exiled from power and citizenship" (655).

Likewise, Lee Smith's mysterious "boy in the cage" is an immediate psychological phenomena and media sensation. He is taught to stand, eat with utensils, play the harmonica, and to speak, but he chooses not to. There is a mystical aura about Pan Otto, who like his mythological counterpart camouflages himself in motley to blend in with the woods and lives in a hidden cave he has built. His gift of night vision and immunity to low temperatures are most likely due to living so many years in a dark, cold cage. Surprisingly, the "most psychotic patients respond to him" (172) when they become delirious or uncontrollable. Unlike his mythological doppelganger whose strident voice causes fear, Pan does not use words, only a calming embrace.

Evalina is fascinated by Pan, who suddenly both appears and disappears, and uses his eyes, gestures, and touch to communicate. He also leaves various types of flora (Pan was the god of fauna) lying across her piano as silent messages. After listening to him play tunes on an old guitar, Evalina realizes that "he had no hesitation with words when he sang, though his regular speech was sparse or halting at best" (259). The Greek god Pan, also fond of music, fashioned a pipe from reeds that grew by the river, hence the flute (a precursor to the harmonica) that bears his name.

A significant element of the novel is the silence necessary to keep secrets. On many occasions, Evalina is observant of the errant ways of others by being drawn into their secrecy. Lee Smith admits that she chose to allow Evalina to narrate the novel since she is "privy to all the other stories" and because she is female, "she's a good listener" (Howard 56). At an early age, she learns the art and importance of discretion. In New Orleans, she keeps secrets for Louise, knowing that the nuns would not approve. Silent and prudent obedience take precedence over her youthful curiosity, and as a result, she becomes an adult caretaker of her emotionally unhinged mother. In spite of Louise's sinful profession, Evalina's Sunday dress of white organdy is symbolic of innocence and purity, surprising attire for one who leaves a brothel to attend mass, and also a sign that Louise wants her daughter to choose a profession far from the likes of her own.

Evalina states, "I did everything I was told at Highland, as I had with the nuns, questioning nothing. I loved rules" (31). She rarely does break the rules, and her lips are sealed after she observes others violating them. She is even praised for her deceptive silence about the guest who pretends to be catatonic. Evalina reports none of these infractions, not even her suspicions about the arsonist who sets fire to the Central Building where Zelda loses her life. Her maturity and discretion are perhaps reasons she is offered a job at Highland, even though she continues to be considered a "guest."

Because of Evalina's ever-changing world, from place to place, from one person to another, she naturally develops a tractable character. She is obedient to those in authority, a good listener, a keeper of secrets, but perhaps her most enduring trait is humility. Evalina is content to be an accompanist, not just on the piano, but in all facets of her life. The repeated trauma she endures not only makes her a survivor, but a compassionate, nonjudgmental woman. She retains her clement nature, no matter what others around her do. An important truth she learns from her years at Highland Hospital is that "in the world of the mad, time is not a continuum, but a fluid, shifting place" (137).

Works Cited

Andrews, William L., ed. *The Literature of the American South.* New York: W.W. Norton, 1998. Print.

Haggas, Carol. "Guests on Earth." *Booklist* 109.22 (2013): 44–45. Literary Reference Center. Web.

Howard, Jason. "Lee Smith." *Appalachian Heritage* 42.1 (2014): 51–64. Print.

McDonagh, Patrick. "The Mute's Voice: The Dramatic Transformations of the Mute and Deaf- Mute in Early-Nineteenth-Century France." *Criticism* 55.4 (2013): 655–75. Academic Search Premier. Web.

Minnick, Lisa Cohen. "Literary Dialect." *The New Encyclopedia of Southern Culture.* Volume 5, *Language.* Ed. Michael Montgomery and Ellen Johnson. Chapel Hill: University of North Carolina Press, 2007. Print.

Smith, Candace. "Guests on Earth." *Booklist* 110.9/10 (2014): 63. Literary Reference Center. Web.

Smith, Lee. *Guests on Earth.* Chapel Hill: Algonquin Books, 2013. Print.

Tekulve, Susan. "Guests on Earth." *Appalachian Heritage* 42.1 (2014): 109–14. Print.

"Z: A Novel of Zelda Fitzgerald." *Publisher's Weekly* 269.7 (2013): 37–38. Literary Reference Center. Web.

Nicky and Angela
The Deer Hunter directed
by Michael Cimino

A film about the brutality of war, loyalty of friendship, and the strength of the human spirit, *The Deer Hunter*, directed by Michael Cimino, debuted in 1978. The main actors are Robert De Niro (Michael), Christopher Walken (Nick), John Savage (Steve) and a young, beautiful Meryl Streep (Linda). Set in the dirty, gritty, blue-collar town of Clairton, Pennsylvania, the men work in the local steel foundry, and the women are either waitresses or grocery store clerks.

The movie opens with the steelworkers leaving their jobs, stopping by the local pub for a round of beer and billiards, and then rushing to make preparations for a wedding. The muddy streets that the wedding attendants and guests walk through are in marked juxtaposition to the aesthetically ornate and pristine church they enter, symbolic of the warmth and happiness inside compared to the cold reality outside. Performed in a Russian Orthodox sanctuary, the sacred ceremony followed by joyful dancing is also a noticeable contrast to an unending supply of alcohol and a raucous celebration in a Veteran's Hall. A uniformed Green Beret, who makes an unobtrusive entrance and sits at the bar, is questioned by the men who will join the war in Vietnam in a few days. One asks, "Hey, Beret, what's it like over there?" but the soldier remains stoic and neither looks at them nor answers, even though they continue to badger him. This scene foreshadows what these ebullient young men will soon encounter and how the war will affect them, especially Nicky.

Later that night on their last deer hunting trip in the majestic Allegheny Mountains, Michael, the principal member of the group, separates himself from the other men as he determines when and where they will hunt. He "detaches himself from his companions in order to perform another ultimate act of dissociation: killing" (Burke 249). His status foreshadows the position of military leadership he will attain. Clearly, hunting is a powerful catharsis for Michael. He proves himself an accomplished marksman when he is the only one to shoot a deer. This skill serves Michael well, not only in his hunting expeditions at home but also in Vietnam.

Michael, the titular character of the film, is analogous to the 19th century American literary figure Natty Bumppo, the creation of James Fenimore Cooper in *The Deerslayer*. Michael, and Natty Bumppo, who is based on Daniel Boone, are archetypes of rugged frontiersmen who display traits of "strength, curiosity, resourcefulness, restlessness, fearlessness, combativeness, independence, and violence" ("Sam Peckinpah's" 22). Cooper's "formula, that of capture and escape" (Alcino) is also seen in Cimino's film. Bumppo's experiences in the wilderness correspond with Michael's experiences in Vietnam. Although they seem able to live in harmony with nature, their rites of passage are paralleled when they kill their first foes—Natty when he slays his first Delaware Indian by Lake Glimmerglass and Michael when he kills his first Vietcong in a village in Southeast Asia. Both men, who gain wisdom but also skepticism, are fearless warriors who need only one shot to take down their targets.

After Michael, Nicky, and Steve are captured by the Vietcong and held with other POW's, Michael establishes himself as the superior man, both physically and mentally. When Steve begins to shake uncontrollably and scream in anticipation of playing Russian Roulette with a .38 service revolver, Michael immediately comforts and assures him he will be able to get through the ordeal. This scene foreshadows Steve sustaining the most egregious war injuries. Michael's ability to overcome the enemy and kill them with their own assault rifles confirms that he is the most trained and prepared for combat among the three men.

Traumatized by the brutal killings he has witnessed, a formerly gregarious Nick becomes unresponsive at a hospital in Saigon. No matter how many times field workers query him, he is able to form only silent, unintelligible words with his mouth and weep. On the other hand, Michael is highly decorated with medals of commendations, but he feels an acute sense of displacement when he comes home alone. Tentatively attempting interaction with his drinking buddies, he fends off greetings and back slaps with silence and a sad countenance. His alienation grows wider, as if he can no longer relate to his former life or companions. The change in his former mindset of indifferent killing is unmistakable during his next hunting trip, also alone. Michael is unable to pull his gun's trigger, although he could easily take down an 8-point buck. Once more, a comparison can be made to Natty Bumppo, who loses his innocence and former name. Metaphorically reborn and renamed Hawkeye, [Natty is described by D.H. Lawrence] as "silent, philosophical … isolate and stoic" (qtd. in "Sam Peckinpah's" 25), adjectives which can also be applied to Michael.

When Michael visits Angela, she is bedridden and unable to speak, even though Michael questions her repeatedly for news of Steve's whereabouts. As proof of her sense of loss and mental oblivion, Angela's unattended toddler cries continuously in a playpen beside her bed, but she seems neither to notice nor care. This scene attests to war's long-reaching psychological trauma not only to those in battle but also to loved ones waiting at home. Unable to utter words, Angela finally writes down an address for Michael, who in a tragic, poignant, and ironic scene finds a legless Steve holding up multiple pairs of socks Nicky has sent him. Perhaps this is a natural inclination for Nicky, since soldiers in the field are warned to keep their feet dry with clean socks to avoid trench foot. (Refer to Lieutenant Dan's words to his troops in the film *Forrest Gump*).

When Michael returns to Vietnam to fulfill his promise to bring Nicky home, he prods him to immediately stop playing Russian Roulette, ironically the same game the terrified men were forced to play when they were initially captured, but the Vietnamese urge Nick to continue, their frenzied shouts suggestive of humanity's primal urge for bloodshed. Nick is unable to speak and his bloodshot eyes do not focus on or recognize Michael, the man who had always commanded and received deference from his friends, yet no amount of pleading reaches Nick. In a twisted ending, Michael fulfills his promise, but he had not planned to bring Nicky home in a flag-draped coffin.

Works Cited

Alcino, Nicholas. "Character Development in Natty Bumppo." SUNY-Oneonta, 1979. Web.

Burke, Frank. "Reading Michael Cimino's 'The Deer Hunter': Interpretation as Melting Pot." *Literature Film Quarterly* 20.3 (1992): 249. Literary Reference Center. Web.

The Deer Hunter. Dir. Michael Cimino. Perf. Robert De Niro, Christopher Walken, John Savage, and Meryl Streep. Universal Pictures, 1978. DVD.
"Natty Bumppo." *Encyclopaedia Britannica.* Web.
"Sam Peckinpah's Heroes: Natty Bumppo and The Myth of the Rugged Individual Still Reign" *Literature Film Quarterly* 16.1 (1998): 22–31. Academic Search Premier. Web.

Sam Bledsoe
Christmas Hope by Leslie Lynch

Another soldier negatively affected by war is Sam Bledsoe in Leslie Lynch's novella *Christmas Hope,* set in Louisville, Kentucky, and published in 2014. Dual protagonists, even though seemingly foils at times, Becca Sweet and Sam Bledsoe meet by happenstance, but there is an immediate connection between them, both physical and emotional. However, pride keeps them silent about their feelings for each other. Shame and guilt about her former life keep Becca humble and reserved. Low self-esteem and guilt cause Sam to avoid all social interaction, as well as responses to queries about his condition.

Even though the writer employs a typical *boy meets girl* plot, there are deeper themes to the story. Both Sam and Becca are outsiders due to their physical markers. Becca is alienated because of her tattoos and her swelling stomach. Although Sam tries to minimize the preponderant scars on his face by covering them with a woolen cap, they often repulse strangers. Sam, a veteran of the war in Afghanistan, suffers from post-traumatic stress disorder (PTSD). "Emotional numbing and a feeling of detachment" (Fry 31) are symptoms common to Sam's condition. An article in the *Journal of Traumatic Stress* reports that PTSD is a common diagnosis of veterans who were deployed to Afghanistan, as well as other Middle East wars. "Peritrauma factors relate to the severity of the trauma exposure and acute reactions" (Wright etal. 310). Support mechanisms include family and social support, yet Sam eschews the assistance he needs to begin his healing process; instead, he prefers an isolated existence. Because he does not explain to Becca the reasons for his aloofness, she feels rebuffed.

Sudden movements and loud noises set off his instinctive mode of *fight or flight.* "Flinching and withdrawal" are other symptoms of PTSD sufferers who demonstrate "hypervigilance" for impending danger and a heightened "startle response" (Fry 32). A major indication of PTSD is reliving experiences in a distinct or disturbing manner, such as the flashbacks and nightmares Sam has. Although he is attracted to Becca, her pregnancy is a constant reminder of the explosion that burned his body when he tried to save a burka-clad pregnant woman.

Other triggers keep Sam on alert. When he mistakes Becca's tattoos for blood, he immediately believes there is a sniper nearby. To calm his anxiety and return to reality, an internal dialogue is necessary. "*Louisville, not Afghanistan. Neighborhood, not war zone. No snipers, no IED's. No suicide bombers*" (Lynch 14). An additional factor of PTSD is avoidance of the reminders of the trauma (Fry 31). Rather than fixate on her pregnancy, his mind repeats, "*Not Afghanistan, Louisville, No suicide bombers. Safe*" (43).

The turning points in both their lives occur when Father Barnabas, the hospital chaplain who has an uncanny perception of the roadblocks to their emotional healing and potential relationship, speaks to them. Father Barnabas' words about forgiving himself and being open to the future finally reach Sam. The wisdom of Father Barnabas is supported by researchers at the Department of Veterans Affairs who report that "self-compassion, characterized by self- kindness, a sense of common humanity when faced with suffering, and mindful awareness of suffering" (Hiroaka etal. 127) are possible factors in the maintenance of PTSD. Currently, military personnel are trained to counsel PTSD veterans because they are more apt to confide in their fellow soldiers than civilians. Only when Sam decides to let go of his guilt and remorse can he move forward to a life with Becca.

Works Cited

Fry, Mandy. "Post-Traumatic Stress Disorder." *Practice Nurse* 46.2 (2016): 30–34. Academic Search Premier. Web.

Lynch, Leslie. *Christmas Hope*. Louisville, 2014. Print.

Hiroaka, Regina, et al. "Self-Compassion as a Prospective Predictor of PTSD Symptom Severity Among Trauma-Exposed U.S. Iraq and Afghanistan War Veterans." *Journal of Traumatic Stress* 28 (2015): 127–33. Web.

Wright, Breanna K., et al. "Support Mechanisms and Vulnerabilities in Relation to PTSD in Veterans of the Gulf War, Iraq War, and Afghanistan Deployments: A Systematic Review." *Journal of Traumatic Stress* 26 (2013): 310–18. Web.

Pip
The Waltons directed
by Earl Hamner

In season Six of Earl Hamner's television series *The Waltons*, an episode titled "The Children's Carol," opens in September of 1940, when Hitler ordered intense bombing of London. In an attempt to gain control of Great Britain, the Germans set fires during the blitz. Many Londoners were either killed or displaced. Two young orphans, Tess and her younger brother Pip, are separated from their parents before being brought to the United States to take refuge on Walton's Mountain, first with "The Sisters" and later with the Waltons. Since the bombing, Pip has been totally mute. He keeps his head down, stands close to his sister, and in his balled-up fist, clutches a cloth held close to his mouth. He gently rubs the cloth back and forth on the side of his face, behavior similar to a baby holding and rubbing a security blanket against its cheek.

In her article about the impact of war on children, Joanna Santa Barbara writes that the most important step is "removing the vector" (891) of war. The displacement and loss of attachment to their parents is part and parcel to their young lives being disrupted by a situation they neither cause nor understand. "Children are dependent on the care, empathy, and attention of adults" in their lives (892). Some children have no protection at all and end up in orphanages or refugee camps. Although Tess and Pip are fortunate to receive humanitarian protection, they have been sent to another continent to live among strangers, so they are understandably confused and frightened.

Traumatized by the war, Pip stops speaking; likewise, pianist Jason Walton stops playing music. Despondency, fear, and silence pervade the inhabitants of the mountain home. The English children are distant and refuse most suggestions of familial kindness, such as playing games, reading books, singing Christmas carols, or eating treats. They maintain their hebetude no matter what the Waltons do to include them.

Jim Hepting recounts his experiences as a child during the London Blitz. His family had heard rumors of evacuation after war was declared on Germany. While at school one day, they heard the air raid sirens and the "intermittent drone of the German bombers" (2). Jim hated the dark, so the black-out requirements only heightened his fear. As the danger escalated, Jim, his mother, and siblings were taken to different parts of the country. When the war ended and his family returned home, "we all felt like strangers to each other as we had been split up for so long" (4). Because of the devastation and destruction of the bombs, Jim stated that it took his family time "to readjust to our virtual slum surroundings" (4).

While outside one day, Tess and Pip are terrified when they see a mail plane, mistaking it for an approaching bomber, fly overhead. Pip sobs uncontrollably as he and Tess crouch low to the ground, behavior they have been taught in London, before running to take cover inside a culvert. Olivia Walton remarks that the fear in the children's eyes is the truest reflection of war. When the children realize that they will soon be reunited with their parents, their faces, formerly devoid of emotions, change to cautious hope. Pip remains stoic and silent until he understands the Waltons actually love him. He finally finds his voice again by crying out, "Mama" to Olivia when all the house lights go out, another moment of familiar terror for Pip.

Works Cited

"The Children's Carol." *The Waltons.* Dir. Earl Hammer. Perf. Richard Thomas, Ralph Waite, and Michael Learned. Warner Bros., 1977. DVD.

Hepting, Jim. "Child of the Blitz: London." *World War II People's War.* BBC Archives, 2003. Web.

Santa Barbara, Joanna. "Impact of War on Children and Imperative to End War." *Croatian Medical Journal* 47.6 (2006): 891–94. U.S. National Library of Medicine National Institutes of health (NIH). Web.

Emma
Breaking the Silence
by Diane Chamberlain

Diane Chamberlain's *Breaking the Silence* contains elements of intrigue, love, science, and historical events. The author "explores psychiatric tensions" (Rotella 336) in this distressing tale of foreboding secrets and eventual atonement. A resident of North Carolina, Chamberlain sets her novel in Virginia where astronomer Laura Brandon resides. She has just lost her elderly father and her husband. To discover the reasons for Ray's suicide and her daughter Emma's sudden muteness, she embarks on a mysterious, complicated trail of investigation.

After Ray' suicide, Emma screams and then ceases to speak. Every measure Laura tries to evoke a response from her daughter fails. Emma has lost her ability to verbalize as if she had "used up all her allotted words and suddenly could find no more" (45). The success that most child therapists have with mute children is through play therapy activities—drawings, dolls, and pointing to or making facial expressions—to determine the root of the child's silence.

During a therapy session, Emma puts a toy gun in a male doll's hand, raises the gun to its head, and makes a "bang' noise. This is indeed a troublesome sign that Emma most likely witnessed Ray's suicide. The longer Emma refuses to speak, "the easier it is for her to stay mute" (75), using only gestures and head nods to communicate. Emma's silence and disdain of men may be caused by Ray, often impatient and irritated by the noisy chatter of this former talkative child, who would shush her when she got on his nerves. When Emma points to a picture that reminds her of Ray, she chooses the angry, yelling face, so "in Emma's mind, men yell" (77) and they kill themselves. No wonder she is reluctant to accept her biological father, a stranger who suddenly appears.

The therapist eventually diagnoses Emma with post-traumatic stress disorder (PTSD). Emma exhibits multiple changes in behavior: she is terrified of the dark, but even with a night light, her sleeplessness and nightmares continue; she also reverts to bedwetting, and for comfort, thumb-sucking; she refuses to go near the water although she has always loved the lake; she also clings to Laura's legs when strangers appear, a sign that she may fear abandonment by her mother. In the journal *Trials*, Tim Dagleish and colleagues report that PTSD is a "deeply distressing and disabling anxiety disorder" (6). Children Emma's age have a restricted capability to communicate "as a result of their limited cognitive and expressive language skills," so therapists must focus on visual signs or "behavioural markers" (6).

The National Child Traumatic Stress Network supports the therapist's diagnosis of Emma's acute lack of speech. It reports that children who suffer from traumatic stress are often unable to "regulate their behaviors and emotions" ("Symptoms and Behavior" 1). In response to stress, children Emma's age may:

- Act withdrawn
- Be anxious and fearful and avoidant
- Be unable to trust others
- Believe they are to blame for the traumatic experience
- Experience nightmares or sleep difficulties
- Fear being separated from parent/caregiver
- Imitate the abusive/traumatic event
- Show sadness and anxiety
- Wet the bed or self after being toilet trained
  [2].

When Emma meets her biological father, she is at first leery of Dylan, responding with "stony silence" (154) to his questions. Unexpectedly, Emma speaks openly with Sarah, yet only when they are alone and perhaps because of their parallel mindsets, for Sarah suffers from the early onset of Alzheimer's. Her childlike demeanor and willingness to play dolls with Emma seem to resonate with the little girl who is comforted by Sarah's welcoming countenance, nonthreatening tenor of voice, and display of genuine compassion. However, this is unlikely, especially during their initial therapy sessions, because Sarah is a complete stranger. Slowly Emma begins to warm up to her father, yet she is "afraid to speak, afraid of the power in her words" (Chamberlain 326).

Laura is surprised to learn that Sarah and her husband had unknowingly been caught in the middle of the secret CIA human experimentations in the U.S. called the MK-Ultra Mind Control Program, depicted in the film *The Manchurian Candidate*. Beginning in 1947 and backed by the U.S. Defense Department, many psychiatrists were recruited to use drugs (mainly LSD), hypnosis, electric shock, eugenics, and in some cases lobotomies on soldiers, prisoners, mental patients, college students, and children to determine the residual effects of biological warfare. Experimentation was carried out in Maryland, South Carolina, Florida, Texas, and California (The Film Archives). In her article "Brainwashing Avatar: The Curious Career of Dr. Ewen Cameron," Lemov reports that Dr. Cameron, portrayed in Diane Chamberlain's novel as Dr. Palimiento, received numerous accolades from the government and from colleagues in his field. As a result, hospital personnel were reluctant to question his unorthodox practices. "Much of the praise for Cameron's personal touch imputed a sense of the noblesse oblige a powerful and well-connected physician-administrator displayed in forbearing to put himself on a pedestal when he easily might have" (Lemov 62). After investigations uncovered the truth, Cameron was perceived as a ruthless, maniacal monster who administered "systematic torture-in-the-name-of science" (6).

Works Cited

Chamberlain, Diane. *Breaking the Silence*. Ontario: Mira, 2009. Print.

Dagleish, Tim, et al. "Trauma-focused Cognitive Behaviour Therapy Versus Treatment as Usual for Post Trauma Stress Disorder (PTSD) in Young Children aged 3 to 8 years: Study Protocol for a Randomised Trial." *Trials* 16.1 (2015): 1–9. Academic Search Premier. Web.

Lemov, Rebecca. "Brainwashing Avatar: The Curious Career of Dr. Ewen Cameron." *Grey-Room* 45 (2011): 61–87. Web.

MK-Ultra Human Experimentation Project. Film Archives. You Tube.

Rotella, Mark, and Sybil Steinberg. "Breaking the Silence." *Publishers Weekly* 246.3 (2009): 336. Academic Search Premier. Web.

"Symptoms and Behaviors Associated with Exposure to Trauma." National Child Traumatic Stress Network (NCTSN). U.S. Department of Health & Human Services jointly coordinated by UCLA and Duke University. Web.

The Jesup Family
"Hell and Ohio" by Chris Holbrook

In his praise of Chris Holbrook's collection of short stories set in Southern Appalachia, Robert Morgan notes that Holbrook "gets the voice right of contemporary life in the mountains" (book jacket). Holbrook says about the genre of his short stories that they must immediately hook the reader with tension, for all words and intense moments are significant.

Holbrook's titular short story opens with a quote from Marvin, the barber who has been cutting the narrator's hair since his childhood. "If I owned both Hell and Ohio, I'd rent out Ohio and live in Hell" (1). This enigmatic statement suggests that the old timers have spent years spinning their wheels in "Nowheresville" and the younger generation leaves town as soon as they are aware of an opportunity. Readers meet Jimmy in the barber's chair and then ride with him in the El Camino to spend Memorial Day weekend with his family, still haunted by the death of Jimmy's younger brother Todd.

An astute reader should discern that the narrative is a study in sensory images, especially the contrast between sounds and silence. Jimmy enjoys the jokes and good-natured barbs traded among the men who frequent the barber shop, but when the subject changes to basketball, Jimmy closes his eyes and listens only to the strop of the razor. Beside the mountain road, while his truck's engine hums, Jimmy recognizes the quietness, symbolic of Todd's death, and he is unable to think (3).

At home, his mother offers a superficial welcome and begins to say something but stops. Both are nervous and sit in silence (5). Jimmy braces himself to face his father, who lowers the television volume when Jimmy enters the room; he starts to shake his son's hand but then decides against it. After engaging in perfunctory small talk, they become silent, and then merely look at each other, an awkward quietness similar to his time with his mother. They all know what is on each other's minds, but they cannot utter it. Outside, Jimmy's father smiles if spoken to or when a joke is told. Otherwise, he remains sullen and silent (8).

At night Jimmy notices the house is so quiet that he cannot sleep. When he joins his snoring father in the den and mutes the television, he dozes off, hearing the whoosh of a basketball net in his dreams, the only way he is able to return to those former days of athletic prowess, for when he awakes, he must suppress those troubling memories and not speak of them.

The noise of the cleaning tools and activities of the men are in sharp contrast to the still, silent cemetery. Jimmy dreads approaching Todd's tombstone when the family gathers there because he feels as if he is being judged. They return to the house where it is "quiet enough for a prayer meeting" (10), and his father isolates himself in a back bedroom.

The reader is not privy to the details of the accident until Jimmy leaves his parents' home and drives back to Cincinnati. Jimmy not only lost his brother that night, but he also lost the will to follow through with plans to play college basketball at the University of Kentucky. He moved away from his hometown rather than face individuals who had pinned their hopes on him and Todd. Significant to note is that for wildcat fans, nothing is more important than University of Kentucky basketball; the pride of having hometown boys on the team would have been paramount for Jimmy, his family and the community. The despondency of Jimmy's father is palpable.

The accident has become the proverbial "elephant in the room" about which neither his parents nor Jimmy can speak. The Jesups, reminded of Todd each time they look at Jimmy's face, relive the events of that tragic night. Mr. Jesup vacillates between resentment toward Jimmy for reckless driving and his own guilt since the Corvette was a gift from him. The disappointment of his hopes and dreams for both boys being dashed that night is a sore that he will not allow to scab over. If he does not move past his emotional withdrawal, he might also lose his only living son. Essentially, Jimmy and his parents have not dealt with unresolved grief, guilt, and blame. Until they break through the barrier of silence, this family will remain prisoners of painful alienation and unfortunately, may never heal.

Works Cited

Holbrook, Chris. "Hell and Ohio." *Hell and Ohio.* Frankfort: Gnomon Press, 1995. Print.

Amanda Cardinal
Wish You Well by David Baldacci

David Baldacci, known for his suspense novels, departs from his usual genre to write the historical fiction *Wish You Well.* Set in the 1940s, the novel begins briefly in New York and then quickly moves to the Appalachian Mountains where many generations of the Cardinal family have lived on a sprawling farmstead atop a mountain in Virginia. A terrible accident causes well-known writer Jake Cardinal, with his family in tow, to swerve his 1936 Lincoln Zephyr to avoid hitting a man standing in the road. The car rolls over multiple times, the driver's door flies open, and ejects Jake onto the road. The side of the car buckles, thrusting sharp, metal pieces into the back of his wife Amanda's head. Prior to losing consciousness, she sees Jake lying in the dirt, his neck at an unnatural angle.

Amanda, confined to a wheelchair, has not opened her eyes since the accident. The doctor contends that her physical body will heal, but "the problem now apparently was only a matter of her soul's having fled" (Baldacci 19). The attending nurse is more pessimistic, telling Lou and Oz their mother is in a "catatonic state" (28), and they should not expect her to ever gain consciousness.

Lou is awed by the Appalachian Mountains where her father had spent his boyhood, but they tower like "menacing hands" (33), an ominous portent, as the train tracks climb higher in elevation. Despite the lack of modern conveniences, the children grow and learn the necessary skills of farm life, but Amanda remains bed-ridden and unconscious. She opens her mouth only to be fed, but she does not speak, although Oz talks to his mother in monologue, and Cotton reads to Amanda. The mountain doctor examines Amanda and pronounces her physically healed, but he taps his forehead to indicate mental trauma and warns about the atrophy of her limbs.

To Lou, Amanda seems a "princess reclining in a deathlike state, and none of them possessed the necessary antidote" (152) to awaken her. After a full year on the mountain, her condition does not change. While reading through all the letters her mother had previously written to Louisa Mae, Lou fears the letters may be "the last words of her mother she would ever have" (342).

A scene at the end of the novel is not quite conceivable. Amanda suddenly regains consciousness to appear before a judge to bar the proceedings of her children being remanded to the courts. It would seem this "princess" has been awakened by the kiss of an unknown prince. This "fairy tale" event weakens the otherwise fine penning of the rest of the novel.

Baldacci's *Wish You Well* is a bildungsroman for protagonist Lou Cardinal. Not only does she move geographically from city life to a stark existence in the mountains, she grows mentally strong. She has no choice—her father is dead and her mother is silent and unresponsive. Lou must be a surrogate mother and protector of her little brother Oz and a co-worker on the farm with her great-grandmother. Over the year's timeframe of the novel, Lou learns how to defend herself, speak up for her brother, and survive life on a mountain where the weather is fickle and the crops are hit and miss.

An important issue Baldacci addresses is race relations. Eugene, the black farm hand for Louisa Mae, is called by some locals "Hell No" because his father, while passing through the town, threw him in the dirt. When asked if he was coming back for the child, he responded, "Hell No," and abandoned Eugene. Louisa Mae takes him in as family, and he proves to be a loyal and hard worker. Lou, who has also learned to love Eugene, defends his honor even though he remains silent when locals taunt him.

Works Cited

Baldacci, David. *Wish You Well*. New York: Warner Books, 2000. Print.

A Sacred Silence

Mary and Reverend William Thompson
A Circuit Rider's Wife
by Corra Mae White Harris

In Corra Mae White Harris' novel *A Circuit Rider's Wife*, protagonist Mary Thompson, the Methodist minister's wife, discovers that marrying her husband William and joining him in his chosen field is less about matrimony and more about itinerancy. She learns by imitating other church women or through their personal exhortations to suppress her feelings and restrain her tongue. Mary is told that any tears she sheds or complaints she expresses will be perceived as dissatisfaction, a negative impression to congregants about their minister. She soon understands that she must acquiesce to these directives to insure that the meager offerings of church members will be enough to meet and sustain William's and her daily needs.

Mary observes the gender segregation of the church's services. She notes the men appear to have a highly developed "Adam clod" (34) which produces in them an oxymoronic expression of muteness, seemingly transporting them back to the Garden of Eden where they try to hide the transparency of their sins from God. She is taken aback during her first revival meeting when a woman springs from her seat, steps into the aisle, claps her hands, and spins around on her toes with unimaginable speed. At specific intervals of time, she emits "a short, staccato squeal" (36) that does not resemble the human voice. Not a word is spoken by the congregation, perhaps unnerved by this strange sight but aware that they are witnesses to a sacred response from a fellow congregant. The church members, well-versed by years of discipleship, are cognizant of the Biblical teaching that warns against hindrance of the working of the Holy Spirit, an unforgivable form of blasphemy. Instead, they maintain a posture of reverent silence.

Mary's husband William is also silenced as he watches the strange scene from the pulpit.

During William's sermon preparation for revivals, Mary suffers periods of unwanted solitude. When William enters the parlor and closes the door behind him, he and Mary are separated physically by being on different spiritual levels. As he passes into a "praying and fasting trance" (46), the separation and loneliness break Mary's heart. While William is earnestly focused on spiritual matters, he refuses to eat with or speak to Mary, who gives into her tears. There is a clear divergence in the maturity of faith between this couple. However, Corra Mae White Harris did not embrace the prevailing principle that "women were unequal to men or incapable of thinking for themselves, but that their highest calling was to lift their husbands and children to a high moral plane through love and service" ("Corra Mae White Harris" 2).

William is moreover silenced when Sister Franny Clark confesses to him that her soul has never been spiritually satisfied in his church with its "easy ways and shiftless doctrines" (Harris 77) concerning baptism and communion. At this point, William recognizes that as a young pastor, he does not yet have the knowledge or strength of conviction to defend Methodism. Rather than oppose a faithful congregant, William is wise to allow Sister Franny to speak her mind. He has been called to the ministry to tend the entire flock, even the aberrant sheep. Showing mindful consideration toward an elderly female of his congregation, he is quietly respectful during her tirade of disapproval.

In a remote mountain church consisting mostly of the impoverished of Celestial Bells community, when wealthy Sister Shaller announces to the women that she feels moved to support a foreign female missionary, "the silence that met this announcement was sad and submissive" (208), for they are already giving all the dues they can afford. Sister Shaller admits that it would mean a sacrifice for them all, but she explains that through sacrifice, they would grow in grace. As the silence continues, it approaches animosity, but the women cannot voice their objections for fear of holy reprisal from a woman who has never been forced to make sacrifices in her world of plenty.

Brother A, also a member of the Celestial Bells congregation, and in spite of his gruff appearance, is a peaceful man who will do any service-related activity for the church, but he is one of "God's dumb saints. He had faith and he had works, but he couldn't pray, that is, not in public" (148). He is so eager to be an active servant that the church is initially unaware of his supplicant muteness. Brother A is willing to use his hands in service, but his tongue is paralyzed with fear at the intimate and humbling act of offering a corporate prayer among fellow worshippers.

A surprising turn of events occurs when Mary discerns her husband is trapped in temporal backsliding, a secret she does not mention to others. William confesses, "I have lost the witness of the Spirit. As if God has forsaken me" (90)! Reluctant to continue preaching, he dreads the possibility that God will not give him the words to say to his congregation, and he feels unworthy to stand at the homiletic platform. One can imagine how distressing this circumstance would be—for a man of God to be struck mute before his flock. Perhaps in these times of spiritual duress and silence, God is simply reminding William that the servant is not greater than the master, and he must first listen to the voice of God before his tongue can be loosed to preach The Word.

Works Cited

Dickey, Charles H. "Something about the Circuit Rider by the Circuit Rider's Wife." *Richmond Then & Now*. Web.
Harris, Corra Mae White. *A Circuit Rider's Wife*. Philadelphia: Curtis, 1910. Print.
"Harris, Cora Mae White." Georgia Women of Achievement. Web.

Uncle Edward
Tales of Chinkapin Creek by Jean Ayer

Jean Ayer, in her 2011 *Tales of Chinkapin Creek*, "strikes gold with these enchanting sketches" (back cover) of the numerous family and community members in West Virginia who touched her mother's life during childhood. Among them was her Uncle Edward, a staid and impassive Methodist itinerary preacher about whom she had heard humorous anecdotes when he was a young boy. Each summer, he drove his horse and buggy from Baltimore to visit the family, but Nellie remembers, "He said not a word to me or my brothers. No hello. Not even a glance in our direction" (Ayers 4). He seemed to have developed his mien from his parents who were described as "oddly quiet" (4). After his arrival, "without a word" he walked through the house to the front porch and took the most comfortable seat. With his black notebook, pen, and Bible concordance in hand, he began his seasonal ritual "that would occupy him for the whole two months of his visit—composing his sermons for the coming year" (4). Uncle Edward understood the necessity of solitude when studying the scriptures.

In contrast to his silence, for the mealtime grace, his "powerful voice" blessed friends, family, and congregations until the food was cold by the time he said "Amen." (4). Focused solely on eating, he never entered conversation at the table, apparently having no affinity for what he deemed trivial chatter. Although the rest of the family was still eating, "abruptly he rose and left the room, with no word of excuse, no farewell, no thanks, nor any compliments to the cooks" (5). Nellie laments that he later blessed them again in evening devotions and ceaseless prayer. The brusque departure from their home by this solemn man was just as unceremonious.

Works Cited

Ayer, Jean. *Tales of Chinkapin Creek.* 2011. Print.

11

Silenced by Fear

Rose-Johnny
"Rose-Johnny" by Barbara Kingsolver

Barbara Kingsolver's short story "Rose-Johnny," her first published work of fiction, appeared in *The Virginia Quarterly Review* in 1987. "Based on her recollections of an eccentric Kentucky woman" (DeMarr 54) and set in the small town of Walnut Knobs, the story focuses on females and shows how their worth in a community can be perceived as insignificant by narrow- minded men. It is also a coming of age experience for the protagonist and highlights "themes of community and place" (56). Even though she grew up middle-class, Kingsolver's "identification with the poor and uneducated was to become a hallmark of her fiction" (51).

Similar to the myth surrounding the legendary "other" character Boo Radley in Harper Lee's *To Kill a Mockingbird*, the people of Walnut Knobs, especially the older women, have conjured up a complete, albeit false, persona for Rose-Johnny. As a result of their misguided fears, misinformation, and misunderstanding, they fill their gullible children's minds with eerie tales of a dangerous woman who will grab and swallow them up if their curiosity tempts them to go near her.

On a chance encounter, narrator eleven-year-old Georgeann Bowles dispels the rumors that have been perpetuated for years. Unlike the race-baited and cynical adults, she meets Rose-Johnny, who is not half woman and half man after all, with an innocent and open mind. In order to continue their friendship, Georgeann understands she must not tell "a living soul about it, and for nearly a year I carried that secret torment" (Kingsolver 140).

Georgann witnesses Rose-Johnny at the counter making quick motions with her hands as if she were unable to talk, but her silence and quick transactions with white customers are prudent on her part. Racism and irrational fear are demonstrated when the man replaces the quarter Georgeann has spent and says her daddy is "not never to send his little girls to Wall's feed store" (143). A moment of humor eases the story's discomforting events when Georgann questions her aunt about Rose-Johnny. In her ignorance, Aunt Minnie labels Rose-Johnny a Lebanese, so Georgeann is surprised to learn from a Bible dictionary that they are seafaring people who build great ships. At this point, she suspects that her family will not tell her the truth about the discrepancies between what the townspeople say about Rose-Johnny and what Georgann actually observes.

She begins to understand the effects of prejudice while she is at the store one evening. Even though Rose-Johnny knows the names of all the customers, she rarely speaks to them and never to the men. Initially, Georgann wonders if she can indeed speak (148). Then she watches Rose-Johnny welcome black families inside after normal store hours, call each one by name, and give them discounts on their purchases. Rose-Johnny teaches Georgann a lesson about racism when she insists that Georgann always speak to them by name in public, no matter who might be around.

Knowing the truth about this woman, Georgann stands alone in defense of Rose-Johnny when a boy at school calls her a pervert. "I knew, in a manner that went beyond words" (152) that she is neither masculine nor lesbian. The reader understands the root cause of Rose-Johnny's unusual appearance and reticence around men when she shares the details of her tragic background. Unfortunately, her sudden disappearance merely gives fodder for wagging tongues to fabricate new stories regarding her whereabouts.

In this agrarian community, and because the Bowles have no sons, Georgann's older sister Mary Etta must labor on the farm alongside her father. After a long day of putting up hay, she comes to the table but neither eats nor speaks. She stares into space, and "even her hair looked tired" (145). That she is described as a dark shadow suggests she is devalued because she is a female. This is not the only burden she must endure, for the assault leaves her with injuries to both body and soul. Certain that the men were looking for her and mistakenly attacked her sister, Georgann recalls, "I took to my bed and would not eat or speak" (146). Sensing that her internal identity has evolved, Georgann cuts her hair as an outward sign and renames herself.

Four distinct issues are woven throughout Kingsolver's fiction: race, gender, social class and sexual orientation. The story is set in the 1950's when prejudice permeated most of The South. "There were separations between races and between economic classes. Blacks and whites moved in different worlds, their distance from each other illustrated" (DeMarr 51) in Kingsolver's short story. This is evident by rumors that Rose-Johnny is a lesbian, that her father was colored, by the lynching of her mother's lover, the drowning of the mixed-race baby, and the subsequent rape of her mother. Additionally, the black families in town feel comfortable buying supplies only after the feed store is closed, for they know they will otherwise be harassed by uneducated, bigoted white men who believe they have a right to run Walnut Knobs their way.

Before she commits suicide, Rose-Johnny's mother is wise to make changes in her daughter's hairstyle and name. Her actions ensure that Rose-Johnny's ambiguous sexual orientation will protect her from the men who had threatened to give her the same treatment her mother received. Figuratively, Rose-Johnny's mother has neutered her daughter and made her sexually mute. As a result, her odd appearance causes men to steer clear of the town's so-called lesbian, and they warn all females to do the same. Even though they ostracize her and add to the rumors about her lifestyle, at least Rose-Johnny does not have to live in fear of being raped. Tragically, Mary Etta Bowles suffers the brunt of their prejudice.

Cutting off her long hair and changing her name to "remake herself into two people" (Parks 2) keeps Georgann connected to Rose-Johnny. When Georgann's mother tells her she will have some explaining to do when she returns to school, her remarks are evidence that intolerant individuals demand an explanation for behavior or appearance that is unusual or does not conform to their standards of appropriateness. However, "in a society where nearly all the citizens condone the hatred and fear of the different and unknown, one person can pass on the more positive value of tolerance in a diverse world" (2). That person is Georgann, aka George-Etta, marginalized by townspeople who believe that she too is a lesbian, but who will continue her coming of age experience as she opposes and exposes the unfounded bias in her community.

Works Cited

DeMarr, Mary Jean. "Barbara Kingsolver: Life and Works." *Contemporary Literary Criticism*. Vol. 269. Ed. Jeffrey Hunter. Detroit: Gale, Cengage Learning, 2009. Web.

Kingsolver, Barbara. "Rose-Johnny." *New Stories from the South*. Ed. Shannon Ravanel. Chapel Hill: Algonquin Books, 1988. Print.

Parks, Joyce M. "Rose-Johnny." *Master Plots II: Short Story Series, Revised Edition* (2004): 1–2. Literary Reference Center. Web.

Wives and Daughters of Coal Miners
Truth Be Told: Perspectives on the Great West Virginia Mine War by Weiss Harris

In the late 1880s, Justus Collins, who had been a superintendent of prison labor in the mines in Alabama, arrived in southern Fayette County in West Virginia where he and his brothers bought acres of land rife with coal. He built and managed three company stores, two of which eventually burned. The third one, the Whipple Colliery Company Store, still stands today, 122 years after its completion. Joy and Chuck Lynn, the current owners, are committed to sustaining the 6000-square-foot structure as a museum and interpretive learning center (Weiss 6–7).

Weiss Harris, aided by William C. Blizzard, Cecil Roberts, and Michael Kline, has gathered information about the West Virginia mine wars during a time of "chaos and looting of the region's natural wealth and environmental splendor" similar to the fervor of "mad dogs in the sheep with blood on their fangs" (8) in his *Truth Be Told: Perspectives on The Great West Virginia Mine War*. The venture capitalists established their own system of "law and order" (8) by keeping the colliers and their families economic hostages, for they owned the mines, tools, housing, and stores. The mines were isolated far from towns, so workers were forced to purchase all essentials from the company stores with wages paid in company scrip.

This totalitarian control bled over into pre-marked election ballots; cheap pay for strenuous labor, such as building the infrastructure before work could begin; and surveillance henchmen planted as spies throughout the entire coal fields, their charge to listen for complaints and squash conversations concerning unions. To deter unionization, Justus Collins hired a diversity of immigrant workers, so-called "hunkies" placed in the most dangerous jobs, who did not speak a common language, so they were disinclined to band together. Because free assembly was strictly prohibited, anyone who was so bold as to "buck the system" was immediately fired and evicted, an impossible situation for immigrants who had no family in the U.S., thus no other recourse save life on the streets.

Black workers suffered the worst injustices. Their housing was directly behind the company store where soot rained down on them from passing trains. On the way to the segregated school, their children walked by white children who harassed them daily. Blacks were not allowed inside the company store except for certain days at limited times. Most of their trading was done at a side window where they would hand in a list and be handed back their purchases. Similarly, in Barbara Kingsolver's short story "Rose-Johnny," fictional storekeeper Rose-Johnny waits until her feed store officially closes to open the doors to black customers, but her goal is to protect them from intimidation by racist white men, not to belittle them. However, this West Virginia debasement of black coal miners was to keep them separate and to send a not- so-subtle message of their worth. In fact, there were tales of the miners being "expendable" (21), because they did not cost anything and there were others who would willingly take their place. On the other hand, valuable mine mules and ponies were expensive to replace.

Every aspect of the miners' lives was controlled by the company owners who knew the uneducated workers, with many mouths to feed, were defenseless against the constraints of their bosses. The unbridled manipulation of the colliers' lives was akin to slavery. Daily, they lived in fear from economic threats that were "palpable," for they had no rights (18–19). The miners knew that a code of solidarity—their silence—was expected if they were to survive in the coal camps. Their wives also learned to remain silent about the most egregious acts perpetrated against them—behind the Coal Curtain.

To be honest, women have always had what men want, and unscrupulous men of wealth, power, and authority have taken advantage of those attributes to meet their own physical needs, disregarding the consequences for women. The second-floor cordoned room at Whipple was the physical counterpart to the mostly political barrier of the Soviet Iron Curtain and "a mantel of darkness and devaluation" (36). Although publicly designated a fitting room where women allegedly went with company guards to try on shoes in private, human rights abuses occurred in this "rape room." It was a place of barter—shoes, clothing, food, extra scrip, and rent—in exchange for sexual servitude. Called the Esau agreement, it required women to sacrifice their bodies so their children had food in their stomachs and roofs over their heads. If their husbands were sick, injured, or laid-off, they had no other choice. To break their silence about these injustices would result in immediate eviction and destitution. Attractive young girls were also lured into the same situation. Called "comfort girls," they were often taken to remote locations to live temporarily with company men who offered them better living conditions in return for sexual favors. If they became pregnant, their babies were sold to orphanages in Tennessee (49). This despicable traumatization of young women also crossed cultural borders. From the early to middle 1900s during World War II Japanese colonization, many girls from Korea were also victimized—forced into sexual bondage within "comfort stations" (Sung 11).

Sons were also not immune to the hardships of life in the coal mines. Many boys, as young as eight years old, were sent underground with their small aluminum dinner pails to do the work of gown men. Michael Kline reports that Emile Zola, in his work *Germinal*, about life in late nineteenth century French coal fields, exposed similar circumstances: "child labor, appalling working conditions, hunger, ever mounting debt at the company store, crippling and maiming from industrial accidents, and early death from industrial diseases" (qtd. in Harris 5). When circumstances required miners to extend their credit, they need only to send their wives or daughters as payment. State officials tried to minimize the "Draconian rule" (202) of coal barons and the atrocities committed against coal mining families, silenced by fear of losing their livelihood, but the mine owners shamelessly held the workers to a life of subjugation; the bottom line was profit at any cost.

Works Cited

Harris, Wess. *Truth Be Told: Perspectives on the Great West Virginia Mine War, 1980 to Present*. West Virginia: Appalachian Community Services, 2015. Print.
Sung, Yoo Kyung. "Hearing the Voices of 'Comfort Women': Confronting Historical Trauma in Korean Children's Literature." *A Journal of International Children's Literature* 50.1 (2012): 20–30. Literary Reference Center. Web.

Walter
The Cove by Ron Rash

Ron Rash, poet, short story writer, and novelist, is a professor of Appalachian Cultural Studies at Western Carolina University in Cullowhee, North Carolina. His fifth novel, *The Cove*, set in 1918 near the end of World War I, is a "dark tale of Appalachian superstition and jingoism so good it gives you chills. ("The Cove" *Kirkus Reviews*). Three miles from the nearest town and "tucked in the Appalachian Mountains is a cursed, shadowy place—the cove" (Anderson 68). Joanne Wilson deemed *The Cove* an efficacious novel that "skillfully overlays its tragic love story with pointed social commentary" (qtd. in "Ron Rash" 6) and stays true to the "local language" (Crowe 67) of Appalachia. The lives of the three main characters—Hank, Laurel, and Walter—are significantly impacted by Rash's trademark themes of loss, alienation, suffering, and redemption.

The Shelton siblings, Hank and Laurel, live alone on remote farmland that locals believe is evil, but "pain and violence here are caused by not a curse, however, but by human cruelty" (Sullivan 78). Interesting to note is that the author gives the female protagonist the reverse name of Shelton Laurel, a North Carolina area of great bloodshed during the Civil War and the cause of its being known as bloody Madison County. The 1863 Shelton Laurel Massacre "personified the hatred, division, and desperation" (Osment) which are replicated in the novel, as evinced by the way people treat the siblings, particularly Laurel. Just as residents are divided by their loyalty to or suspicions of Hank and Laurel, during the Civil War, inhabitants were deeply divided by their loyalty to either the Confederacy or the Union. The end result is the same—the loss of innocent lives. In fact, Ron Rash remarked in an interview with Digital Heritage that at the end of the Shelton Laurel struggle over allegiance, the youngest soldier was the last to die by firing squad, even though he begged for mercy. The fifteen-year-old boy lost his life due to association with the "wrong side" as do Laurel and Hank because they have unknowingly harbored a German hun.

While serving in the war, Hank loses his right hand, a visual symbol that he is damaged goods; his loss also foreshadows that he will not be able to fully protect himself or his sister. Laurel's distinguishing feature, an unusual purple birthmark, is most likely a vascular birthmark, a "port-wine stain made of dilated blood capillaries" (WebMD) that often appear on the face. It makes her an easy target for superstitions and prompts false rumors that she caused her father's death.

The literary traditions concerning natural body markings run the gamut regarding size, color, location, shape, and meaning. In Genesis 4:10–15, after Cain, who like the Sheltons is a tiller of the soil, murders his brother Abel, he initially receives a verbal curse from God but then a mark which designates forgiveness, mercy, and protection. Revelation 13:16 of the New Testament warns of the dangers of the mark of the beast, the number 666 which is the symbol of man. Over time, myths about birthmarks have interpreted them as ominous signs. In some cultures, people with birthmarks have been isolated from the rest of the community, as is Laurel. In Nathaniel Hawthorne's short story "The Birthmark," the beautiful Georgina also has a birthmark on her face. Although she has always considered it a charm, her scientist husband perceives it as a repugnant flaw, and because it is in the shape of a tiny hand, her female detractors deem it a bloody hand, connoting a murderous act, relative to both Biblical Cain and the superstitions surrounding Laurel. The birthmarks of both women indirectly cause their deaths—Georgina's by her husband's botched removal and Laurel's because the coward who kills her has no sympathy for such a cursed woman.

"The gripping plot, Gothic atmosphere, and striking descriptions, in particular of the dismal cove, make this a top-notch story of an unusual place and its fated and fearful denizens" ("The Cove" *Publishers Weekly*). Ostracized and branded a witch by townspeople who dare not step foot in the isolated cove, Laurel's presence in the area makes it seem even more mysterious and forbidding. Colored bottles hanging from trees just outside their property alert strangers, if they dare to proceed farther, to the presence of an evil woman.

The song Walter plays from his silver flute is a wistful ballad that needs no words, for it seems to find its origins solely in pain and loss. Nonetheless, Walter is comparable to a female siren, for Laurel is drawn to this stranger, as well as his symbolic mouthpiece, since he claims to be mute. Additionally, the mournful notes of the flute seem to speak for Laurel words that she cannot express in her sadness, caused by unwanted estrangement from a community that treats her like a pariah. She truly is the "other," shunned by her community.

The cabin is described as always smelling of "suffering" (Rash 44), but after a lifetime of isolation, and because Walter is a stranger with no knowledge of the superstitions about her, Laurel is hopeful that the cabin will soon smell like blossoming love. She prays that perhaps her life will finally be fulfilled with the friendship, companionship, and love for which she has so desperately yearned. Her own past "experience of suffering … encourages the development of empathy and compassion" (Lang 102), so she reaches out to Walter even though the townspeople have mistreated her like a stranger in her own hometown.

A shift in tone occurs as a relationship grows between Laurel and Walter. At this point, the novel progresses from a "mountain mystery" to a "love story … with restrained libido" (Crowe 67). After enduring so many people looking past her as if she were invisible, she is thankful that he looks her in the eyes and smiles. Mentally, she observes that he is enigmatic; he cannot speak, read, or write, but his music brings levity to her life. Laurel reckons that not being able to talk would be a fault that most women would not accept, but she is accustomed to quietness: no one "to share the silence … that was the terrible thing" (Rash 84). She has grown accustomed to silence, so she is grateful to have someone to listen. "What you say with your head nods is enough. I'd not ever want more" (107). She vows that his music is communication enough for her, and when Walter first covers her hands with his, she wonders about what has been left unspoken; after he comes to her room to lie with her, she knows.

When Walter finally admits his identity, he does so in a voice that has grown rusty and raspy from disuse. Ironically, because locals avoid the cove, it has become a symbolic sanctuary for Walter. Similar to a "mountain western" (Crowe 67), the men of Mars Hill are led by a "cowardly recruiting officer of great political ambition and devious means" ("Bloody Madison" 170). The posse of men literally ascribes to the notion of "shoot first and ask questions later." Emphasis on setting is evident in Ron Rash's mesmerizing narrative. For Laurel, the cove is an ominous place of alienation but paradoxically a silent refuge from outside judgment. After meeting Walter, it is a haven of budding love but tragically also her ultimate tomb. The author unfolds his story expertly; his characterization is superb, especially the "xenophobia that accompanies the war" and he weaves "narrative threads together with formidable strength and pathos" (Sullivan 78). The novel begins with a prologue in which a bloated head is drawn from a well on the homestead. Readers might forget that detail until toward the end when the identity of the submerged head is revealed—ah, sweet irony!

Works Cited

Anderson, Lisa. "The Cove." *Library Journal* 137.14 (2012): 68. Literary Reference Center. Web.

"Bloody Madison." *Thomas Wolfe Review* 36 (Annual 2012): 170. Literature Resource Center. Web.

"The Cove." *Kirkus Reviews* (2012): 35. Literary Reference Center. Web.

"The Cove." *Publishers Weekly* 259.2 (2012): 1. Literary Reference Center. Web.

Crowe, Thomas. "The Cove." *Now & Then: The Appalachian Magazine* 29.1 (2013): 67. Print.

Lang, John. *Understanding Ron Rash*. Columbia: University of South Carolina Press, 2014. Print.

Osment, Timothy N. "Shelton Laurel Massacre." Digital Heritage, 2010.

Rash, Ron. *The Cove*. New York: HarperCollins, 2012. Print.

"Red Birthmarks, Hemangiomas, and Your skin." WebMD, 2010.

"Ron Rash." *Contemporary Authors Online*. Detroit: Gale, 2013. Biography in Context. Web.

Sullivan, Patrick. "The Cove." *Library Journal* 136.17 (2011): 78. Literary Reference Center. Web.

Rachel Harmon, Mrs. Galloway and McIntyre
Serena by Ron Rash

In his essay "The Gift of Silence," also used as a corporate press release, Ron Rash muses about his experiences with quietude. As a child, he had difficulty pronouncing certain words, so his parents sent him to a speech therapist when he was five years old. However, "certain habits of silence had taken hold" until he believed that as long as he "listened attentively enough to others my own tongue would be able to mimic their words.... I became comfortable with silence" (Rash "The Gift"). One of his most treasured memories was of sitting on the porch in the evenings with relatives as their "tongues set free words I could not master" (Rash). When he began school, he learned that the written word could be a powerful tool of communication; thus commenced his career as a writer.

Most readers and critics alike would agree that *Serena* is a masterpiece in the literary canon of Ron Rash. Mark Powell claims, "While *Serena* stands alone, it simultaneously stands on the shoulders of all that has come before it" (204). The Gothic novel is set in the Depression era of the 1920s and 1930s in the Appalachian Mountains near Waynesville, North Carolina. As the government works to designate the land for the Great Smoky Mountains National Park, a historically accurate event, the greedy, fictional Pembertons are timber barons who do their best to "scalp the better part of the Southern Appalachians" (201). The ruthless Pembertons wield their power over both friend and foe, for they are as passionate about killing, whether animal or human, as they are about coupling.

Both "alluring and repellant" (Charles), Serena, the central character and emasculator of all male characters, is so self-confident and authoritative that the rugged men in the logging camp respect but also fear her. She is merciless, the "penultimate amoral force ... villain, a *belle dame sans merci*" (Brown 62). Although not a silent character, Serena refuses to speak about her past, which is of no consequence to her. Her concern is for the present, and she will "silence" anyone who tries to deter her from her quest. The only occasion of vulnerability in this woman is when she miscarries Pemberton's son. When told she cannot have more children, she is silent, unable to find words of response to the devastating news.

Two of the relatively silent characters in the novel are Abe Harmon and his daughter Rachel, a young camp girl whom George Pemberton had bedded before he wed Serena and who becomes pregnant with his child. She and her father sit on a bench at the train station, "watchful and silent as actors awaiting their cues" (Rash 7). To seek revenge and to preserve the honor of his daughter, Abe Harmon plans to kill Pemberton with his bowie knife, but he is no match for Pemberton, "a man in power, a man with power, and a man of power" (Willis 14) and Pemberton's new hunting knife. Bending over her dead father, Rachel's tears and sorrow do not elicit any sounds (10). The reader should note that Serena will regret returning the bowie knife to Rachel.

Immediately after Rachel's mother left them, her father threatened to slap her if she ever spoke again about her mother; Rachel eventually forgets the sound of her voice. Harmon was a quiet, bitter man, awkward with words and showing his emotions, but before he died he placed a cradle by her bed, "not speaking a single word acknowledging he'd made it for the child" (50). With her stomach growing larger each day, Rachel receives disdainful looks and judgmental stares from the women in town who abruptly stop talking when they see her.

When Rachel sees Pemberton later, she lowers her head and does not make eye contact. After a time of silence lapses, she merely nods her head toward him. Other camp women steer clear of Rachel because they will not eat with a whore. In her loneliness, Rachel believes that "being starved for words was the same as being starved for food, because both left a hollow place inside you" (130).

Galloway's mother rarely speaks, and her few words "are imbued with irony and foreshadowing" (Brown 62). When Pemberton inquires if she ever speaks, Galloway replies, "Only if she's got something worth listening to" (119). A blind seer, Mrs. Galloway is analogous to the Theban Tiresias who has visions of the future although his prophesies are not believed. The loggers themselves are likened to a Greek chorus that "serves as one of the novel's centers of moral conscience" (Lang 91). In Greek tragedy, the function of the chorus is to add commentary and to warn the protagonists of their fallacies in logic or reactions. Like Oedipus, George Pemberton is unaware of his fate, so he could use words of advice, but although the logging men do make predictions and comments about the camp environment, they never speak their concerns in the presence of Pemberton or the vindictive Serena.

After Serena saves his life, Galloway reveals that his mother has prophesied that her son will be saved by a woman, and then he will be "honor bound to protect that woman and do her bidding for the rest of his life" (181), an interesting element of foreshadowing of his role as her guard dog and henchman. He mutes Dr. Cheney by cutting out his tongue, but the slow and excruciating death of George Pemberton is Serena and Galloway's most calculated killing. Years later, while Serena and Galloway are in Brazil, Rachel's son Jacob hunts them down and uses his grandfather's knife to silence Serena; he does the same to Galloway, who has terrorized his mother for years in his unrelenting efforts to track her down.

McIntyre, an uneducated lay preacher, misquotes scripture as a warning to the other workers about the end times. Straight from the book of Revelation is the moniker he gives Serena, "the whore of Babylon ...

brazen as Jezebel" (30). When he regains consciousness from the snake incident, he tries "to speak, but only a few inarticulate sounds came from his throat" (105). Eventually rehired, he does not utter a word, so the men surmise several reasons for his muteness. Some say he has taken a "vow of silence" (322) and others believe he is expecting a sign before he will speak again. As the men discuss the many deaths ordered by Serena and carried out by "Stub" Galloway, McIntyre speaks one last line, "I think this is what the end of the world will be like" (336), perhaps representative of the novel's theme that man is "fast destroying nature ... the last ties that bind us to a recognizable humanity" (Powell 203).

Works Cited

Brown, Joyce Compton. "*Serena.*" *Appalachian Heritage* 37.1 (2009): 61–64. Print.
Charles, Ron. "The Murderess of Smoky Mountain." *Washington Post*, 12 Oct. 2008. Web.
Powell, Mark. "*Serena.*" *Southern Quarterly.* 47.3 (2010): 202–04. Literary Reference Center. Web.
Rash, Ron. "The Gift of Silence." Corporate Press Release. HarperCollins. Web.
Rash, Ron. *Serena*. New York: HarperCollins, 2008. Print.
Willis, Rachel. "Masculinities and Murder: George Pemberton in Ron Rash's *Serena.*" *James Dickey Review* 29.2 (2013): 13–34. Literary Reference Center. Web.

Daleen Leigh
Sister of Silence by Daleen Berry

In appreciation for Daleen Berry's memoir *Sister of Silence*, first-place winner of the West Virginia Writer's Competition: Appalachian Theme, Lori Green Supinski stated that the memoir "speaks for all of us who couldn't, or didn't, have the words to express what we were going through" (foreword). Berry, an investigative journalist from West Virginia, recounts her childhood experiences living with an abusive, alcoholic father and a weak, passive mother. The fear and pain Berry held inside allowed her own terror to happen when at age thirteen, she was molested by Eddie Leigh, a twenty-year-old pedophile and friend of the family. He made young Daleen promise not to tell anyone, so she "unwittingly became a co-conspirator in the secrecy that would shroud" (Berry 19) her life for many years. As a result of her silence, Eddie's sexual aggression and abuse continued until the day she finally found the strength to divorce him.

Like the typical con artist, Eddie knew all the subtle ways to ingratiate himself with Daleen and her family, by generous compliments to her and an eagerness to assist her mother with necessary chores around their home. Eddie worked hard at his job, was not an excessive drinker, did not use drugs, and regularly attended Bible study with her, so Daleen's family and friends would not have suspected him of abuse. However, like most domestic abuse and rape, Eddie's violent acts toward Daleen occurred in private, so there were no witnesses to the crimes. She kept telling herself to "keep the secret, keep silent, be the good little girl" (104).

Why did Daleen stay with Eddie? She often wondered that herself, but her mother, who accepted her father's drinking and abuse, was the only role model she had known, so Daleen learned a scurrilous lifestyle from childhood. She stated that "survival is something that seems to come natural to Appalachian people" (41), and she believes this attitude, which has been perpetuated for generations, made her doubt her ability to provide for her children (180). Why did she marry him despite knowing that he was violent before their marriage? Probably because she felt that Eddie had ruined her chances of being with anyone else. Why did she remain silently compliant for thirteen years? Unfortunately, Daleen, like many other domestic violence victims, had to choose between "physical safety and financial security" (Carey 201).

Most female victims refuse to report and press charges because their batterers, especially if they are husbands, could become incarcerated and leave the victims with no means of financial support. Daleen was still young, had not finished high school, and had no marketable skills at that time. She also had four children, so the cost of child care would far outweigh any money she could earn at menial jobs. Eddie virtually held her in emotional and financial helotry:

> Domestic violence is a problem of enormous consequence. The ramifications of a violent relationship for a woman and her children are numerous and severe. While statistics indicate that many women are victims of domestic violence, it is impossible to quantify the actual pain and degradation many women endure at the hands of their abusive partners. Equally unquantifiable are the fear and terror they and their families suffer as they anticipate the next assault.... Battering is the single largest cause of injury to women, and physical abuse is usually accompanied by emotional or psychological abuse [McCormick 427].

This was certainly true for Daleen, who "walked on eggshells" around Eddie and often gave in to his voracious sexual urges, leaving her with unresolved guilt and shame. Like many abused women, Daleen began to believe his accusations that she was to blame, that she had provoked his wrath. She wanted her marriage to work, so she sacrificed herself—her body, her needs, her happiness—to either please him or assuage his anger, but she hated herself for obliging him. His pattern of lies and blame continued when he denied putting his hands all over her thirteen-year-old sister Carla, but Daleen knew Carla's accusations were true because he had done the same to her.

The potential danger to Daleen's four children, who were born within five years, was most worrisome. While she was pregnant, she faced the risk of Eddie's battering causing damage to her children *in utero*, but once again she remained silent. "More babies are born with birth defects as a result of pregnant mothers being battered than from all diseases and illnesses we now immunize pregnant women against combined" (427). Eddie's *modus operandi* ranged from neglect to abuse to terror, so they all lived in constant fear of what he might to do.

Although Eddie would leave and be gone for days, she allowed him to come home, thus prolonging the abuse. She reasoned, "We lived in the Bible Belt, that part of Appalachia filled with God-fearing church folk where the Ten Commandments were still revered" (Berry 91). Daleen's strong religious beliefs deterred her from leaving her husband, so she hid her shameful secrets behind false smiles, far easier than disclosing them. She had made her bed—now she had to lie in it. Like many women before her, Daleen believed it was her fate to suffer in silence.

Daleen's opportunity to write for *The Preston County Journal* empowered her with the confidence to stand up to Eddie after years of his mental, verbal, and physical abuse. Ready to stop hiding her secrets, Daleen decided to tell them by writing her memoir, *Sister of Silence*.

Works Cited

Berry, Daleen. *Sister of Silence*. Morgantown: Nellie Bly Books, 2011. Print.

Carey, Camille, and Robert A. Solomon. "Impossible Choices: Balancing Safety and Security in Domestic Violence Representation." *Clinical Law Review* 21.1 (2014): 201–54. Academic Search Premier. Web.

McCormick, Tonya. "Convicting Domestic Violence Abusers When the Victim Remains silent." *BYU Journal of Public Law* 13.2 (1999): 427. Academic Search Premier. Web.

Chris Allen
Milton's Child by Kit Thornton

West Virginia native Kit Thornton claims his novel *Milton's Child* is fictional, but he does admit that most of the events happened to him, though not necessarily in the same manner or time sequence. The repeated, brutal beatings that Chris Allen, the ten-year-old protagonist endures from his father Clark, a Pentecostal minister, and the church authorities, make this book difficult to finish. As I read, my intense anger and loathing toward this so-called man of the cloth caused me to put the book down several times to regain a sense of emotional normalcy. This is a testament to Thornton's ability to capture and sustain his reader's attention.

Child abuse administered by people who embrace distorted Biblical doctrines is not a new phenomenon. In October of 2015, at The Word of Life Christian Church, two teenagers were savagely beaten by their parents and other members of the secretive sect in upstate New York. Police Chief Michael Inserra stated that "both brothers were continually sub-jected to physical punishment over the course of several hours, in hopes that each would confess to prior sins and ask for forgiveness" (McKinley and Mueller A1). During the intervention session, which turned into an assault, the boys were beaten with a cord and received punches and kicks to their stomachs, groins, backs, and legs. The next day, the nineteen-year-old died, and his seventeen- year-old brother remained hospitalized in critical condition. The Associated Press reported that the fatal beating was a result of the older brother's intention to leave the church (Fox News).

Neighbors nearby the secluded church building had observed strange behavior beyond the locked fence of the "immersive religious environ-ment" (McKinley and Mueller A4) but kept silent about their suspicions. Reverend Esper of the church next door "rejected the assertion" that the cult was a real church. He opined, "This is not of God. If this was of God, there would be growth, not destruction" (A4). Unfortunately, the people in New York did not want to become involved, and as in the past, their silence caused the loss of innocent lives. Likewise, the silence of bystanders in the novel almost cost Chris Allen his life.

A major circumstance of the novel is the 1974 West Virginia Kanawha County textbook crisis between two opposing social classes. The stark contrast between these two factions are described by the author: the hillers, educated professionals who live in the suburbs of Charleston are "liquor-drinkin,' rock-and-roll listenin,' pot-smokin, pornographic, homo-sexual, dirty book readin' fancy folk." The crikkers, coal miners, blue-collar factory workers, and welfare takers who live in the hollers, are so loved by God that He allows them to be "crushed in roof falls, cough their lungs out black with dust, break their necks, and let the hillers send them around the world to fight their damned little wars" (Thornton 190–191).

Traditionally, narrow-minded religious groups, like the Pentecostals hillers and congregants of other local conservative churches are adamant that the sin-riddled textbooks adopted by state education officials must be banned and burned, so they organize a boycott and multiple protests, carrying signs that read and prove their ignorance, "WE DON'T NEED NO NIGER [sic] LOVING JEW BOOKS OUR CHILDREN BELONGS TO GOD" (72). They, in effect, mute the words of the textbooks and stunt the learning of their children. Advocating that young people should not be asked, in other words follow blindly and silently, but be told what to think and believe (120), they become emboldened and establish their own church schools until the state concedes to their demands.

Biblioclasm can be traced as far back as 210BC in China and was continued historically during the Holocaust when the Nazis burned books written by Jewish authors. It is a familiar theme of literary works such as Nathaniel Hawthorne's *Mosses from an Old Manse*, as well as the dystopian novels *1984* by George Orwell and *Fahrenheit 451* by Ray Bradbury. Popular films with similar themes include *Footloose, Pleasantville, The Book of Eli, and The Book Thief.* Book banning and burning still occur intermittently due to fear and dissenting points of view in ultra- conservative areas. Proponents seem oblivious to the dangers of erasing or destroying realities of culture—good, bad, or ugly. As a result, an annual Banned Book Week has been established in the U.S. During this week, individuals are encouraged to publicly read and champion books that have appeared on past banned book lists.

Trouble seems to follow Chris Allen. His life eventually becomes smothered in silence: an electric silence, a pressurized silence, a humiliating silence, an oppressive silence, a silence in fear of retribution. Originally, his simple, truthful responses to his parents and teachers are misconstrued as showing off or talking back, but the reader can sense their fear at not being in complete control. Chris is puzzled by the lies told about him and the punitive measures they mete out, so he begins to remain silent to their questions and stoic during the beatings. Their reactions to his silence go beyond being sadistic, for they have misconstrued Proverbs 13:24: "He that spareth his rod hateth his son, but he who loveth him chasteneth him betimes." The adults are intimidated by this Appalachian child's intelligence and calm demeanor. Frustrated that they cannot break his independent spirit, they believe corporal punishment will prove their authority and domination over the boy. Chris' superior knowledge and logical thinking are useless against his large, vitriolic father, who wishes to tame his spiritually errant son and" beat the devil" out of him with lashes from a leather belt. The church school principal uses his thick "board of education," to send the message that Chris is to obey his rule, but these devices of instruction only leave Chris choking for breath, unable to speak out, and mark him with severe bruises.

Irrational fear is pervasive in this community. Besides the physical harm to his body, Chris' heart also takes a beating when he realizes the adults are in collusion and will eventually betray him—medical professionals, social workers, and local police officials (due to pressure from church leaders and Ku Klux Klansmen). "Chris sat as still as a stone. He did not think his heart could break more, but it had turned to cold fire in his chest. He felt tears welling up in his chest, but he forced them down. He would never cry for them again" (132). Tragically, Chris cannot even trust his own mother who professes to love him but supports his father rather than intervenes on his behalf. The horrific attempt at exorcism, which almost kills Chris, and the absurd religious zeal and mindset are comparable to the fatal exorcism of Stump Hall by his evil pastor and deacons in Wiley Cash's *A Land More Kind than Home*. They, too, tried to drive out demons from the silent boy.

The title of Thornton's 2011 novel refers to John Milton's *Paradise Lost*, which captivates Chris' imagination in his effort to understand the wide gap between Biblical tenets and the rejection and violence from his father, who claims to be a man of God. Even though his parents do not explain what he has done to receive such despicable treatment, they reassure him it is for his own benefit—to teach him to listen, to obey, and to break his stubborn will—a notion he cannot reconcile with his father's vile name-calling and "righteous" wrath. Milton's epic work has appropriate relevance to Chris' relationship with his father, for Book III of *Paradise Lost* addresses the "tension between justice and mercy," a theme of medieval morality plays in which Merritt Hughes noted the "Son is superior in love, wisdom" and kindness, and "challenges the Father to be better, more merciful, and less destructively violent" (qtd. in Graves 352–353), but Chris' attempts to change his father's ability to reason are futile.

Besides *Paradise Lost*, the scientific and psychology journals Chris peruses help him to speculate about the cause of his father's rage toward him. Through his limited knowledge, research, and personal interviews, Chris becomes aware that his father had learned familial abuse from his own father. Chris' pent-up anger frightens him at the possibility of his own violent tendencies. Research has determined the "empirical relationship between experiencing childhood physical abuse and becoming perpetrators of violence in adulthood" (Maxwell et al. 251), and that psychotherapy can reduce the chances of this trend continuing. Despite a determination to stop the cruel cycle and not spread the toxic infection like a "plague rat" (Thornton 94) or become a "vector for the disease of anger and pain" (92), Chris is astonished that his own internal rage toward his father is nearly impossible to contain. Within the heritage of this family, one can understand that the cycle of abuse is profound and a learned behavior that is difficult to unlearn.

Works Cited

Graves, Neil D. "Pedagogy or Gerontagogy: The Education of the Miltonic Deity." *Texas Studies in Literature & Language* 50.4 (2008): 352–84. Literary Reference Center. Web.

The King James Study Bible. Nashville: Thomas Nelson, 1988. Print.

"Parents of Teen Beaten to Death in New York Court." Associated Press. Fox News, October 16, 2015. Web.

Maxwell, Kendal, et al. "Breaking the Cycle: Association of Attending Therapy Following Childhood Abuse and Subsequent Perpetration of Violence." *Journal of Family Violence* 31.2 (2016): 251–58. Springer Link. Web.

McKinley, Jesse, and Benjamin Mueller. "Glimpses Inside Secretive Sect after Killing at Upstate New York Church." *New York Times*, 14 October 2015. Web.

Thornton, Kit. *Milton's Child*. Huntington: Mid-Atlantic Highlands, 2011. Print.

Bea Todd
Appalachian Child: The Chronicles of an Abused Child and Her Journey to Survival by Bea Todd

Like Chris Allen in *Milton's Child*, Bea B. Todd also endured a childhood of constant threats and beatings from her father. The major difference is that Chris Allen's father Clark was a so-called man of God who learned violence from his father. Bea's father, Vince Brown, was an angry, spiteful, self-centered, distant, lazy individual who learned violence from his mother. The major similarity is that both men tried to make up for their emotional weaknesses by using verbal and physical cruelty to control their families. In her 2010 memoir, *Appalachian Child: The Chronicles of an Abused Child and Her Journey to Survival*, native West Virginian Bea Todd breaks her silence to reveal the multiple layers and years of her father's abuse.

Bea grew up in Nicholas County, an impoverished rural area of West Virginia. Money and household amenities were few, but abuse from Vince Brown's mouth spewing vile names and his hands, feet, and belt were plentiful and frequent. Similar to Chris Allen, Bea could not understand why her father seemed to loathe her, as she was the main target of his most volatile rage. Although Bea felt responsible for intervening on her mother's behalf, Jean rarely reciprocated, for if Bea told on her father, her mother would confront him, and then the abuse would be worse, thus her silence about her father's misdeeds. Because the violence was a never- ending cycle in their home, Bea cannot recall a single time when her father showed her affection. She wrote that "he simply didn't love me" (152). Bea was convinced that he would kill her if she didn't leave home as soon as possible, but living in an area with no means of public assistance or support, Bea believed that her silence was the best way to avoid provoking her father's wrath and to lessen the number and severity of the beatings. Her memoir is as emotionally difficult to read as *Milton's Child*, for the level and means of constant abuse are barbarous.

Although Chris Allen's mother was not sympathetic about the abuse he suffered, Bea has many fond memories of Jean working hard and loving her children. However, the only thing Vince accomplished was to lie in bed spewing contemptuous epithets until he heaved himself up to administer his daily dose of self-pleasure. He had no empathy for any of them after he "kicked their asses or beat the hell out of them" (Todd 64–70), often for accidents or perceived offenses that were beyond their control. He iterated, "You kids aren't worth a goddamn!" (79). It is no wonder that he made them feel like animals or his slaves rather than his children. As a child, Bea knew of no other recourse but to silently endure the constant debasement in her home. If she could not depend on her own mother to come to her defense, who would?

In her book, Todd shares statistical evidence about child and spousal abuse but does not specifically cite all of her sources. She notes:

> On the average in the United States alone, four children die of abuse each day. Their ages range from just days old to adulthood. They come from every facet of life; across all social and economic barriers; and are from all races, religions and ethnic backgrounds (44). Male abusers are more likely to use deathly violence (108). Child abuse damages the self-esteem of the victim. This damage can result in hundreds of behavioral problems such as anger, rage, fighting, bullying, use of abusive language, inability to handle peer pressure positively, shyness, unwillingness to participate in activities with others, bouts of depression, self- inflicted wounds, suicide, torture, murder, and use of illegal drugs [111].

There is one satisfactory scene for both Bea and the reader. When Vince angrily told Bea to pack her things and leave, Jean retorted, "If she leaves, then so will you. I will see a lawyer tomorrow and I will divorce you. You will get out of this house and never come back!" Fearful of his wife's threats, Vince said to Bea, and not in his usual arrogant voice, "I don't want you to leave, 'cause if you do, your mommy will make me leave too, and I ain't got no place to go" (126)! He was willing to evict his sixteen-year-old daughter, but when the tables were turned, he could not bear the same treatment. There was no apology, so his out-of-character words and sudden humility were merely to evoke pity from his wife.

The origin of Vince's irrational rage toward his wife and children, especially Bea, is difficult to pinpoint, but there are several possibilities. His own mother, who modeled abusive behavior, was a harsh taskmaster with her other children and her husband, but she coddled Vince; perhaps he was in an emotional rut concerning repressed relationships. Targeting two females in his household also implies misogyny. He appeared to blame Jean and Bea for his bad luck, so he lashed out at them in frustration. His narcissistic attitude was most likely a cover for his low self-esteem. Narcissists "tend to be manipulative, selfish, entitled, vain, arrogant, hostile, [and] overly dominant" (Carlson 259). These traits would certainly suggest an inclination toward egocentrism in Vince's personality.

Manipulating his family's lives gave him a measure of power and control that he lacked otherwise. Jean was the hardworking breadwinner of the family, a position he forced her to usurp due to his lack of motivation, and Bea was an educated girl with potential for future success. Neither of these positive traits were part of his personality, so perhaps self-loathing was instrumental. When Bea left home, Vince would have one less slave to do the work he should have been doing himself. Why Jean stayed with her abusive husband until the day he died is a mystery that only she can reveal.

As she matured, Bea acknowledged the abuse "had left my soul less innocent, more saddened, and deeply scarred" (99–100), but she was mindful not to become bitter. After the account of Todd's father's criminal behavior, she includes family photos and important resources available to survivors of abuse. However, she ends the memoir with a disordered mishmash of topics which tends to lessen the value of her book.

Works Cited

Carlson, Erika N. "Honestly Arrogant or Simply Misunderstood? Narcissists' Awareness of their Narcissism." *Self & Identity* 12.3 (2013): 259–277. Academic Search Premier. Web.

Todd, Bea. *Appalachian Child: The Chronicles of an Abused Child and Her Journey to Survival.* 2010.

Patience Murphy
The Midwife of Hope River
by Patricia Harman

Set between 1929 and 1930 during the Depression era in West Virginia, Patricia Harman's *The Midwife of Hope River* introduces Patience Murphy, a bold and resilient woman who becomes a resourceful and compassionate midwife to women, no matter their color or social status. As a former nurse-midwife, the author is not only knowledgeable about the history of midwifery, but also the "sustaining power of community, human connectedness, and love" (Brown preface). Because of the subject of this novel, an interesting contrast is noted between the loud and chaotic period of labor and the anticipatory silence at the moment when presentation of an infant's head occurs.

The author piques the reader's interest early in the historical fiction when the narrator reveals that she is "wanted by the law in two states" (Harman 12), and that her name, Patience Murphy, is an alias. The emotional and social walls she constructs are for her own protection. She refrains from talking about her personal life, so "the habit of hiding my past is a part of me" (62).Throughout the novel, Patience freezes when she notices marshals in her vicinity, always fearful that she will be arrested by federal agents who have seen her face on wanted posters. She is like a modern day motorist who speeds, and therefore must vigilantly watch for a blue light to appear in the rearview mirror.

Murphy's involvement in the march at Blair Mountain demonstrates her belief in equality and justice for people of all colors, and her compassion is duly noted when she offers a home, companionship and eventually an apprenticeship to a young servant girl. Murphy's past life as a "worthy adversary" ("Midwife" 395) segues well to her present, when a black granny midwife turns over to Patience the care of her patients. Although initially leery of how she will be received, she does not hesitate to minister to pregnant women in the impoverished community surrounding the coal mines, underscoring that "midwives are warriors in this beautifully sweeping tale" (395).

In 1925, West Virginia Midwifery statutes required that women were "of good moral character" (23), an attribute Patience questions about herself because of her past activities. Midwives were also forbidden to perform vaginal exams; however, this examination is vital for Patience to determine the progression of labor. A third requirement was a ban on using any type of artificial means to facilitate delivery, but Patience breaks this law only when she assists in a difficult or life-threatening birth. Although midwifery was considered a "noble and respected" (Nurse-Midwifery" 17) practice, some medical professionals were not advocates and even called midwives barbarian. Between midwifery and obstetrics, the most glaring difference was that midwives patiently waited for labor to develop naturally, even if it took days. On the other hand, many impatient medical practitioners used "excessive intervention" (Feldhusen 4) to expedite the process. By 1935, nearly 40 percent of births took place in hospitals, and by the end of the 1930s, "twilight sleep" was used almost exclusively (4).

Two specific scenes depict both humor and humility for Patience Murphy. First, after Patience declares a baby stillborn, minutes later the infant mews, and she is embarrassed by her misdiagnosis. Secondly, Patience assists the veterinarian with a neighbor's horse. After their success with the unusual delivery, she remarks, "Nice colt," to which he replies, "It's a filly" (46). Understandably, both experiences render her silent.

In brief increments, Patience exposes details of her past, like pieces of a jigsaw puzzle slowly being connected. Because of indiscretions in her youth she must remain silent lest she be found by authorities. Patricia Harman infuses her fiction with historical significance as she relates Patience's experiences to "suffragettes, radicals, and union organizers" (77), as well as Sid Hatfield, John Lewis and Mother Jones. At the core of the protagonist's troubles is her involvement in the battle at Blair Mountain. The memory of what she did that night during the riots is too painful to utter; consequently, she carries with her a "rusted tin box of guilt" (34).

Works Cited

Feldhusen, Adrian. "The History of Midwifery and Childbirth—A Time Line." *Midwifery Today*, 2000. Web.
Harman, Patricia. *The Midwife of Hope River*. New York: HarperCollins, 2012. Print.
"The Midwife of Hope River." *Kirkus Reviews* 80.15 (2012): 395. Literary Reference Center. Web.
"Nurse-Midwifery: Yesterday, Today, and Tomorrow." *Nurse Practitioner*, 2005: 17–18. Academic Search Premier. Web.

The MacPherson Family
The Silent Sister by Diane Chamberlain

In Diane Chamberlain's *The Silent Sister*, once again trauma and fear are the overarching themes, but in this novel for an entire family who lives in North Carolina; along with the fear, are numerous lies told and kept over a twenty-year span. The silence and secrecy of patriarch Frank MacPherson is as tight as wet shoelaces tied twice. He has multiple secrets which he chooses to reveal only to select individuals. The trouble begins when Frank's seventeen-year-old daughter Lisa, a child prodigy, kills her violin teacher, Steve Davis, with her father's gun.

Lisa, who does not speak about the repeated abuse and rape that has occurred for over two years, is a shy, petite girl with wispy, blond hair—she looks like an angel. Both she and her teacher share a passion for classical music, but for Steve Davis, Lisa is a mark of his success. He parades her around the world to perform in major concerts, usually among adult musicians, so she stands out and he takes credit for her mastery of the violin. She is a "true love object" (Begley 48); he not only desires companionship from her but also a sexual relationship. Because Davis and his wife have been unable to procreate, he feels compelled to prove his virility, so he chooses a younger partner.

"Offenders typically groom their targets, gradually seducing them by creating the appearance of caring for them," but there is a "power imbalance" (Hendrie 16) between this teacher of renown and his vulnerable student. Their relationship is almost *Lolita*-like with perhaps a bit of *Pygmalion* added to the mix, as Lisa is unable to free herself from Davis' tutelage as well as his oppression. She needs to stay in his good graces to guarantee her acceptance into Juilliard, and he needs her to stroke his ego and showcase his teaching ability. Similar to many pedophiles, Davis has an outstanding reputation that he can rely on for protection if Lisa makes accusations against him. He has "rationalize[d] their sexual activity as educational" (16) and identifies himself as a mentor, "that having sex with a minor isn't damaging. Rather, it's therapeutic … a way for a child to be mentored and empowered" (Wilkinson 47) by someone who is trustworthy.

Other secrets include Lisa being whisked away to have Davis' child; a mean-tempered old man who, in return for a monthly pay-off, keeps his lips seals about abetting Frank and Lisa; and Riley MacPherson discovering at age twenty-five that she is Lisa's daughter, not younger sister. The secret of greatest magnitude is that in order to avoid a trial and probable conviction, Frank helps his daughter to fake her drowning and sends her to California to live with a new identity. The shoelaces are eventually unknotted, and the novel ends in a true denouement, but the real tragedy is Lisa's loss of her true self.

Works Cited

Begley, Sharon, and Rod Nordland. "What is a Pedophile?" *Newsweek* 137.12 (2001): 48. Academic Search Premier. Web.

Chamberlain, Diane. *The Silent Sister*. New York: St. Martin's Press, 2014. Print.

Hendrie, Caroline. "Labels Like 'Pedophile' Don't Explain the Many Faces of Child Sexual Abuse." *Education Week* 18.14 (1998): 16. Academic Search Premier. Web.

Wilkinson, Peter. "To Catch a Pedophile." *Rolling Stone* 3/4.943 (2004): 46–49. Academic Search Premier. Web.

Liz, Bean and Earl
The Silver Star by Jeanette Walls

Jeanette Walls' novel *The Silver Star* opens in Lost Lake, California, and ends in Byler, Virginia. Sisters Liz and Bean must care for themselves due to their mother's bohemian lifestyle, for Charlotte Holladay fancies herself a singer/songwriter/actress with her "big break right around the corner" (Walls 5); however, all of her "leads" for work in Los Angeles lead to dead ends. Her world of pretense and restless spirit take her away from home days on end while Liz and Bean must fend for themselves. When the police snoop around their silent bungalow, the girls steal away in darkness and board a bus that takes them to Charlotte's Virginia hometown, which holds secrets, lies, and painful memories for her and where she says, "we were all experts at pretending" (69).

Because Liz and Bean have been left alone so often, they are independent, resourceful girls. They shed no tears, feel no fright, and show no hesitation to make their own decisions. They are actually more nurturing than their emotionally fragile mother. Even though they recognize that she is a negligent parent, they make excuses for Charlotte in order to protect her. They take a "vow of silence" and do not divulge any unnecessary information about their mother or the reason for their traveling alone across the country. Liz and Bean's intelligence and imagination help them to cope with all external interference.

When Bean visits her deceased father's family, she meets her cousin Earl, a five-year-old who isn't "quite right" (115), "different, not much strength, and he'd never really learned to talk" (55). He does not walk either, so he has to be carried everywhere. He is content to sit quietly at the kitchen table and watch his mother work.

Injustice of working conditions in sweatshops, factories, and the mines is a significant theme of the novel. Since Northern investors bought out the Holladay's cotton mill, they have lowered the quality of goods, rule with heavy hands, and offer paltry paychecks to harried workers who fear losing their jobs if they expose the owners. They feel trapped, with no voice to make right the order of their lives. They understand that if they speak out against the owners, they will be terminated. This is a typical scenario when amoral people are driven by greed and feel no sympathy for those who make possible their lives of wealth and ease.

Unfortunately, the mill superintendent is a megalomaniac, black-mailer, and narcissist— not only with mill workers but also his wife who quietly and obediently endures his abuse. He also has law enforcement "in his back pocket." When he accosts Liz, she refuses to report the incident, fearing embarrassment, shame, and possible repercussions. Although her younger sister encourages her to break her silence, it is to no avail. That one man can wield so much power to silence the hardworking people of a small town is both a travesty and an unfortunate reality in some areas.

Works Cited

Walls, Jeanette. *The Silver Star*. New York: Scribner, 2013. Print.

Ruby Pickett and Iris Stevens
Secret City by Julia Watts

"When the U.S. Army came to what is now Oak Ridge, TN in 1942 with the Manhattan Project, one thousand families on 56,000 plus acres had to be moved" (Tabler). Set in 1944, Julia Watts' novel *Secret City* demonstrates the guarded secrecy maintained by the U.S. government in Oak Ridge while the atomic bomb was being developed during World War II. This is not the only secret in Watts' book, for a forbidden and clandestine affair develops between a high school girl, who is originally from Kentucky, and the wife of a highly respected scientist.

From the introductory pages of the novel, the reader is made aware of the seriousness of the government work in Oak Ridge, the gated city "with eight-foot-high chain link fences topped with barbed wire" (Carey 3). A poster on the guard house states: "What you see here, what you do here, what you hear here, when you leave here, let it stay here" (Watts 2). The warning comes with teeth, for any suspicions, unfounded or otherwise, about employees might result in their immediate firing and the entire family being escorted out of the city. To acknowledge that any seemingly benign individual could have treasonous intentions, posters of young, pretty housewives are captioned, "People died because she talked" (13) and "Loose lips sink ships" (23). Newcomers are taught to be wary, for "anybody could be a Jap spy" (23). This ominous environment would also encourage residents to report neighbors or even family members they mistrust. Other historically accurate elements in the novel are identification badges required at all times and vehicles being routinely searched when entering and leaving the city.

The purpose of the Manhattan Project was to build the first atomic bombs to defeat the Axis. Each part of the project was compartmentalized to reduce overall knowledge of the work being done. The Oak Ridge assignment was to enrich isotopes U-235. Secrecy was so important that the U.S. Army, whose "priorities were security and pacification" (Carey 6) patrolled, monitored, and restricted communication and activities inside and around the perimeter of the city, which had previously been a sparsely populated farm area near the Clinch River. During the initial phase, the "isolated Tennessee community life was difficult for newcomers, who included many scientists and engineers from distant states. They lived among strangers in a strange place, working on a project they were ordered not to discuss" (2).

Because so many of the Kentucky coal workers have secured jobs in Oak Ridge after long stretches of unemployment, they are actually held in financial servitude. Instability due to the war, intimidation from the government, and loyalty to America guarantees their silence; they are told only that what they do each day is of benefit to the country. They most likely feel a sense of accomplishment in a joint effort, since young soldiers are fighting while they are working at home, and their patriotic duty is to support the war.

Americans often tend to romanticize war. We use euphemisms to dismiss its pernicious consequences, for war is a traditional part of our history: "the nation was forged in war (American Revolution), divided by war (Civil War), emboldened by war (WW II), and radicalized by war (Vietnam)" (McCarthy 1). To speak of war with patriotic phrases, such as "freedom" and "protecting America" causes us to palliate the "hellish aspects" such as daily casualties, loss of loved ones by family members, traumatic experiences, and destruction of the war-torn landscape (1).

Julia Watts paints a stereotypical picture of the mountain mindset in the mid–1900s. An avid reader, protagonist Ruby Pickett needs to "escape into words," away from her Appalachian life where teachers warned her she was "getting above her raisin'" (Watts 4) and that she should forget her hopes of graduating since she would soon drop out of school, marry, and have children. Unable to envision life outside of a Kentucky coal mining camp, Ruby's displaced mother, who often stares off into the distance in silence, also urges her to quit school and find a job. The reader should not underestimate the culture shock of living in a coal-mining town and then moving to a new city among people from differing social classes and levels of education, particularly the research scientists, military personnel, and upper level government officials. Allusions to Hollywood stars include Tyrone Power, Barbara Stanwyck, and Rita Hayworth, their films shown at the local theatre as amusement and diversions from the worries of war. For Ruby's friend Virgie, who speaks about the actors in a sacred voice, the movies have become her pseudo religion (70). Budding love is another theme in Watt's book, for Virgie's painfully shy brother Aaron shows interest in Ruby, but her indifference toward him foreshadows her preference for females. She does go with him to a dance, but since he does not initiate conversation, it becomes a "silent night" (138).

After Virgie's father is accused of sharing government secrets, Ruby asks Virgie to write to her from West Virginia, but her hesitation stems from believing the government goes through all correspondence from the outside and determines whether or not it will be delivered. In fact, some government mail addresses were factious to maintain secrecy. Other forms of communication, such as telephones and radio, were also heavily monitored.

The purpose of the city's first newspaper, *The Oak Ridge Journal*, was to keep residents informed and to build a sense of community, especially for those homesick individuals whose collective morale had declined. Patriotic messages accompanied each issue, and every article had to be submitted for approval by Army officials. Fran Gates, a former editor, recalled that it was difficult to publish an interesting paper and omit what residents wanted to know most of all— "what we were really doing in Oak Ridge" (qtd. in Carey 3). Secrecy in the early years is illustrated by the newspaper's birth announcements, which included only the infants' first and middle names; the parents' names were omitted altogether.

What begins as a babysitting job and innocent friendship between Ruby Pickett and Iris Stevens becomes a scandalous affair. After an affectionate moment between them is reported and Iris is immediately sent away for psychiatric treatment, Ruby laments that people she cared about "disappeared and were replaced as if they had never been born" (187). This scene highlights the level of control the government wields over Oak Ridge residents for the sake of national security. It also underscores the societal perception about homosexuality in the conservative South of the 1940s.

Although The Society for Human Rights was established in 1924, it soon disbanded, and the subject of homosexuality was not on the radar of "mainstream media" until after WW II ended. "When the national silence was first broken in the late 1940s, homosexuality was condemned on all fronts. All of the major religions considered it sinful and immoral, psychiatrists regarded it a serious mental disorder that needed to be treated, and nearly every state had laws criminalizing it, many calling for prison terms for 'convicted' homosexuals" ("Straight"). From his extensive research, pioneer Alfred Kinsey reported in his 1948 book *Sexual Behavior in the Human Male* that homosexual behavior is "not restricted to people who identify themselves" ("Milestones"1) with that sexual preference. In 1950, the first national gay rights organization was established "to eliminate discrimination, derision, prejudice, and bigotry" (1), but homosexuality was considered by the general public as a form of perversion and continued to be listed as a mental illness by the psychological community. Thus the reader can understand why a lesbian relationship, in particular between a minor and an adult, was perceived as a grievous sin during this time period.

Similar to Watts' work is the YA novel *The War at Home* by Connie Jordan Green. It is also about a Kentucky family that relocates to Oak Ridge for employment and discovers the restrictions and rigid security in the city. The specific details are significant because they inform young readers of today about the history of making and dropping the atomic bombs during World War II, and the ambivalent morale of workers, especially after they learned that the bombs had been dropped.

Works Cited

Carey, Michael Clay. "Community Journalism in a Secret City." *Journalism History* 39.1 (2013): 2–14. Academic Search Premier. Web.

Green, Connie Jordan. *The War at Home*. New York: Margaret K. McElderry Books, 1989. Print.

McCarthy, Timothy Patrick. "War Is Still Hell." *The Nation*, September 2012. Web.

"Milestones in the American Gay Rights Movement." *American Experience*, PBS.

"Straight from the Closet." *The Thistle* 12.2 (2000): 1–4. MIT. Web.

Tabler, Dave. "Wheat, TN Disappears at the Hands of The Manhattan Project." Center for Oak Ridge Oral History Panel Discussion. *Appalachian History*, 2016. Web.

Watts, Julia. *Secret City*. Tallahassee: Bella Books, 2013. Print.

The Silence of Deference

Gertie Nevels
The Dollmaker
by Harriette Simpson Arnow

Tillie Olsen lamented that "women's books of great worth suffer the death of being unknown, or at best an eclipsing" (40), and she counts Harriette Simpson Arnow's *The Dollmaker* among those works. Arnow's novel authentically portrays mountain people like Gertie Nevels as "particularly complex and resilient characters" ("Harriette Simpson Arnow" 37). Kristina Groover claims the novel "posits the domestic values of child rearing, housekeeping, and gardening against the canonical male story of quest and war" (219). Harriette Simpson Arnow's novels share the same compelling force: to draw marginalized mountain women to the forefront and underscore their depth of character, "their genius as well as their ignorance and fatalism" (Whitehead 67–68) within the confines of their limited power.

Arnow, who was most often confident and defiant, had a "quick wit and a sharp tongue" (Surface 63) and was bold in expressing her opinions. However, throughout her masterpiece *The Dollmaker*, the self-deprecating protagonist, Gertie Nevels, spends a lifetime of silence, in deference to most everyone in her world, no matter their gender, age, or position in life. The novel focuses on "human beings to whom language is not a means of changing or even expressing reality" (Oates 59). Like Robert Morgan's Julie Richards in *Gap Creek* and Ginny Powell in *The Truest Pleasure*, Gertie is only one of several female Appalachian characters who faces "daunting circumstances" (Drewitz-Crockett 118) with courage.

The only situations about which Gertie is not reticent to speak up are those concerning the health and safety of her children. This fact is proven when she uses her knife to perform a manual tracheotomy on Amos and when she screams for help as she witnesses a train severing both legs of her beloved daughter Cassie. The reader will observe in this work that master storyteller Arnow is gifted with the ability to fashion characters that are "achingly true to life, vivid and unforgettable" (Cortner 56). She addresses Appalachian themes such as "pride, honor, love, betrayal, grief ... alienation, powerlessness, and despair" (Whitehead 71).

The narrative begins with the Nevels' agrarian lifestyle in Kentucky, but ends in an industrialized Detroit where Clovis follows the pattern of outmigration during the 1930–1940s and leaves his family behind to work in a factory. A preference for life on the farm was echoed by the Southern Agrarians, twelve writers who collaborated on the 1930 text of essays called *I'll Take My Stand: The South and the Agrarian Tradition*:

> Their thesis was that human beings, and particularly southerners, functioned better under an agrarian, as opposed to an industrial, way of life and that if the agrarian way, characteristic of the Old World before the Industrial Revolution, were to be realized in the Western world in the twentieth century it would have to be in the American South. What the agrarians, more specifically, were protesting was the industrializing of the South as well as the general liberalizing of its intellectual life in the 1920s [Andrews 389].

This group believed that the South was being altered too quickly with no consideration of its loss or the cost in yielding its cultural identity (391). However, Appalachians, no matter how "firmly rooted" in their heritage, were on the "threshold" of a new existence—the "beginnings of the extinction of their traditional culture" (Miller 125).

Gertie is happiest staying busy on the farm, which relieves her stress and becomes her quiet manner of expression, but Clovis accuses Gertie of being jealous of his "machine fixen" (Arnow 88), and as their yearnings do not mesh, the schism grows wider, for there is a "great gulf of silence and secrecy" (Miller 151) between them. Although both are talented with their hands, Gertie has viewed her husband's tinkering as insignificant but fails to recognize that his affinity for mechanical things is as serious a gift as her whittling (Branham 6). After Cassie's death, Gertie turns her back to him when Clovis finally confesses his reasons for moving the family to Detroit, but his rationalization is misguided, and the travails they have endured might have been prevented if not for the lack of communication between them.

A large woman with low self-esteem but a spirit of fortitude, Gertie is deferential to her mother, a self-proclaimed victim and hypochondriac who stings her daughter with words of disapproval. Her mother is one "that even a daughter cannot love ... with her sniveling character and whining ways" (Kitch 70). Never a kind comment from her lips, she judges, upbraids, and disapproves of every aspect of Gertie's life. She justifies her harsh reproaches by quoting Scripture, telling Gertie she is nearly an infidel, yet her mother's punitive Christ is much different than the loving one Gertie envisions for her wood sculpture. Her mother's insistence that she renege on the purchase of the farm destroys Gertie's dream, for she is "dumb as ever under her mother's words" (Arnow 154). Her wishes disregarded, she boards the train for a guilt trip to Detroit. Disappointed that Gertie will not speak up, Reuben glares at her "filled with the contempt of the strong for the weak" (156). Gertie, who has learned meekness and diffidence from her father, opens her mouth to speak, closes it, and then stands silent under Reuben's scrutiny, nervously cracking her knuckles.

The train ride of "steerage on wheels" leaves Gertie silent and agape as it takes the family on a foray through a "Dantesque industrial hell" (Branham 3). The locomotive, a major "symbol of modernity" (Locklear 187), is the antithesis of a *deus ex machina*, for there is nothing or no one to intervene and reverse her destiny, except Gertie herself, for although she is under great duress, she makes the final decision to acquiesce and go to Detroit, so "her portrayal also concedes the necessity of conforming" (Locklear 51) to some extent. The train is the means by which Gertie and her children leave their home and heritage to travel toward an unfamiliar way of life, one to which Gertie is oppositional. The train is also a vehicle of death, as it takes Reuben away from her and then takes Cassie's life. Although her older children gradually become ashamed of their mountain culture and more easily assimilate to life in Detroit, Reuben and Cassie, who decline to do the same, share Gertie's yearning to return home.

Gertie is like many mountain women, who have an "affinity" for the "cyclic patterns" of nature and take comfort in the mundane tasks of an ordinary life. They endure harsh conditions, struggling against constraints that "victimize" them, and in their personal lives they face isolation, both physical and emotional disconnects from spouses, loss of loved ones, and a "subservient role in the patriarchal system" (Miller 6–7). Nevertheless, these women are to be admired for the sacrifices they make for their families, and often without complaint. Gertie immediately feels intense displacement in cramped migrant housing, and she is most resistant to the industrialized environment, for there is a marked contrast between Gertie's quiet demeanor and the constant noise of the factory and trains. In fact, the novel is a long series of contrasts: the pastoral, bucolic tradition vs. the urban, industrialized new world; established roots vs. migration; "freedom [vs.] constriction, democracy [vs.] hierarchy, and innocence and simplicity [vs.] experience and complexity" (Parker 204). Other contrasts include ownership of the Tipton farm, which would have afforded her "autonomy and a legacy of security" (204) vs. rental housing at Merry Hill, which provides no acreage for her gardening and posits Clovis at the mercy of the factory owners; the sustenance of the farm vs. purchasing food at the grocery; the safety of rural Kentucky vs. the dangers of the streets and railroad tracks of Detroit; and the natural inclination of Gertie's art vs. the profitability of the jig saw.

Apprehensive due to the strangeness of the crowded school and intimidated by the teacher's authoritative aloofness, Gertie cannot express the reason for her presence. She is docile and stands quietly like a child while a store clerk tries to explain about paying grocery tax. She offers no rebuttal to the hurtful comments by a neighbor who calls her a "big nigger-loven communist hillbilly" (Arrow 349), but her son is both angry and embarrassed by the verbal attack with no reprisal. She trembles and searches for words, but in her humility and timidity she cannot find appropriate ones (381). On the few occasions that Gertie is able to speak, she offers only vague responses. Ironically, Gertie often quotes Scripture, a long-standing pattern she has learned from her mother, although Gertie neither distorts its interpretation nor uses it for condemnation.

Gertie is deferential to Clovis, especially when he is angry. When he scolds and rebukes her, she is "silenced by his blazing eyes" (536) then rueful of her distrust. Gertie's beleaguered mind falters, "picking up words [and] laying them down" (606), indicators of her indecision and self-doubt. Clovis reprimands Gertie for her discontent, and as a result, both Reuben and Cassie adopt the same sullen attitude of taciturnity. Rather than interfere when Reuben fends off neighborhood bullies, she remains "stony-faced and silent" (380), acknowledging that she has erected the wall between them. After a withdrawn Reuben steals away to Kentucky, Gertie wishes her volition were as strong and courageous, for losing Reuben is a major blow to Gertie's confidence as a mother.

Clovis admonishes Gertie for allowing Cassie to talk to her make-believe friend, claiming that the neighborhood children will think she is "quair," but Gertie merely turns away and keeps her lips tightly clamped together; Cassie responds likewise when the children taunt her. After Gertie finally asserts that Callie Lou is make believe, she regrets her words, for Cassie pulls away from her mother, does not speak for a week, and loses her life because she is hiding from Gertie while she plays with her doll. After Cassie's death, Gertie rebuffs sympathy and refuses communication with others, her only words an inner dialogue of chastisement and self-blame.

Unlike most women in Appalachian fiction, Gertie Nevels is both a loving mother and an "accomplished, productive artist" (Hobbs 169). The time devoted to rearing children or developing an artistic talent pulls on both "energies and emotions" (171) and is a difficult balance to achieve simultaneously. Harriette Arnow knew this truth in her own life, as she was a farm wife, mother and writer, often forced to compromise in one area. This dilemma is often blamed on husbands who have domestic expectations for their wives or on a social construct that deems "marriage alone a woman's career" (172). Gertie "grapples with the distractions and obstructions" (172) that deter her from sculpting the block of cherry wood, but she turns to her carving during times of contrition, remorse, and desperation.

In her grief, Gertie uses her knife, a tool which has become an extension of her deft hands and has served her well on many occasions. She symbolically becomes a carpenter like the Savior whose face she imagined on the treasured block of wood. Ironically similar, just as she tries in vain to carve out an identity of her own in unfamiliar surroundings, her treasured block of wood never receives a face. Instead, Gertie becomes a female Christ figure, a scapegoat, a sacrificial lamb that goes quietly to the slaughter, and the splintering of the cherry is representative of the fracturing of her family unit.

This final act ends Gertie's true nature as a primitive artist, for her artistry has become her voice and stipulates her new identity as the doll maker. She must come to terms with a craftsman's "perennial dilemma of maintaining one's artistic integrity or prostituting" (178) her talents. Gertie's acceptance of her changed world is symbolic of our country's conceding to the imposition of "modern industrial society" (Parker 206) that occurred between the 1920s and 1950s. Clovis' partiality for machinery is also a sign of that subtle shift.

Oates states that "exploited free-lance factory workers," Gertie among them, are not given a face or voice. "They remain mute, unborn" (61). Wondering at the purpose of her life, an unvocal Gertie, laboring with "her hands in silence" (65) is forced to make ugly, mass-produced, painted dolls, and consequently feels as if she were a betraying Judas, but the reader might ask if assent in Gertie's oppressed condition equals "betrayal or victimization" (Walsh 185). Rigney believes the merit of Arnow's novel rests in its depiction of the austerity of existence and the "futility of the human predicament" (qtd. in Walsh 186). Gertie, however, is merely one of many displaced women in Detroit, and each must discover her own path to adjustment, a capacity for contentment, and most of all her usefulness.

After all the sacrifices Gertie has made by uprooting her family, she has lost two of her children. If only she had found the words to stand up to her captious mother's demands! If only she had been bold enough to tell Clovis she had money to buy the Tipton place! However, because Gertie is passive, her downfall is a surrender to prevailing gender role perceptions, believing that "her subservience catalyzed a long, unfortunate chain of events" (Locklear 54) for her family. Consequently, Gertie endures a miserable life in Detroit. Unlike Langston's Hughes' "dream deferred," Gertie's is a dream denied.

Works Cited

Andrews, William L., ed. "The Southern Agrarians." *The Literature of the American South.* New York: W.W. Norton, 1998. Print.

Arnow, Harriette Simpson. *The Dollmaker.* New York: Scribner, 1954. Print.

Branham, Harold. "The Dollmaker." *Master Plots II: American Fiction Series.* Detroit: Salem Press, 2000. Web.

Cortner, Amy Tipton. "Why the America of Mattie Ross Needs to Read Harriette Simpson Arnow." *Appalachian Heritage* 40.2 (2012): 56–58. Print.

Drewitz-Crockett, Nicole. "Authority, Details, and Intimacy: Southern Appalachian Women in Robert Morgan's Family Novels." *Southern Quarterly* 47.3 (2010): 117–28. Literary Reference Center. Web.

Groover, Kristina K. "Domestic Novel." *The Companion to Southern Literature.* Baton Rouge: Louisiana State University Press, 2002. Print.

"Harriet Simpson Arnow." *Listen Here: Women Writing in Appalachia.* Ed. Sandra L. Ballard and Patricia L. Hudson. Lexington: University Press of Kentucky, 2003. Print.

Hobbs, Glenda. "A Portrait of the Artist as Mother: Hariette Arnow and *The Dollmaker.*" *Hariette Arnow: Critical Essays on Her Work.* Ed. Haeja K. Chung. East Lansing: Michigan State University Press, 2012. ProQuest ebrary. Web.

Kitch, Sally L. "Gender and Language: Dialect, Silence, and the Disruption of Discourse." *Women's Studies.* 14.1 (1987): 65. Literary Reference Center. Web.

Locklear, Erica Abrams. *Negotiating a Perilous Empowerment: Appalachian Women's Literacies.* Athens: Ohio University Press, 2011. Print.

Locklear, Erica Abrams. "On Teaching Hariette Simpson Arnow." *Appalachian Heritage* 40.2 (2012): 53–55. Print.

Miller, Danny L. *Wingless Flights: Appalachian Women in Fiction.* Bowling Green: Bowling Green State University Popular Press, 1996. Print.

Oates, Joyce Carol. "On Hariette Arnow's *The Dollmaker.*" *An American Vein.* Ed. Danny L. Miller, Sharon Hatfield, and Gurney Norman. Athens: Ohio University Press, 2005. Print.

Olsen, Tillie. *Silences.* New York: The Feminist Press at the City University of New York, 2003. Print.

Parker, Kathleen R. "American Migration Tableau in Exaggerated Relief: *The Dollmaker.*" *Harriett Arnow: Critical Essays on Her Work.* Ed. Haeja K. Chung. East Lansing: Michigan State University Press, 2012. ProQuest ebrary. Web.

Surface, Amber. "Through the Eye of the Needle." *Appalachian Heritage* 40.2 (2012): 63–64. Print.

Walsh, Kathleen. "Free Will and Determinism in Hariette Arnow's *The Dollmaker*." *Hariette Simpson Arnow: Critical Essays on Her Work*. Ed. Haeja K. Chung. East Lansing: Michigan State University Press, 2012. ProQuest ebrary. Web.

Whitehead, Sharon Faye. "Hariette Simpson Arnow: Out of the Shadows." *Appalachian Heritage* 40.2 (2012): 67–71. Print.

The Women
Oral History by Lee Smith

Lee Smith's 1983 novel *Oral History* is set in West Virginia, spans one hundred years, and is narrated by many characters, most by oral tradition but also from "Richard and Jennifer [who] both give us a journal rather than the interior monologue of the other characters; they are both immersed in the written language" (Dale 186); Jennifer's research notes frame the novel's beginning and end. Interspersed between sections is an updated family tree that aids readers in connecting the various characters and their genealogy. Smith acknowledges about her settings of Southern Appalachia, "Place determines who my characters are, how they live, what they believe and think, how they speak—often determining the narrative voice and tone of the whole novel" (qtd. in Werris 54), and in *Oral History*, the Hurricane and Snowman Mountains surrounding Hoot Owl Holler keep the Cantrell family isolated and protected from the rest of the community. The genesis of the story is patriarch Almarine Cantrell's infatuation with Red Emmy, a sorceress whose curse touches each generation of his family. Her power lends a "mythical quality" (Cassada 760) to the story, for her father has pawned her to the devil. The mystery surrounding Red Emmy both fascinates and keeps at bay curious outsiders. For example, her spit causes Granny Younger seven days of pain, and to get rid of her, Almarine must mark her chest with a cross of blood and her forehead with ashes, then loudly recite the names of the Trinity. She cavorts with an invisible barking ghost dog, and her intermittent laughter heard across the haunted holler is a symbolic reminder of her immortality.

Ironically, although female characters dominate Smith's book, they are sometimes silent and deferential to their weaker male counterparts, for "it's a woman's duty and her burden" (71). Throughout the novel, generations of Cantrell women, who have opportunities to leave home for relationships and better lifestyles, will not or cannot go, for the emotional gravity of the holler keeps them bound between the mountains.

On the train, Richard observes that the men "spoke little, mostly to each other and rarely to the wives. The women were a sad, downtrodden species ... quite subservient to the men, speaking only when spoken to. My few attempts at conversation were repulsed and I sat in silence" (120–21). Sadly, he also notes the instinctive affability of the mountain children changes suddenly to "poker-faced taciturnity" (158) when they become adults.

In church, he watches these normally impassive people letting loose to avoid the "fiery pit of hell" (159), speaking in tongues, using snakes to determine faith (one woman allowed a snake to slither across her bare breast), "wailing [and] screeching like Banshees" (175), flailing their arms and legs, and fainting. His surprise that they leave worship services with genuine spiritual joy parallels Aristotle's theory about Greek tragedy. He averred that audiences, after contemplating the gamut of the tragic hero's life—exaltation, hubris, error, and bathos— experienced an emotional catharsis of their own.

The "other" character is Rose Hibbits, an ugly, pock-marked girl who at the least provocation cries. Her skin condition worsens, her hair falls out, and eventually she loses all mental faculties, "slobbering and mumbling" (246) with gibberish sounds until she becomes merely an object of pity.

The novel is full of mountain folklore and superstitions. For example, during the Civil War, family loyalties were so divisive that a church in Abingdon had one door for the supporters of the Union and another for the Confederates. For traveling safely through the holler, one must keep a buckeye in a pocket; seeing a redbird gives one a wish; when a human or animal dies, ravens will eat out the eyes; "a witch will ride a man" (49) to death while he is asleep; for luck, sprinkle a newborn with chimney ashes; wetting one's face with the first spring rain will make it beautiful (this did not work for Rose Hibbits); "three shrieks are the universal indicator for foreigners" (150) in the holler, to warn moonshiners about possible revenuers; and killing a "hog on the new of the moon" (218) will not render lard.

Healing practices are also highlighted including laying a spider web, held in place with "soot and lard" (Smith 21) on an amputated leg to stop oozing; quoting Ezekiel 16:6 to stop bleeding; placing blood from a wart on a penny, then putting it in the road until someone picks it up; and curing thrush, which must be performed by a woman who never knew her father, by breathing in a baby's mouth while saying the "three most powerful names" (246).

Works Cited

Cassada, Jackie. "Smith Lee." *Library Journal* 108.7 (1983): 760. Literary Reference Center. Web.

Dale, Corinne. "The Power of Language in Lee Smith's *Oral History*." *An American Vein*. Ed. Danny Miller, Sharon Hatfield and Gurney Norman. Athens: Ohio University Press, 2005. Print.

Smith, Lee. *Oral History*. New York: Berkley Books, 1983. Print.

Weiss, Wendy. "PW Talks with Lee Smith: Appalachian Queen." *Publishers Weekly*, 2016: 54. Literary Reference Center. Web.

Julie Richards
Gap Creek by Robert Morgan

Robert Morgan stated that his novel *Gap Creek* originated from his wish to tell a story loosely based on his maternal grandmother who not only took care of him while his mother worked but also performed heavy farm work and tended to the sick in her community (Morgan 329). *Kirkus Reviews* noted that *Gap Creek* is essentially about suffering and misfortune, for the landscape and forces of nature wreak havoc and bring relentless conflict into the lives of Gap Creek residents. Morgan believes that a writer "has to touch quick and draw blood" (Wogan 371). Typical of his prose and a tale of survival in which characters must "push against" (371) the elements of the unforgiving environment, *Gap Creek,* chosen for Oprah Winfrey's Book Club, became an immediate best seller.

In *Gap Creek*, the female protagonist Julie is unable to express herself distinctly. Her "voice is not eloquent but simple and direct" (Bruccoli and Baugman). Morgan admits that Julie, is neither well-educated nor much of a talker. "In fact she feels inarticulate. She expresses herself best with her hands, with her work" (Morgan 329–30), her life's purpose as a support to her family. Julie explains the "empowering potential" of work, which satisfies her need for a semblance of control, a mechanism to deal with stressful situations, and an opportunity "to center and express herself" (Drewitz-Crockett 118). Morgan's use of a female point of view highlights that "women's experiences ... had much to offer contemporary readers about everyday life in the southern mountains" after the Civil War, and his "transformative decision" (117) makes these characters more endearing.

In an early scene of this rite of passage novel, Julie helps with Masenier, her ill brother whose body stiffens from a seizure, and his mouth draws back to scream, but he only gnashes his teeth as worms crawl from his throat; then he is silent and still (Morgan 15). When Julie's father becomes bedridden and she refuses to shoulder his work, her mother questions her, but she has no response. "There wasn't no words that fit how I felt" (28), acknowledging that complaints are futile—the work must be done.

The first time Julie sees Hank Richards, she is too embarrassed to speak. After Julie timidly announces her engagement, her mother becomes angry, but Julie does not offer a rebuttal. "I never was good with talk ... besides, there was nothing I could say to convince Mama" (48), for Julie is accustomed to silently obeying her parents' wishes. Although Mr. Pendergast complains about her cooking and cleaning, Julie determines that it is best to remain quiet (58), for she feels at the mercy of the old man while living in his home. She avoids quarreling with him because they have nowhere else go to. When Hank angrily reminds the old man that no one gives her orders except him, Julie starts to say that no one gives her orders, but instead she holds her tongue again (65).

Deferring to Hank is one issue, but Julie soon finds out that she is expected to do the same to his mother. Julie wants to defend herself to this haughty and demanding woman, but out of respect says nothing, for she is unaccustomed to talking back to her elders. Urged by his mother to show who "wears the britches" in the family, Hank snaps at Julie, but she can think of no reply. Her usual reaction to pent-up frustration and stress is to clean house, because work helps her think clearly. She states, "It was with my hands and with my back and shoulders that I could say how I felt. I had to talk with my arms and with my strong hands" (122), illustrating that "the ritual of work helps Julie ground her feelings and clarify her identity" (Bruccoli and Baughman).

After Julie gives a stranger their money and Hank calls her a stupid heifer, her heart becomes icy cold but she barely notices the physical pain of his slap to her cheek. "It was Hank's words that burned right into my heart" (Morgan129) and cause her silent shame. Julie has learned that refusing verbal payback to Hank's outbursts gives her a sense of power and control, for he is perplexed by her lack of resistance. She allows Hank to talk all he wants to, since she realizes that having the last word is of utmost importance to him (Morgan 140). Julie's passivity and quiet demeanor are additional steps in her rite of passage as a deferential mountain wife. She acknowledges that the hardships they endure are burdens on Hank's shoulders, but illogically, she willingly shoulders the brunt of the blame, even for incidences that she does not cause. Both she and Hank believe the stereotypical notion that a woman's lot is to suffer and she should do that suffering in silence.

Like Hank Richards, some of "Morgan's male characters occasionally threaten violence and often do not recognize or speak about the strength and personal beauty of their wives" (Conway 292). Hank is a prime example when he proves himself a weak coward during the flood. At this point Julie realizes she is emotionally stronger than her sullen husband who is despondent, yet she is determined to fight for their survival.

"Although Julie is initially reluctant to speak up for herself, she begins to set limits and define her own identity" (Bruccoli and Baugman). Julie is unresponsive after Hank admits that he was fired from his job, for she finally understands Hank's volatile "anger, sulking, and inarticulate fears" are more about him and less about her or her actions (Bruccoli and Baugman). After they are evicted and climb back up Painter Mountain, Julie utters no words of complaint about her struggles with morning sickness and cramps. She trudges alongside her husband in silence, resolved to face future trials together.

Works Cited

Bruccoli, Matthew J., and Judith S. Baugman. "Julie Harmon." *Student's Encyclopedia of American Literary Characters*. New York: Facts on File, 2009. Bloom's Literature.

Conway, Cecilia. "Robert Morgan's Mountain Voice and Lucid Prose." *An American Vein: Critical Readings in Appalachian Literature*. Ed. Danny L. Miller, Gurney Norman, and Sharon Hatfield. Athens: Ohio University Press, 2005.

Morgan, Robert. *Gap Creek*. Chapel Hill: Algonquin Books, 1999.

Wogan, Hicks. "Morgan, Robert." *Literature: The New Encyclopedia of Southern Culture*. Ed. Thomas Inge. Chapel Hill: University of North Carolina Press, 2008. Print

Lonnie Sawyer O'Riley
Be Still My Soul by Joanne Bichof

Be Still My Soul is set in Virginia in the Appalachian hollow called Rocky Knob where seventeen-year-old Lonnie has learned "to survive by fading into the background" (Hill). Lonnie Sawyer O'Riley is deferential first to her abusive father, who has never accepted her as his biological daughter, and like Julie Richards in Robert Morgan's novel *Gap Creek*, to her husband Gideon. Joanne Bischof opens her novel with a recurring situation for Lonnie—she rubs her bruised wrists where welts from her father's hands have left their imprint. She starts to question him, but bites "her tongue at the tremble in her voice" (Bischof 1). After Gideon O'Riley, a mandolin-playing rogue gives Lonnie an indecorous kiss, both of their lives are altered drastically. Lonnie's bitter, alcoholic father declares that like her mother, she has been soiled by sexual impropriety, so he demands that Lonnie and Gideon marry immediately.

This scenario is a page right out of Lil Abner's Dogpatch with an angry father coercing the reluctant groom to take part in a shotgun wedding. The purpose of this measure is to minimize the embarrassment and stigma of an unplanned pregnancy, yet Lonnie has only been kissed by Gideon. Joel Sawyer's insistence on this marriage may be twofold: to restore the honor of his household and to be rid of a daughter he has never loved.

Lonnie's father has judged and condemned her and Gideon to a loveless, arranged marriage, certainly not the autonomous commitment most couples choose. Multiple studies of American couples "shed light on factors that strengthen love, among them self- disclosure ... commitment, and communication" (Epstein etal. 342), but Lonnie and Gideon have had no time to develop a relationship. They speak only when necessary and without looking at each other, so love has not materialized, much less had an opportunity to grow. Epstein also reports that "other influences are family support and social values" (342). However, Lonnie's family support consists of a cruel, domineering father and a spineless mother, and Gideon's father quietly acquiesces to Joel Sawyer's gun-fortified demands. Additionally, Lonnie's conservative principles do not mesh with Gideon's moonshine-drinking, girl-chasing habits.

Shocked by the abrupt change in her life, Lonnie tries "to mute the thundering of her heart" (Bischof 50), for she is barely able to speak to anyone in the church or to Gideon's family after he takes her to his home. When she walks into a room, conversation comes to an impetuous end as his family merely stares at her in silence. Tearfully, she feels abandoned because "no one had saved her. Her ma, her pa—they were all silent" (52).

Lonnie has never challenged her father who treats her like a hindrance that he must tolerate, and she maintains that same quiet demeanor around her husband. Most marriages in the 1800s assumed fixed gender roles and societal expectations. Wives were to passively comply with their husbands' wishes, and the men were charged with providing for their families. When Gideon informs Lonnie that they will leave the next morning and she asks him why, he does not answer, so Lonnie soon realizes that "he only spoke when he had something to gain" (29).

Emotions inflamed, they walk in silence. Lonnie's stubbornness and pride keep her from complaining or asking Gideon for help on the rugged terrain, and he does not offer any. Ironically, this is quite opposite to his chivalry on the night he stole the kiss. When she lags behind, Gideon's irritation is apparent in his voice, but she is unable to respond because "her throat was so tight not a single word could slip through" (82). She utters not a word to him even after suspecting she is with child because she neither expects nor wants his pity. Even when Gideon eats most of their rations, her protest fails for she "opened her mouth to speak, then closed it" (96).

Although the young couple observes the attributes of a loving marriage through the wisdom and maturity of the Bennetts, Gideon is reluctant to let down his guard and speak to Lonnie with kindness and concern. Lying in bed together, they search "the darkness for words to assign" their thoughts, but the silence between them continues (140).

In contrast, Gideon had no trouble speaking boldly to the girls back in Rocky Knob, but his flirtatious intentions were based solely on his own amusement and selfish pleasure. His wife is of quite a different ilk. Her integrity as a woman and her proper deportment demand his respect, something he has never proffered to a female other than his mother. His cocky attitude and fleeting attention had broken many girls' hearts, but so far he has been unable to reach Lonnie's. Not used to having his charm rebuffed by women, Gideon is unsure of how to proceed with Lonnie, and he knows his past indiscretions are strikes against him in winning her acceptance.

In a childish snit, Gideon decides to leave, but realizing his folly, he soon returns. As they face each other "words did not come [but] were weighed down by silence and disappointment" (171). The wall of silence between them slowly begins to come down when Lonnie discovers the beautiful cradle Gideon has fashioned. However, the emotional barrier returns when Lonnie gives birth while Gideon is away. Lonnie shuns Gideon's attempts at reconciliation, and Gideon is tormented by "the silence, the sleepless nights" (327). Luckily, like many couples forced into arranged marriages, Lonnie and Gideon eventually admit that love has grown between them.

Works Cited

Bischof, Joanne. *Be Still My Soul*. Colorado Springs: Multnomah Books, 2012. Print.
Epstein, Robert etal. "How Love Emerges in Arranged Marriages." *Journal of Comparative Family Studies* 44.3 (2013): 341–360. Academic Search Premier. Web.

13

A Legacy of Silence

Eugene Gant
Look Homeward Angel
by Thomas Wolfe

One finds it difficult to capture the exact genre of Thomas Wolfe's epic novel *Look Homeward Angel*. Memoir, autobiography, confessional, Jeremiad, bildungsroman, lyrical narrative, and so much more, the verbose work spans the years of 1837–1920. Wolfe appeared unable to employ "self-discipline … he simply wrote too much" (Andrews 500), but he was determined to narrate the character of America (501), and as a result, he was accused of attempting a "Herculean transformation" of his own experiences into 'fiction of bardic proportions" (Inge 8). Wolfe's explicit details of people, events, and landscapes are numerous and phenomenal. William Faulkner noted that Wolfe endeavored that which was most improbable, "to reduce all human experience to literature" (qtd. in Andrews 500).

The life of Eugene Gant, the protagonist based on Wolfe himself, "is buried because he has little outlet at home for the energy—emotional, intellectual, and creative—with which he has been gifted" (Higby 4), thus the subtitle *A Story of the Buried Life*, an allusion to Matthew Arnold's poem. Like Eugene Gant, Wolfe was "the product of two strong egotisms: his mother, ambitious and inbrooding … his father, an extroverted and self-indulgent Northerner" (Cornis-Pope 1153). Their origins and oppositional values of this dysfunctional marriage produced the "cultural tug and pull" (Idol 468) of the backdrop of his writing. Narrated in third person omniscient, the book allows the reader to know Eugene through his sustained internal dialogue.

Varied reasons for the continuous moments of silence in Eugene's life are also difficult to categorize. Most of his family members are expressive, sometimes boisterously so, except Eugene and his brother Ben, called the quiet one, and with whom Eugene shares the "spirit of acquiescence" (Wolfe 38). Eugene is a complex character with intense sadness, loneliness (mostly self-willed), confusion, hopelessness, grief, and unfulfilled desires. Intense pathos from the reader is evoked by Eugene's tale of woe.

Eugene's father W.O. Gant, a chronic alcoholic, is at times a self-reflective man, but bellows drunken diatribes at his wife Eliza until they reach such a deafening climax that there is "nothing but the white living silence" (24) to follow, for all have retreated to their rooms and bolted the doors. W.O. silently plans an acroama which he delivers to his family just before they sit down at the dinner table. Gant "checks in" with Eugene to inquire how he is doing in school and if he needs money, but their relationship is remote. Eliza Gant, Eugene's mother and a contradistinction to her husband, is at least partially responsible for his lack of social confidence. After quietly observing her niggardly ways with possessions and money, Eugene asks nothing of her.

Except for Ben, Eugene's siblings do not share his academic interests, so their interactions are intermittent unless they are charged with taking care of him. As a child, he receives their chiding and cuffs, although painful, in silence. At the early stages of boyhood, a precocious Eugene learns by way of his keen abilities to listen and observe the world around him. Learning to read by age three, he is fascinated by the "structure of language" (71) and "the power of words" (Broadus), both verbal and written, so he labors tirelessly over his schoolwork. An easy target for bullying by classmates who think him queer, Eugene, who fears the taunting will escalate, keeps the verbal and physical abuse a secret. He is so timid that he does not ask his teacher to be excused; he feels shame at admitting natural bodily functions. Sick with nausea, "but locked in silence" (72), he vomits in his hands rather than ask to go to the lavatory. After school, Eugene yearns to spend the rest of his day quietly reading at the library, but his mother insists he work, although as her pawn, Eugene has a "silent horror of selling for money" (130) only to satisfy her greed.

Eugene's time at Pulpit Hill merely extends his isolation. He recognizes himself as the "Other" when he is taunted for his lack of knowledge about university traditions and his preference to live in a single room. His naiveté during an Exeter excursion to visit whores, who also taunt him, causes his mortification when he must reveal to the doctor his severe case of crabs. Articulation continues to be elusive for Eugene. When Gant asks his son about college, "speech choked in Eugene's throat. He stammered a few answers" (337) and then ran from the room.

At age sixteen, Eugene learns painful lessons about loss, first that of his beloved brother Ben, his only family ally in shyness and quiet demeanor. When he falls in love, he initially speaks to the woman in fear and timidity, alternating between halting gaps and spurts of conversation. After professing his love and being spurned, his mother dismisses his pain and regret as merely trivial, but he is unable to rebut her insensitive and hurtful words.

Eugene remarks that his family has endured a "splintered existence" (219) between residences, which Eugene despises because of a lack of dignity, privacy, and quiet repose. At this point, Eugene slowly gains an understanding of "how to reconcile his passionate nature with his perpetual loneliness through self-reflection and artistic expression" (Rohan 37). Of the Gant family Wolfe wrote, "they were a life unto themselves—how lonely they were they did not know, but they were known to everyone and friended by almost no one" (53). By the end of the tome, the reader will understand the accuracy of the phrase "O Lost," a lament which is repeated at times of despair throughout Wolfe's narrative.

Works Cited

Andrews, William L., ed. *The Literature of the American South*. New York: W.W. Norton, 1998. Print.

Broadus, J.R. "Look Homeward Angel." Magill's Survey of American Literature, 2006. Web.

Cornis-Pope, Marcel. "Wolfe, Thomas Clayton." *Benet's Reader's Encyclopedia of American Literature*. Ed. Barbara Perkins and Phillip Leininger. New York: HarperCollins, 1991, Print.

Higby, John. "Look Homeward Angel." *Masterplots, Fourth Edition*, 2010, 1–4. Literary Reference Center. Web.

Idol, John L., Jr. "Wolfe, Thomas." *Literature: The New Encyclopedia of Southern Culture*. Ed. W. Thomas Inge. Chapel Hill: University of North Carolina Press, 2008. Print.

Inge, M. Thomas, ed. "Southern Literary Renaissance." *Literature: The New Encyclopedia of Southern Culture*. Chapel Hill: University of North Carolina Press, 2008. Print.

Rohan, Joanne Joy. "Reconciliation of Opposites: Excess and Deprivation in Thomas Wolfe's Look Homeward Angel." *Thomas Wolfe Review*. 36.1/2 (2012): 37–44. Literary Reference Center. Web.

Tomkins, David. "Look Homeward Angel." *The Facts on File Companion to the American Novel*. New York: Facts on File, 2006. Blooms Literary Reference. Web.

Wolfe, Thomas. *Look Homeward Angel*. New York: Scribner, 1929. Print.

The Follett Family
A Death in the Family by James Agee

James Agee's *A Death in the Family* is the "only novel set entirely in the Appalachian South" (Brosi 45) to win a Pulitzer Prize. One of the major "prose stylists" of his era, Agee's *A Death in the Family* is a "poised and brilliantly detailed study" (McHugh 16) of familial interaction. Agee's work and life, both in "furious pace and brevity" ("James Agee" *Literature* 575) have often been compared to that of Thomas Wolfe. The setting of Agee's novel is Knoxville, Tennessee, in the summer of 1915. The autobiographical work, with its "keen sensitivity to adolescence" (Inge 8), centers on Agee's relationship with his parents and the car accident that took his father's life when he was only six years old. Numerous flashbacks of memories are embedded throughout the main storyline, which spans only a few days, as this Southern family mourns the death of its favored son, Jay. The Follett's suffer "an initiation story of the most painful" kind, addressing "the ultimate meaning of family" (575). The strained relationships forged among family members are the result of years of forbearance of speech and spiritual divide.

Throughout Agee's book, the Follett family display perpetual stretches of quietness in moments of both "tension and tenderness" ("James Agee" *Critical Survey* 3); they believe silence should be treated with dignity and respect. Although they are often described as lonely, they prefer solitude, recognizing it as essential to their well-being and perceiving it as properly intimate. They ascribe to the rhetoric of silence, which for them, is natural and pleasant, much easier than conversation or confrontation. Cheryl Glenn claims that a rhetoric of silence offers an "imaginative space that can open up possibilities" (160) between groups of people. However, the Follett's secrets and silence have caused them to accept a false notion of family. Several relationships are detached and empty, the origins from overdrinking by the men, especially gauche Uncle Ralph about whom no one dares to speak, and overzealous religious beliefs of the women, which are tolerated but not discussed. They rely on cursory glances, occasional eye contact, body posturing, and gestures to relay messages but struggle to express themselves verbally. Repeatedly, Agee's characters reflect, remember, wonder, think, carry on inner dialogues, strive in vain to find appropriate words, and wish to or should speak, but they censor themselves. Perhaps this is what Agee alluded to when he used the phrase "expressive pockets of dead silence" (qtd. in Baxter 176).

Sharing similarities to Joseph Conrad's novel *The Secret Agent*, Agee's work includes secret feelings, thus "silence is essential ... sound functions as a disruptive force," and to reveal those secrets would be "destructive" (McLeod 117). The Folletts' lack of disclosure is "manifest ... in fragmentations" (Yearley 3) and results in wider distance and dysfunctionality. Most often when the Folletts do speak, their responses are vacuous, and they appear in darkness or in shadows, their voices barely audible whispers or somber "grave" words that suggest a pall and foreshadow impending death.

Even the movements of the characters are restrained. They pass from room to room, go up and down stairs, and in and out of doors with discreetness, careful not to disturb the stillness that surrounds them. Like the character Verloc in Conrad's novel, the Folletts are locked in a "virtual fortress of silence" where not even a "whisper" from outside can permeate their world. As a result, they have become "indoctrinated with the necessity of silence" (McLeod 118).

After receiving news of her father's death, Catherine sits at the kitchen table, listening to the "whole quietness which was so much stronger than the sounds" (Agee 232). When Jay and his son Rufus (Agee's childhood sobriquet) walk through the streets, their steps are silential while they observe the rush of swirling wind and leaves falling from trees. As they rest outside on a large rock, Jay gently touches his son's head and shoulders, but he cannot bring himself to fully embrace Rufus, and he offers no words of affection. Later, when Rufus gazes at his father lying in the coffin, he notices his unexpressive mouth and determines that silence must be a standard for "strength ... manhood, and indifferent contentment" (282). The major elements that disturb perpetual silence in the Follett's world are external and mundane—the streetcars as they travel back and forth through the city and as Jay backs out of his driveway, the scroop of the old Ford, "a prime symbol of modernization" (Yearley 1).

Rufus and Catherine are frequently reprimanded and shushed for their innocent questions or comments. As if in a silent tableau, the children have been taught to equate quietly sitting still with being good. If they follow the rules of this disciplinary silence, they can expect to gain their parents' approval. Their sensitivity to a harsh word or warning look restricts their verbal urges, so they retain a calm, albeit uncomfortable, demeanor. Nonetheless, this "remoteness from humanity" (Agee 272) is troublesome. For generations, the adults in this family have squelched their own voices—their wills defy a desire or need to express themselves freely—and they have passed down this quiescent tradition to their progeny.

Although James Agee was educated at Exeter and Harvard, he always thought of himself as a "hillbilly" marooned in the realm of academe. Writing this novel "shaped his sensibility and imagination" (Fabre 163) to provide him both contentment and grief, as well as solitary moments of reflection after his father's death.

Works Cited

Agee, James. *A Death in the Family*. Centennial ed. New York: Penguin, 2008. Print.

Baxter, Charles. "Stillness." *Burning Down the House*. Minneapolis: Graywolf Press, 2008. Print.

Brosi, George. "Appalachian Literature." *The Companion to Southern Literature*. Ed. Joseph M. Flora and Lucinda Hardwick MacKethan. Baton Rouge: Louisiana State University Press, 2002. Print.

Fabre, Genevieve. "James Agee." *Literature: The New Encyclopedia of Southern Culture*. Chapel Hill: University of North Carolina Press, 2008. Print.

Glenn, Cheryl. *Unspoken: A Rhetoric of Silence*. Carbondale: Southern Illinois University Press, 2004. Print.

Inge, M. Thomas. "Southern Literary Renaissance." *Literature: The New Encyclopedia of Southern Culture*. Chapel Hill: University of North Carolina Press, 2008. Print.

"James Agee." *Critical Survey of Long Fiction*, 4th edition. January 2010. Literary Reference Center. Web.

"James Agee." *The Literature of the American South*. Ed. William L. Andrews et al. New York: W.W. Norton, 1998. Print.

McHugh, Frank K. "Agee, James." *Benet's Reader's Encyclopedia of American Literature*. Ed. Barbara Perkins and Phillip Leininger. New York: HarperCollins, 1991. Print.

McLeod, Deborah. "Disturbing the Silence: Sound Imagery in Conrad's *The Secret Agent*." *Journal of Modern Literature* 33.1 (2009): 117–31. Literary Reference Center. Web.

Yearley, Clifton K. "A Death in the Family." *Masterplots, Fourth Edition*, 2010. Literary Reference Center. Web.

The Stargill Family
The Rosewood Casket by Sharyn McCrumb

The title of Sharyn McCrumb's *The Rosewood Casket* comes from a 19th century song, made popular by Dolly Parton, Linda Ronstadt, and Emmy Lou Harris (McCrumb "Keepers" 182). The novel centers on the Stargill family, who for generations has perpetuated a legacy of silence. The novel "explores characteristic McCrumb themes: family ties, love of the land, and individuals' links to family and community history" (Mosby 4). McCrumb quotes playwright and actor Pinero who claimed "the future is simply the past, entered through another gate" (McCrumb *Appalachia* 45). She says that the more she writes, the more she is drawn to "the idea of the past as prologue" ("Keepers" 181), relevant to this work as she parallels, through the voice of Daniel Boone, the plight of the Cherokees and Shawnees who were the original owners of the land the farmers now possess. Then she reaches back at the end of the Ice Age to describe the mountain landscape when the first humans appeared in Appalachia. The point the author makes is that land being exchanged through various hands is a constant.

Set in Powell Valley of the Smoky Mountains near the point where

Tennessee, Virginia, and North Carolina merge, the novel's theme is about the "passing of land from one group to another, as a preface to the modern story of farm families losing their land to developers in today's Appalachia" (McCrumb 303). Concerning the disappearance of so many Appalachian farms, Jim Wayne Miller notes that families sometimes "awake in a close dark place over a motor's hum to find their farm's been rolled up like a rug with them inside it" (qtd. in McCrumb).

Current patriarch Randall Stargill has modeled for his sons a lifelong detached demeanor, stubbornly withholding emotions regarding both family members and outside relationships. His insistence that his four living sons come home to construct a rosewood casket allows the reader to immediately surmise that his request is only the means to an end—to physically unite these geographically scattered brothers in order to improve relationships among them while they work together. His secondary motive is that rather than sell the land after his death, his sons will realize how important the farm has been, and as the author notes, "to celebrate the land and to understand its power" (McCrumb *Appalachia* 19) for generations of family.

Randall's wish to keep the land in the Stargill family is similar to the situation of Wang Lung in *The Good Earth*, a novel written by Pearl S. Buck, a native West Virginian. Chinese peasants Wang Lung and his wife Olan have worked the fields of their land for many years, prospering as each son is born until they are able to purchase additional land. They battle "drought and devastating floods" (Yearley 2) as well as covetous neighbors and bandits to retain their property. At one point, they even have to eat the land to survive by mixing the dirt with water to make a thin gruel. After Olan's death, Wang Lung accidentally hears his sons agreeing to give up their "inheritance and spend the money they will get from selling their father's property" (Cutler 3). On his deathbed, he realizes that his greedy sons care neither for him nor the land, which will be divided and sold once Wang Lung is interred under it. This too is Randall Stargill's fear. Although well-meaning, his sons do not honor his request to die at home, so the reader might assume that they will not honor his love of the land but will eventually sell it.

Cognizant of his past, Randall's neighbors are cautious and steer clear of him, for he makes them uneasy. His wife Clarsie was the neighborly one, but Randall always remained quiet and unfriendly. When their son Dwayne died, Randall shed no tears and showed no emotions, and since Clarsie's death, he has continued to distance himself by rarely venturing past the confines of his farm, thereby being perceived as a recluse.

The oldest son Robert Lee acknowledges that he has never won his father's approval; it appears that he carries lingering guilt for not doing more with his life. He often turns away and leaves his wife listening to "empty air" (42). She claims the Stargill boys "learned early on not to show their wounds" (247) even if they ache from personal affronts. Upon news of his father's death, when Robert Lee emits a "loud, wordless cry" (255), he surprises his silent brothers. Ironically, he "takes it the hardest" because his father had loved him "the least" (275). Complex family dynamics are enacted by this common birth order circumstance. First-borns are normally saddled with high expectations, and if they are not met, affection and attention are often diverted to the youngest.

The second son Charles Martin displays his moodiness and "dark silences" (34) and does not invite others into his world of fame. During casual conversations, he can find few words and turns red-faced trying to talk about "anything more personal than his public life on a stage" (165), proving that he is comfortable only as his onstage persona. Third son Garrett has his own demons to overcome. Guilt from his past makes him feel a loss of his own virility, not a subject he wishes to broach with his brothers. In fact, the first meal the Stargill brothers share at the farmhouse table is "consumed in a strained silence" (89). This causes the youngest son Clayt to reason that he should be able to say something "to these strangers with whom he shared ... bloodlines" (89), but the words never come.

If the land is indeed to be kept in the family, it will probably be through Clayt, a lifelong nemophilist and Daniel Boone re-enactor, for he loves the history of the region and never tires of exploring the surrounding forest. He enjoys the silence of the natural world much more than the company of humans. In this respect, he is like his hero Daniel Boone who loved the "wilderness [that] had made him almost a changeling among his village-dwelling kinfolk" (29). Like both Daniel Boone and his father, Clayt shares a similar independence and aloofness to the people in his community.

A character who would like to divest the Stargill's of their farm is an unscrupulous realtor who holds to an interesting mountain tradition called "helloing the house." Mountaineers, who were leery of outsiders and watchful of revenuers, did not appreciate people boldly approaching their homes. Those visitors might receive a shotgun to the face, so it was best to announce their presence from afar.

Both history and heritage may explain the tendency toward silence that the Stargills prefer. The early German and Scots-Irish immigrants to Appalachia were spirited planters in a new agrarian environment. Those tight-knit clans might have harbored resentment toward outsiders regarding power and property rights for the land, which offered an abundance of natural resources and soil conducive to farming. In fact, they were often referred to as "sons of the soil" due to their strong connection to the land. The geographic isolation of the mountains made them socially remote. Additionally, they struggled to find words of easy conversation with others due to their limited education. Provincial, hard-scrabble lives led to their self-sufficiency and determination to manage problems on their own, so these proud mountaineers were reluctant to ask for or accept charity. Conversely, they were most willing to offer a meal, usually eaten in silence, and a bed for the night to those traveling through their areas.

Works Cited

Buck, Pearl S. *The Good Earth*. New York: Washington Square Press, 2004. Print.

Cutler, Constance A. *Masterplots, Fourth Edition*, 2010. Literary Reference Center. Web.

Mosby, Charmaine Allmon. "Sharyn McCrumb." *Critical Survey of Mystery & Detective Fiction*. (2008): 1–4. Literary Reference Center. Web.

McCrumb, Sharyn. "Keepers of the Legend." *Bloodroot: Reflections on Place by Appalachian Women Writers*. Ed. Joyce Dyer. Lexington: University Press of Kentucky, 1998. Print.

McCrumb, Sharyn. *The Rosewood Casket*. New York: St. Martin's Press, 1996. Print.

McCrumb, Sharyn. *Sharyn McCrumb's Appalachia*. Oconee Spirit Press, 2011. Print.

Yearley, Clifton. *Masterplots II: Women's Literature Series*, 1995. Literary Reference Center. Web.

The Arnette Family
Pretending to Dance by Diane Chamberlain

Diane Chamberlain's novel *Pretending to Dance* spans twenty-four years, from 1990 in the Morrison Ridge Community of Swannanoa, North Carolina, where the family owns 100 acres in the Blue Ridge Mountains, to San Diego, California, in 2014. The book is structured with alternating chapters in the voice of Molly Arnette in the present and flashbacks to Molly in her early teens. She reveals her family's pretense, lies, secrets, regrets, and finally forgiveness. By her own admission, Molly opens the novel with her words, "I'm a good liar."

Concerning family dynamics, her psychologist father Graham tells her that "everyone comes from a dysfunctional family ... one day you will create one of your own and it will be messy and crazy and full of love" (Chamberlain 324). Too young for those words to embed in her heart and because of all the secrets gradually revealed, Molly nurses her anger for years.

There are two main threads of deception in the Arnette family. The first is that Molly is the child of Graham Arnette and his former lover. The second one is that Graham is dying, trapped inside a wheelchair so that he cannot literally dance, and inside a body that has stopped functioning except for his voice and sight, which also begin to diminish. Progressively, he "woke up several mornings unable to speak … he was so short of breath, he'd panic" (315). Addressed are also two societal issues concerning life and death: adoption, related to Molly's barrenness, and euthanasia, requested by Graham.

Pretending to Dance is a true coming of age story for Molly. While the adults withhold truths from her, she has her own pubescent secrets—about marijuana, love, and sex. A naïve Molly also experiences painful disillusionment and the foolishness of being judgmental. As an adult, she also learns that withholding truths about the past can be destructive to marriage.

Chamberlain suffused the novel with many references to pop culture that might fill readers with nostalgia. From Twisted Sister to Rachmaninoff, Johnny Depp to Patsy Cline, and the Carolina Shag to Footloose, the author runs the gamut of interests of both young and adult characters. An interesting allusion is made to Highland Hospital in Asheville, an important location in Lee Smith's novel, *Guests on Earth*. Graham Arnette, who espouses Pretend Therapy, had once worked there, and he explains to Molly its unorthodox treatments, specifically the holistic approach combining music, dance, art, and nature. This type of therapy was beneficial to Highland's most famous patient, the multi-talented Zelda Fitzgerald, who died in the hospital's fire.

Characterization is the writing forte of Chamberlain. In this novel, Graham's loyal caretaker Russell is the most endearing character, both physically and emotionally strong, for it is he who abets in the euthanasia and admits, "We counted on silence" (309). About Chamberlain's work, Bobbye Terry states that her "stories are filled with twists and evoke the reader's emotions" (1), but Kirkus Reviews begs to differ. It reports that *Pretending to Dance* is "marred by excessive sentimentality and superfluous exposition that dilutes the drama" (10); therefore, the reader must be his or her own judge.

Works Cited

Chamberlain, Diane. *Pretending to Dance*. New York: St. Martin's Press, 2015. Print.
"Pretending to Dance." *Kirkus Reviews* 83.15 (2015): 10. Literary Reference Center. Web.
Terry, Bobbye R. "Diane Chamberlain." *Guide to Literary Masters & Their Works* (2007): 1. Literary Reference Center. Web.

PART III

Social Hindrances

14

Silenced by Hardship

The Women
Spirit of the Mountains
by Emma Bell Miles

In the memoir *Spirit of the Mountains*, Emma Bell Miles, "one of Appalachia's first feminist authors" (Brooks 160), attempts to convey the essence of early mountain life, people, places, religion, literature and music. Miles struggled "to straddle two worlds: the world of the mountains she loved, and the world of intellectual society she needed" (161). After marriage, her adult life was spent traveling back and forth between Rabbit Hash, Kentucky, and Walden's Ridge near Chattanooga, Tennessee.

In the chapter titled "Cabin Homes," Miles writes, "solitude is deep water, and small boats do not ride well in it" (17). She alludes to a lack of understanding by outsiders that mountain people prefer their wilderness existence and pioneer spirit as they live off the land. She also adds that mountaineers naturally demand solitude for personal growth.

Brooks notes that Emma Bell Miles' writing focuses on women being dependent on, submissive to, and suffering for their men (169). Edith Summers Kelley supports this claim: men were "safe and aloof" in their masculinity, but women were expected to be "passive, obedient, and docile" (qtd. in Miller 59). Miles explained the differences between mountain men and women. The men spent most of their time outdoors working the crops, hunting, journeying, trading, drinking and fighting. They came inside the house only to eat and sleep. The women spent their time indoors cleaning, cooking, canning, quilting, spinning, knitting, and tending to children. They carried on the traditions of the females who came before them with long nights of nursing the sick and weary nights waiting for the men to return home. She also adds that "they are so silent. They know so pathetically little of each other's lives" (Miles 70).

This observation is verisimilar in Miles' section titled "Grandmothers and Sons," especially about seventeen-year-old pregnant Mary Burns, with uncombed hair, bare feet, and a faded dress. She spoke in a sweet, hushed monotone about the hardships she faced from her husband who was cruel to her beyond what was expected and tolerated from mountain men. No one knew if he hit her; Mary rarely complained, for there was no end to her "capacity for doglike devotion" (43–47). If a mountain woman's husband mistreated her, she was to withstand it without response. Her lot was one of "service and suffering ... sweetly borne ... a sublime silent courage and patience" (66–67). The women were not to speak words of protest about their men.

Wilma Dykeman observed about Miles' work, "She saw the younger women who were exploited ... mistreated. She saw the older women who gathered such strength" (qtd. in Miller 81). Both observations are illustrated by young Mary and wise Aunty Genevy, whose most striking character is her dignity as a "mountain matriarch" and her "stoic acceptance" (Miller 81–84) of her life of hardship, for complaining would not change a situation, and she knew not to pry in other women's lives.

At most mountain churches, the men and women sat on opposite sides of the aisle. It was improper for a woman to speak in church, and she also was not allowed to uncover her head. After the sermon and on the way home, the men made comments about Scripture while the women and children "remained meekly and decorously silent" (57) as if their opinions were of no consequence.

One chapter begins with a quote by Joe Winchester, "The less a man talks, the fewer lies he tells" (83), since "terse and piquant proverbs" (176) were common in daily conversation inside mountain cabins. Almost Indian–like, mountaineer men were laconic, teaching their sons to establish a quiet and composed mien in deference to privacy and to accept hardships in their lives. When approached with news from others, they often only nodded with a cursory glance and a muttered response (85).

Brooks stated that Emma Bell Miles' body of work, especially her aptitude to convey messages through silence, makes powerful statements about the circumscribed life of women in mountain culture. The Appalachian women of the past suffered because of the choices they made and were plagued with a life of exclusionary discourse and unacknowledged voices (163–165). Even though socially unjust, to eschew traditional, restrictive roles, they could risk both judgement and ostracism.

Works Cited

Brooks, Shannon. "Coming Home: Finding My Appalachian Mothers through Emma Bell Miles." *NWSA Journal* 11.3 (1999): 157. Literary Reference Center. Web.

Miles, Emma Bell. *The Spirit of the Mountains*. New York: James Pott & Company, 1905. Print.

Miller, Danny L. "Mountain Gloom." *Wingless Flights: Appalachian Women in Fiction*. Bowling Green: Bowling Green State University Popular Press, 1996. Print.

Almeda, Amos and Jonah
Tales of Chinkapin Creek, Volume II by Jean Ayer

In 2012, Jean Ayer published a sequel to the first volume of collected stories from her mother's memories in *Chinkapin Creek Volume II*, "sparkling sketches of rural West Virginians who lived by their hands, hearts, and wits before the age of machines. Life in the Mountain State in the early 1900's was blessed but hard" ("Tales of Chinkapin Creek, Volume II" 278). The residents knew how to be efficient with their time, so they worked diligently instead of engaging in unnecessary or idle talk. Customary communication included head nods and gestures. Often, rather than acknowledge information or instructions, they responded only with silence. This volume of Ayer's memoir describes multiple silent characters.

Mrs. Almeda Pope, a woman who assisted on hog butchering days, "never spoke and never smiled" (56), and when she threw crackling treats to the children, she never looked up at them. One year she merely gazed at the tortoiseshell combs in Mrs. Wister's hair, and "Mama took the combs from her hair and handed them to Mrs. Pope, who nodded gravely and never said a word" (7). Years later, Mrs. Almeda's daughter, who asked for home-butchered meat, (9) left without a word of thanks. Almeda and her husband were probably in awe of the Wister land, home, buildings, and livestock, so this most likely attributed to their reticence around the Wister family, whom they viewed as "out of their league." Additionally, they might have reasoned that since the Wisters had so much, they would not mind sharing, for the family's benevolent reputation was well known throughout the Chinkapin Creek community.

Carrie Wister learned a lesson about speaking before knowing all the facts when she insinuated that Amos was not working as hard as the other men. Unusually silent, he left the farm at noon without saying a word. Upon learning that Amos was incapable of sweating, she apologized for her hurtful words, but he did not acknowledge her presence. He said nothing (12) because of his position as a hired employee; Amos could not dispute Mrs. Wister or defend himself against her misspoken comments.

After Jack Wister approached Robert E. Lee Kilgore about working as a blacksmith on the homestead, the powerful man gave him a quick glance and resumed his work without a word (98). There was no verbal agreement or even a handshake. Kilgore, who merely showed up one morning, was oddly disoriented and silent (99). When Carrie went to help his wife with a new baby, she sensed something was amiss—the infant did not cry and Mrs. Kilgore said not a word of thanks. After Carrie shared scripture with the woman, she offered no response except to turn away her face marked with apparent pain and hardship.

The Kilgore family obviously carried around a great deal of emotional baggage. The description of the blacksmith's jet black hair and dark eyes is a hint to the reader that he may have been at least part Native American, so his lack of work in Minerva could have been due to his being shunned by townspeople, rather than the fact that there were already two blacksmiths working there. A man who has a specialized skill but is impeded from plying his trade because of prejudice would, of course, be frustrated with a situation over which he has no control. His being named after a famous Civil War general suggests that his parents had high hopes for their son, but he felt guilty for the less than prosperous life he had eked out so far. Perhaps Kilgore tried to abate his anger with alcohol and by lashing out at the closest thing in his path. Unfortunately, it was his wife.

Hired man Jonah Smith, so bashful that he would leave a room whenever Mrs. Wister entered, was unable to make eye contact even with the children, and strangers made his face turn "as red as his bandana," such a pitiful dark red that everyone else suffered too. (141). Brothers Arthur and Albert, were also painfully shy. When they were in the kitchen with Jonah, all three of them sat, "silent as owls" (141).

Years later, just after Jonah and equally bashful Sadie married (which made Nellie wonder if they ever talked to each other), he went outside, still in his good suit, to slop the hogs instead of joining the wedding party. Jonah's behavior made it apparent that his bashfulness hindered him from being a social creature. Among a crowd, whether a small one at a kitchen table or a large one of wedding guests, Jonah was too far from his comfort zone. He was much more content to be outside doing familiar farm chores around the animals.

The reticence of the mountain people is a result of many factors, among them perhaps a lack of education and a lack of conversational skills, both initiation and response. Their lives revolved around survival, and that was accomplished by working sunup to sundown, with no time for conversation. Instead, they spoke with their strong bodies out in the fields or down in the coal mines.

Works Cited

Ayer, Jean. *Tales of Chinkapin Creek, Volume II*. North Charleston, South Carolina: CreateSpace, 2012. Print.

"Tales of Chinkapin Creek, Volume II." *Kirkus Reviews* 80.17 (2012): 278. Literary Reference Center. Web

The Walls Family
The Glass Castle by Jeannette Walls

A contemporary story of hardship and poverty, Jeannette Walls' memoir *The Glass Castle* is a tale of nomadic existence that leads to a period of darkness in the lives of the author and her siblings. Although they cannot rely on their parents to rear them properly, the children's independence and resilience provide a hopeful ending. "A portrait of bohemian, artsy, kooky, and sometimes feckless parents" (Bartkevicius 150), the book sends the reader on a journey with the Walls family from California, to Arizona, West Virginia, and finally New York.

Rex Walls is a brilliant, lazy, violent alcoholic who constantly pontificates about his plan to build a glass castle for the family, hence the title. His delusional dreams, "constant pursuit of gold and other get-rich-quick schemes provide the backdrop for Walls' coming-of-age memoir" (Rogers and Marshall 728). He and his free-spirited wife Rose Mary are too immature to provide a stable home and steady nurturing for the children. As a result, the Walls siblings are always hungry, suffer neglect, abuse and destitution at the hands of their parents, but there is not "a trace of self-pity" (Masserman 2) in Walls' account. Their self-indulgence forces a young Jeannette to arrogate her father's role as the family provider.

The initial silence mentioned in the memoir occurs in the hospital where three-year-old Jeannette receives treatment for burns sustained from cooking while her oblivious mother is in another room. Because of the hushed whispers of the doctors about the severity of her condition, she remains silent, worried that she is a bother to everyone around her. Despite her pain, she is cognizant of the hospital environment. "I wasn't used to quiet and order and I liked it" (Walls 11). Later in the story, Jeannette is exposed once again to fire but only she is aware of it. "I tried to scream to warn them, but nothing came out of my throat" (33). A third fire is caused by her drunk father's negligence to which the children respond by "shutting down and closing off" (115). They learn that complaining about their ever-changing situation is futile, so they live quiet lives without basic necessities.

The National Alliance to End Homeless reported in 2007:

> The number of estimated homeless youths (age 18 and under) in the U.S. ranges anywhere from 52,000 to more than one million…. Definitions of what it means to be homeless vary across institutions; but in general they refer to people who are temporarily or more permanently without shelter. Prior to the 1980's in North America, the homeless were commonly referred to as vagabonds, hobos, and itinerants. As terminologies change, so do the representations of homelessness in various kinds of mass-produced cultural texts, such as novels, memoirs, and film, in ways that uphold certain kinds of truths about what it means to live without a permanent home [Rogers and Marshall 725].

The four Walls children certainly qualify to be included among these numbers, but they do not self-report. The children's formal education is sporadic, but they quickly learn how to survive the game of life. Jeanette's eloquence protects them from trouble with officials from the Child Welfare Office, for they are impressed by her elevated speech and embellished information. When Jeannette does speak to outsiders, she does not tell the truth.

When they move deep into the mountains of West Virginia, the stillness and darkness cause the children to grow even quieter (Walls 130). Viewed as outsiders, when Jeannette smiles and nods to townspeople, they do not look at her, reciprocate her nod, or speak. School officials, who cannot understand the children's accent, conclude that they have speech impairments and assign them to special education classes.

Jeannette endures months of torture from her classmates, but she does not reveal the bullying. One incident causes her father to rail against his children, for he will not listen to their side of the story. He shakes his head at Jeannette, who has always been a daddy's girl, as if he "could keep out the sound of my voice. He wouldn't even look at me" (148). The children do not say a word of defense but go to bed in "silent darkness" (148).

Because Jeannette has been reared to be polite and considerate of those in authority, many times during her childhood, she must be silent rather than rebuff adults who do not deserve her respect. Her parents had always urged the children to be bold and speak up, "but now we were supposed to bite our tongues" (143–44). They cannot challenge adults, including their indifferent parents and others who try to take advantage of their gullibility. Even when men make sexual advances toward Jeanette, she merely removes their hands and says nothing. She does not share these incidents with her mother because it would be futile.

Jeanette also knows that revealing abuse by their grandmother will elicit no sympathy or help from her parents, so she never mentions it. She finally realizes that as a young girl, she has no voice to make a difference in her life, for her concerns are dismissed by the very people who should protect their children and provide their basic needs. Even when she tries to explain to her mother that the family can receive government assistance for both housing and food, Rose Mary listens to Jeannette's "tirade in silence" (194) and refuses to consider receiving charity from any source.

Although Jeannette is dumbfounded by memories of her life in poverty, shame, and despair, she does not harbor ill-will toward her incorrigible parents. "Oscar Wilde wrote, 'Children begin by loving their parents; as they grow older they judge them; sometimes they forgive them'" (qtd. in Ferris 220). In order to move forward in her life of contentment with her husband, this is exactly what Jeannette does. Today she and husband John live in the suburbs of New York where she is a journalist for MSNBC.

Works Cited

Bartkevicius, Jocelyn. "The Glass Castle." *Fourth Genre: Exploration in Nonfiction* 8.1 (2006): 150–52. Literary Reference Center. Web.

Ferris, Lucy. "Sharpening Teeth." *Southern Review* 42.1 (2006): 215–220. Literary Reference Center. Web.

Masserman, Patricia. "The Glass Castle." *Magill's Literary Annual* (2006): 1–3. Literary Reference Center. Web.

Rogers, Theresa, and Elizabeth Marshall. "On the Road: Examining Self-Representation and Discourses of Homelessness in Young Adult Texts." *Journal of Adolescent and Adult Literacy.* 55.8. 1–3. Literary Reference Center. Web.

Walls, Jeannette. *The Glass Castle.* New York: Scribner, 2005. Print.

Lydia Hawkins
Child of the Mountains
by Marilyn Sue Shank

Set in 1953 in the small, impoverished communities of Paradise and Confidence near Charleston, West Virginia, *Child of the Mountains*, a YA novel by Marilyn Sue Shank, contains a wealth of information, from mountain ballads to folk remedies, Appalachian crafts, coal mining traditions, conservative religious practices, medical terminology, legal proceedings, and the Civil Rights movement. In her Appalachian dialect, protagonist Lydia Hawkins reveals, through flashbacks, the hardships of living in poverty, compounded by an alcoholic father, incarcerated mother, and dying brother. The strength of this book, however, is its underscore of the misunderstanding and disrespect from outsiders, especially government officials, whose intrusion is unwelcome by mountain people.

Instead of speaking up or speaking out, Lydia, who "has a strong sense of right and wrong" (Scott 73), chronicles her pain in a spiral notebook she purchases at the company store. Her writing is a tool to gain perspective of her predicaments and the individuals in her world. Realizing that she is judged before people get to know her, Lydia tries to imagine how her literary idol, Anne Shirley, a "strong, willful, and brilliant character" (Barratt 3) from Lucy Maud Montgomery's *Anne of Green Gables,* would react to her circumstances. Anne is impetuous and outspoken, unlike the quiet Lydia, but in her heart she wishes to be bold like Anne. When older, gossipy women from the church make disparaging remarks about Lydia's mother, she knows what Anne would say, for initially she too had to deal with judgmental church women, but Lydia "didn't say nary a word" (Shank 30), only looked down at the hole in her shoe. In response to spiritual urgings by the preacher, who expects her to "spit out some words" (31), she bites her lip, cracks her knuckles, and remains silent.

Most all obstacles Lydia and her family face are from wealthy professionals who are powerful enough to control those they deem below them, as if moving chess pieces on a game board. When Lydia's mother uncovers the deceit from doctors at the research hospital, she has neither a voice nor the words to right the situation, so her only recourse is to defer to those in authority who will make decisions about her son's fate.

At school, when Lydia is taunted by classmates about her worn, faded dress, she says nothing, even though Anne Shirley would have used strong words of rebuttal, and she does with her arch-rival Gilbert. Both girls, whose parentage is veiled by half-truths, also share similar circumstances with teachers. The compassion Mr. Hinkle and his lawyer fiancé show Lydia is one of the most poignant sections of the book. Lydia is reluctant to disclose her problems to Mr. Hinkle, but she finds him trustworthy, one of the few adults she can rely on to follow through with promises, for even her family members have kept important secrets about her birth from her.

Likewise, Anne Shirley finds in her teacher Miss Stacy "a kindred spirit who is able to nurture Anne intellectually and emotionally, providing the role model" (Barratt 2) she seeks. Additionally, the minister's wife Mrs. Allan is a "paradigm of moral excellence and unselfish sympathy" (3) for Anne, just as Mr. Hinkle's fiancé is for Lydia. Eventually, Mr. Hinkle and his fiancé help Lydia to find her voice, and when she does, it sounds uncannily like the spunky one of Anne Shirley!

Works Cited

Barratt, David. "Anne of Green Gables." *Masterplots II: American Fiction Series*, 2000. Literary Reference Center. Web.

Scott, Karen. "Child of the Mountains." *Library Media Connection* 31.1 (2012): 73. Literary Reference Center. Web.

Shank, Marilyn Sue. *Child of the Mountains*. New York: Random House, 2012. Print.

15

A Shunning Silence

Mary
A Circuit Rider's Wife
by Corra Mae White Harris

Mary Thompson, the narrator of Corra Mae White Harris' novel *A Circuit Rider's Wife*, wonders if the outcome of the prodigal son parable in Luke 15 would have been different if the account involved a wayward daughter. Would the father have welcomed her home with outstretched arms, draped a robe around her shoulders, and placed a ring on her finger? Would he have ordered the fatted calf to be killed for a celebratory feast? Mary doubts it. She believes that if a prodigal daughter had returned home to her father, he would have said to her, "Go and sin no more. But go" (Harris 85–86). Mary points out the double standards in perception and judgment of men and women who have committed the same sins. From Biblical times to the present, this mindset seems to prevail.

Narrator Mary considers the plight of a devalued woman, also named Mary, an unwed mother who lives in a deteriorating shack situated in a huge field, which Harris described in an excellent metaphor for Mary's personal life: "The field was her desert" (86). To provide for herself and her child, she offers sewing services but must walk fourteen miles to the nearest town to gather and then return the clothing. Although Mary has lived there for eight years, no respectable woman has crossed the field or spoken to her.

When the circuit rider and his wife arrive at her door, Mary appears as a gaunt figure, hardened by a life that has totally erased the softness of her womanhood. Her clothes are dirty and torn; her shriveled face hides condemned eyes. The couple announces that they have come to take dinner with Mary, but she exclaims, "Oh, not with sech as me" (86). She has been vilified by the townswomen for so long she feels unworthy to sit at her own table with the minister and his wife, choosing instead to stand behind their chairs, ready to serve them. The meal is scant, but the minister's wife feels that of all the food she has ever tasted, it is the "most nearly sanctified" (87).

Mary is eventually persuaded to attend worship services, where she sits silently on her bench and humbly creeps forward to receive communion. Alas, she is not received by others. "They would have none of her" (87) or her child.

The self-righteousness and condemning silence of the so-called Christian women at Redwine Church speak volumes of judgment. Their sharp rebuff of this frail, shadow of a female and her child is the height of hypocrisy. By debasing those who have overt sins, they can keep their own sins hidden while they inwardly elevate themselves spiritually. Apparently, they choose not to recall the account of the Good Samaritan or heed the warnings Jesus gives to individuals who are quick to point fingers and blame others, "Judge not lest you be judged" (Matthew 7:1) and "Ye who are without sin, cast the first stone" (John 8:7). These "pious" women have decided to be judge and jury, similar to the Pharisees who lived their lives strictly according to the law, eschewing grace and compassion.

The circuit rider's wife reasons that this poor soul is actually free since she has no reputation to earn, defend, or lose. Thus, she goes about doing good deeds. Symbolic of this young woman's redemption and acceptance by God, the field around her hovel becomes a garden of color, and her cabin is highlighted by beautiful blossoms (88).

Works Cited

Harris, Corra Mae White. *The Circuit Rider's Wife*. Philadelphia: Henry Altemus Company, 1910. Print.

16

The Silence of Ignorance and Poverty

Emma McClure
To Make My Bread by Grace Lumpkin

Grace Lumpkin's novel *To Make My Bread* was published in 1932 and won the Maxim Gorky Award for best labor novel of the year. Scholars of Depression-era literature will discover Lumpkin's work is a "radical novel [which] represents a significant part of literary history" (Kirby 661). Readers meet the extended McClure clan in the Southern Appalachian settlement of Swain's Crossing and follow them on foot down the mountain to Leesville. Tired, dirty, ragged, and weak with hunger, the farmers have been promised war-time employment in a textile mill, pitched as Paradise where money grows on trees. Desperate for an easier life than they have had while barely eking out an existence on the farm, the McClures, who believe these falsehoods, sell their homes and land.

The title's origin is most likely from lines spoken by the Giant in the children's tale "Jack and the Beanstalk": "Fee, fi, fo, fum. I smell the blood of an Englishman. Be he alive or be he dead, I'll grind his bones to make my bread." Unfortunately, the grinding of bones is the very lifeblood of the millworkers who toil long hours for only a pittance while the factory owners, symbolic of the Giant in Lumpkin's novel, grow increasingly rich. However, just as young Jack is able to fool the Giant, the millworkers walk away from their jobs to organize a labor union against the poor conditions in the mill. Nevertheless, there is no beanstalk to cut down to prevent the mill bosses from retaliation. Another reference to the title is a worker's comment that the mill's weave room machines make the "sound of sinners' teeth grinding in hell" (Lumpkin 219), a noise with which they soon become familiar.

The constant sound of the machines is in stark contrast to the silence of the women who must work or risk losing their jobs when they are ill or their children need them at home. At one point Emma remarks, "I don't run the machines anymore. They run me" (330). The results of the strike are brutal—the proletariats are evicted or murdered.

This inhumane treatment might have been avoided, or at least lessened, if the people were educated and not gullible to the lies of the smooth-talking wealthy. The majority of the benighted inhabitants of Swain's Crossing cannot read, so mail must be read aloud to them by the store owner who speaks "smoothly like a preacher and with confidence" (Lumpkin 81); they listen quietly and respectfully to his voice. They have no voice except a collective, weak one made up primarily of women and children, for many of the men are either dead or have gone to war.

Moments of quietude include disciplinary silence toward children for talking back or misbehaving. Another is the hush that moves over an entire household when a stranger approaches; even the dogs lie still until they get a scent of the one coming over the mountain. Sometimes those strangers want to talk yet "seemed to be holding in words" (36). When the men hear that one among them has discovered his wife in a back shed with another man, they do not speak about the adultery out of respect for a neighbor. As the men mull over their options and whether or not to sell their farms, they "hold their words of counsel a secret" (137) from the women who are not consulted about the life-changing decision. However, in matters concerning her children, protagonist Emma McClure finds her voice to silence her father, Grandpap, with words of scorn for his poor example to her sons. She disapproves of his moonshine running to make money, yet Grandpap responds in like kind, for he knows "the best way to close a scolding woman's mouth" (71) is with silence. Emma checks her tongue when her son Kirk invites his pregnant girlfriend Minnie to live with them; otherwise she is fearful he will leave and never return. When her husband dies and Grandpap is in jail for two years, Emma quietly worries about providing for additional mouths.

When Grandpap is denied a factory job due to his age, Emma fears he will make a scene, yet she remains "hushed and strained" (151) in deference to her father. The entire clan is silently glum after they are told to return the next day to make an X in the "Doomsday Book," of which they have no knowledge. Abject from vulnerability and hopelessness, they endure silent shame.

After Emma's daughter Bonnie approaches a group of females at school recess wanting to ask if she can join them, "her tongue was dumb" (241) and the girls ignore her. Her son is taunted by bullies in his class who "resented John's silence" (211), for he neither cries nor responds in any way to their mockery and hateful words. Their lack of reading and writing skills, as well as their backward ways make them outcasts.

The former mountain farmers abruptly find themselves away from their agrarian existence and thrown into a foreign industrial town. Socially inept, they are slow to make friends in town or with their co-workers at the mill. They often want to initiate conversation, but they keep their heads down, mute in their awkwardness, especially the young men and girls who are ready for courting. The women, assigned work that men will not do, are "required to sacrifice their personal lives and seldom permitted a voice in policy making" (Jeansonne qtd. in Kirby 665). While their mother Emma is slowly dying of pellagra, Bonnie and John watch "over her in silence" (Lumpkin 307), unable to help her. Although Bonnie's own child contracts pneumonia, she cannot stay home from work to tend to him. As a result, the doctor reprimands her for not calling him sooner, but survival is at the forefront for the poor, and the choices they must make are compromises in other aspects of their livers. They are damned no matter what they do. In the stillness of the shack and looking down at her lifeless son, Bonnie cannot explain her lack of attention to the child. "There were words that came up in her ... but she could not speak them" (329).

Eventually, Bonnie and John acknowledge that their weakness of deferring to those with clout and money will never insure a better future for their families. After a number of merciless affronts to the millworkers, Bonnie's courage to speak from a makeshift platform and deliver a passionate plea for continued unity is a result of her resolve to no longer be silent, but a sniper makes sure that she will not speak out again.

Works Cited

Kirby, Lisa A. "'How it Grieves the Heart of a Mother ...': The Intersections of Gender, Class, and Politics in Grace Lumpkin's *To Make My Bread*." *Women's Studies* 37.661–677 (2008). Web.

Lumpkin, Grace. *To Make My Bread*. The Macaulay Company, 1932. Lanham: Rowman & Littlefield, 2014. Print.

Tom Powell
The Truest Pleasure by Robert Morgan

In his novel *The Truest Pleasure*, Robert Morgan does not follow the traditions of characterization in Appalachian literature with a silent wife who is submissive to her husband. Ginny Powell, the protagonist of this tale, is bold and quite vocal, whereas her husband Tom is the silent character. Tom Powell is mostly reticent due to his lack of education and general knowledge of the world. As a result, when Ginny, her father, and her brothers, discuss current events they have read about in the local newspaper, Tom is content to only listen and reflect while the others talk. Uncomfortable in crowds and embarrassed to answer questions about himself, Tom responds with monosyllabic responses or goes outside to avoid speaking. He is much more comfortable communicating physically through his extraordinary hard work on the farm.

Ginny notes that her unconventionally laconic husband's silence is often frightening and sharper than any words he might speak. His withdrawal and silent moods are also painful for her, as she relies on touch for a connection with her husband and a path to healing and wholeness. Only in the dark, when being face-to-face is not required, is Tom able to communicate, yet he is still unsure and silent as he expresses his emotions with the hard work of lovemaking.

Although he struggles to gain acceptance by Ginny's family, his truest pleasure is recognition as the future and sole owner of the homestead he loves and has worked so diligently to improve. Determined to compensate for his lack of learning, Tom proves to the family his worth as an excellent provider. His strong back, arms, and hands become his loudest mouthpiece.

Works Cited

Morgan, Robert. *The Truest Pleasure*. Chapel Hill: Algonquin Books, 1998. Print.

Barle McCorkle
"Mother Yaws" by Tennessee Williams

Yes, it is true that Tennessee Williams was not an Appalachian writer, but his short story "Mother Yaws," published in 1977 in *Esquire*, is set in Appalachia. It demonstrates how a life of ignorance can lead to an unnecessary death sentence. The gist of the story is of an uneducated woman who is treated as an outcast by her own family, strangers, medical personnel, and the townspeople of Triumph, Tennessee. Williams experienced first-hand the emotional pain of ostracism, first from his father, then a conservative South when he made public his homosexuality, and finally by American theater critics who turned their backs on and vilified him in the press. Although flamboyant and demanding at times, he suffered from low self-esteem and was forever haunted by death and fear that he might follow his sister Rose's path to insanity. The reader should recognize the lack of resources and options the protagonist has due to her lack of mental acuity. This Southern Gothic narrative is a sad commentary on the lives of the silent poor and uneducated who can be victims of cruelty when they do not receive compassion and assistance they need so badly.

Tom McCorkle, rather than refer to his wife by her first name, Barle, calls her the Luther'n minister's daughter, an indication of his lack of love and respect for her, as well as a symptom of their dysfunctional relationship. Barle has an unusual sore on her face, and because of its embarrassing appearance, she tries to cover it with her hand and does not respond to her husband's question about its origin. His insistence that she look in the mirror has double significance. First, it connotes identity, how she perceives herself in contrast to the way others see her. Secondly, since her husband does not recognize her as his spouse, it is his attempt to further debase her, by making her face the ugliness of the sore. He describes it as an affront to the eyes and that she looks like a "half-butchered hawg" (579). Lifting his leg and purposefully farting in her direction further deprecates this defenseless woman.

Nauseous, Barle stumbles out to the yard to vomit and is called back inside only to feed the dog, which her lazy children do not consider doing themselves. Their behavior proves that they have adopted their father's disdainful attitude toward Barle, for when she returns inside, no one will touch her, and she cowers in a corner of the kitchen in a submissive position, an indication of her vulnerability. McCorkle, who sends her to a doctor in Gatlinburg, tells Barle that if she is contagious, she must move back in with the Luther'n minister, but Barle knows that her father is no more kindhearted than her husband, and he will not welcome her.

At the doctor's office, other patients stare at her "despite the silence that had prevailed" (581) before she enters the room. Sent outside to wait because of a vocal patient's threats of "undisguised repugnance," Barle says nothing in protest, but meekly complies, faltering in the sweltering heat and losing consciousness. In the examination room, the doctor keeps his distance. When he inquires if she has Blue Cross, she asks, "I got blue cross?" (581). In her ignorance, she thinks this is a diagnosis. When he inquires if she has mental problems, she says both her husband and father think so, but she is not aware that these are insults spoken about her.

Her condition is diagnosed as yaws, a "tropical infection of the skin caused by a spirochete" (*Columbia Electronic Encyclopedia*) which can be treated successfully. When she returns home and McCorkle asks about her disease, "she made a baffled noise in her throat" (584) as nothing intelligible will come from her mouth. Ordered to sleep on an old pallet in the basement, she breaks down and cries but again obeys her husband's command, for speaking up would be futile.

This financially and mentally poor soul is shunned by everyone in town, even by her minister father, who posts a sign forbidding her to enter his home. Neighbors stare at her as she walks by, but no one initiates conversation or shows pity. Although she lacks book knowledge, she uses the basest survival skills to live on Cat's Back Mountain surrounded by forest animals that do not care about her yaws, and ironically, respond positively to her childish chattering.

Gore Vidal noted about Tennessee Williams that a sense of "otherness" is crucial to his literary works because he was fixated on characters who were outsiders (xxiii–xxiv). This is evident in his short story "Mother Yaws." There is also a double-entendre at play here. Literally, time after time, Barle is allowed inside for only brief moments, but she finds herself mostly relegated to the outside—banished from her home, the waiting room, and her father's home. Even the doctor treats this illiterate woman with disrespect. Instead of addressing her properly and in a humane manner, he sends Barle back to a community that condemns her.

Living outside among animals is an appropriate place for Barle who has been treated like one. In her own home, she crouches in the corner, like a dog that has been cornered or treed. Because of her ignorance, she *is* "treed," for she cannot speak in her own defense against the cruelty she endures. Instead, she merely does as she is told without comment. Barle finds herself in the same situation when the mother wildcat attacks her. Although living outside has become her lot, she is only temporarily welcome, as she is also the "other" in the animals' habitat.

Works Cited

Columbia Electronic Encyclopedia, 6th Edition, Q1 (2014): pp. 1–1. Web.
Tennessee Williams: Collected Stories. New York: Ballantine, 1986. Print.

Rinthy and the Nameless One
Outer Dark by Cormac McCarthy

In Gothic literature, anxiety, fear, and terror are often "in tandem" with destructive "brutality, rampant sexual impulses, and death" (Fisher 145). Southern Gothic writers present evil as a compelling, forceful, unavoidable, and "irreducible" reality (Moore 142) in their psychologically aberrant characters. During the time that Cormac McCarthy wrote literature set in Appalachia, he drew on stereotypes of poverty, ignorance, and aimlessness. Many of his characters are poor whites in destructive situations who exemplify "the dark corners of the southern landscape" and whose lives are void of the slightest "humanistic affirmation" (Grammer 360). Because he grew up in Tennessee, McCarthy was familiar with the natural features of the region and the attitudes and speech patterns of the local people. In *Outer Dark*, one of his Southern Gothic novels, protagonists Culla and Rinthy Holme, siblings whose incest produces a child, are "mountaineers driven or drawn out of their isolated home places into the modern world" (Cawelti 306).

After Culla, whose name means "fool or dupe," wordlessly steals away and abandons the infant, an evil and tatterdemalion tinker finds and hides it. When Rinthy discovers Culla's covert actions, she looks at him with incrimination, a "silent and inarguable female invective" which causes him to flee.

Due to their lack of socialization, those who befriend Rinthy, in her quest to find the ragged tinker who has her son, offer her meals that are eaten in silence. Their attention is on one task at a time, for they do not engage in idle talk. Often they make no eye contact or respond when asked a question. Likewise, Rinthy can think of nothing to say, a result of her many years of isolation, lack of education, and social skills. This is evidenced by her behavior at one of her stops when she asks for medical advice about her painful "paps" which have wept milk since bearing her child. She hesitantly approaches the doctor with a "curtsying nod [being] ragged, shoeless, deferential and half deranged" (151).

Suggestive of the consequences of his shameful sin, Culla is not as fortunate, for trouble eventually befalls him. When he is offered work on the land surrounding a squire's large house, he encounters a mute negro worker who uses his long dark arms to communicate. He scuttles around the barn and works in silence, ever suspicious of Culla, and rightly so, for Culla steals the squire's boots. When Culla arrives in the town of Cheatham, no one speaks a word but suspicious eyes turn toward him, and he is quickly chased for miles by a horde of angry men.

Among the chapters that alternate between Rinthy and Culla, McCarthy interjects brief, italicized text that gradually introduces a trio of abominable men, "lawless, asocial, drifters who have gone totally beyond the pale into the 'outer dark'" (Branham and Huffman 5). Similar to the remorseless Misfit and his murderous companions in Flannery O'Connor's Southern Gothic short story "A Good Man Is Hard to Find," for no apparent reason, they accost, rob, and kill most everyone with whom they cross paths. These unconscionable characters "reveal a primordial savagery that lurks beneath the surface of civilized society" (Cawleti 310). Among the three night riders is a nameless man who stares at Culla with a "benign imbecility" and about whom the bearded leader claims, "If you cain't name something, you cain't talk about it. You cain't say what it is" (McCarthy177), suggesting that the nameless one is almost subhuman and for whom there are no words to describe. At the novel's gruesome end, the three men slit the throat of Rinthy's son, who has an empty eye socket and multiple burn scars on his body. The nameless mute, in the lowest crassitude, kneels, drools, and makes primeval whimpering sounds as he "buried his moaning face" (236) inside the wound to suck the blood and eviscerate the child's body. The reader can now name the mute one—a degenerate cannibal.

In the Faulkner-esque style of long, convoluted passages, McCarthy describes the beauty, silence and sounds of the animals, the woods, the river, the sky, and the seasons. Some critics charge that this style "serves to obscure rather than enrich his work" (Arnold 3). Nevertheless, with such precise delineation, these elements seem to the reader additional characters, albeit composite ones. As a result, during the early years of his writing, McCarthy could certainly be labeled an Appalachian regionalist.

Works Cited

Arnold, Edwin T. "Outer Dark." *Master Plots II: American Fiction Series*, 2000. *EBSCO Host*. Web.

Branham, Harold and William Huffman. "Outer Dark." *Critical Survey of Long Fiction*, 4th edition, 2010. Literary Reference Center. Web.

Cawleti, John G. "Cormac McCarthy: Restless Seekers." *An American Vein: Critical Readings in Appalachian Literature*. Athens" Ohio University Press, 2005. Print.

Fisher, Benjamin F. IV. "Southern Gothic." *Literature: The New Encyclopedia of Southern Culture*. Chapel hill: University of North Carolina Press, 2008. Print.

Grammer, John. "McCarthy, Cormac." *Literature: The New Encyclopedia of Southern Culture*. Ed. Thomas Inge. Chapel Hill: The University of North Carolina Press, 2008. Print.

McCarthy, Cormac. *Outer Dark*. New York: Vintage Books, 1968. Print.

Moore, Robert R. "Religion and Literature." *Literature: The New Encyclopedia of Southern Culture*. Chapel Hill: University of North Carolina Press, 2008. Print.

Joe
"The Lost Dog"
by Chris Holbrook

In Chris Holbrook's *Hell and Ohio*, a collection of short stories of Southern Appalachia, "The Lost Dog," is a rite of passage tale about a young boy named Joe who has lost his dog Queenie. In fact, the story's theme is one of loss. Parallel to the lost dog, Joe's father loses his means of income after quitting his job, and Joe loses a degree of innocence, ignorance, and fear when he and his father travel to Hyram Bennett's farm to search for Queenie.

When Joe finally joins him in the car, impatience and aggravation are evident on his father's face and in his voice. He does not care why his son was deterred, so Joe does not try to explain. After announcing his intention to stop at Clayton's store, Joe's father does not speak again. All of Joe's movements indicate uneasiness and fear of his father. After he pumps the gas, he is unsure if his father expects him to come inside or wait in the car. Noticing the embarrassment on his father's face while he stands at the counter opposite a clearly exasperated proprietor who requires Joe's father to sign an account book, Joe decides it is best to wait in the cold. From past experiences, he knows not to ask about what transpired in the store. For no reason except his own frustration, Joe's father snaps at him about wanting candy or soda although Joe asks for neither. Silent until they are back inside the car, his father "let go with what Joe had seen on his face" (20), so he merely cringes when his father swears. Joe's thoughts reveal that he wishes his father were still out on the road in his rig. When Joe makes an innocent comment, his father interprets it wrongly, and the tension between them escalates.

The scene at the hog farm indicates how naïve Joe is of rural life. Startled by the huge hog that butts the fence and the sound of the rifle which breaks the prolonged silence, Joe cries out and falls into the mud, embarrassed by the laughter of others and his father's scolding. Afraid, he stands off to the side and says nothing. To add to Joe's quiet anguish, when Lonnie, who sees an easy target in Joe, puts hog bristles down his shirt, he is uncertain of how to react to this painful prank.

On the ride home with Queenie (30), his father finally admits that Joe knows so little about life because he has not been taught, but Joe does not reply. In a rare moment of affection, Joe's father decides to teach him a driving lesson immediately. When Joe gingerly takes the wheel, once again he is unsure of himself and fearful of his father's wrath if he does something wrong. However, his father speaks to him with a temperate voice (32), so Joe cautiously relaxes and gains confidence

Joe's father has his own rite of passage experience when he realizes the importance of interaction with his son, especially via verbal communication. Because he has spent long stretches on the road, he and Joe do not know each other, thus the silent awkwardness between them. Joe has known only irritation and disapproval; as a result, his fear has trained him to be silent and wary around his father since he does not know what might trigger a volatile outburst. Joe gradually begins to understand that the financial adversity this man has faced makes him bitter, angry, and short-tempered. Lonnie Bennett's accusation that Joe's father was fired instead of quitting his job indicates that it might be factual, but Joe's father would be much too proud to confess that fault in his work ethic. On the other hand, he may feel foolish for quitting his job after hearing and believing false rumors of new jobs in the mines. Either way, his ego would be bruised. By the story's end, with both Queenie and his father at home, Joe has reason to hope that he and his father will begin to communicate more easily.

Works Cited

Holbrook, Chris. "Hell and Ohio." *Hell and Ohio: Stories of Southern Appalachia.* Frankfort: Gnomon Press, 1995.
_____. "The Lost Dog." *Hell and Ohio: Stories of Southern Appalachia.* Frankfort: Gnomon Press, 1995.

The Lamb Family
Bloodroot by Amy Greene

Amy Greene's *Bloodroot*, which won the Weatherford Award for outstanding depiction of the Appalachian South in 2010, is so well written that the reader will be surprised to know it is her debut novel. The setting in eastern Tennessee on Bloodroot Mountain, a symbol of the hardscrabble lives of the characters (Schuster 31), could also be considered a character itself, for it seems to occupy the bodies and souls of several generations of the Lamb family who have been gifted with "the touch." Beginning with Byrdie's grandmother and great aunts living in Chickweed Holler, their heightened awareness causes them to experience unusual sensations and visions, which are passed down to their offspring.

In his article about Amy Greene's work, Joseph Schuster commented that *Bloodroot* has all the attributes of a well-written novel: "densely populated by characters who seem living, breathing human beings and not fictional constructions; centered on narrative events that are of consequence; profound without being pedantic set in a place that has substance" (30).

The characters are so varied and complex that they cannot be pigeon holed into one category, yet they have in common a love for the mountain. The book opens during the Depression when families endeavored to eke an existence, so poverty is an endemic and perpetual state. Their bleak financial condition does not change over almost a century of living in the mountainous area. Ignorance is another negative trait of this family, for most of its members either drop out of school early or do not attend at all.

Byrdie's daughter Clio harbors a deep, hidden resentment about being pent up at home, especially when the snow makes it impossible to descend the mountain. Her frustration manifests itself in violence and screams, for she is incapable of uttering explanatory words. Byrdie remembers her scream "liked to froze my blood" (Greene 66).

Clio's daughter Myra, around whom all the other characters' lives revolve, is loved by all who narrate the novel—Doug, a childhood friend; her grandmother Byrdie; her children Laura and Johnny; and finally Myra herself. The tone of the novel changes from freedom, to despair, to resignation, and then finally a glint of hope as "the characters struggle to achieve some healthy relationship to the past" (Montgomery 89).

Because old-fashioned notions of marriage prevail on the mountain, the men are bullies, demanding complete control of their wives. They use threats to instill fear in the women, and then deliver cruel and violent punishments to those who do not obey. For example, on a visit with her granddaughter after Myra marries John, Byrdie observes Myra's horrible life, both physically and emotionally. When she begs Myra to go back up the mountain with her, Myra's sad response is, "I can't Granny. I made my bed" (Greene 96), believing that her predicament is her own fault due to the wrong choices she has made.

Gender roles are rigid on Bloodroot Mountain. When John finds out Myra has gone to the pool hall, he reminds her that he expects "a woman to keep her ass at home ... and I ain't the only one who believes that way" (299). He decides to humiliate Myra to make sure she abides by his rules, and a vivid scene imparts his declaration when he orders his brother Hollis to bend Myra over a table, pull up her dress, and hold her arms down while he beats her with his belt. In ignominious words Myra reveals, "when it was over, I fell silent and still" (300). His stomping her pet rabbit to death is a figurative parallel of what he hopes to do her spirit. Further debasement occurs when he shoves her under the house and locks the door to the crawl space, forcing her to spend the night lying prone among bugs, rats, and dead snakes, her face against the damp, fetid dirt. The degradation continues when she is locked there a second time after John drags her by her hair across the yard and rapes her outside and then threatens to burn down her grandmother's house if Myra does not obey. There is no compassion or reverence for humanity in the deepest recesses of his heart, and Myra's silence and resigned obedience embolden John to continue the abuse. She becomes almost helpless to regain her own life.

However, with renewed strength, Myra is determined to escape her evil warden while he is passed out drunk. After she maims John with a hatchet, she quickly returns to her grandmother's cabin, and with Granny's help delivers twins, Laura and Johnny, whom she adores. Like most twins, Laura and Johnny develop their own mode of communication. Johnny recalls a time when they were small, and if he wanted his sister, he could "call her back without words." He read the "set of her mouth and the line of her shoulders" (108) to understand what she could not speak.

The mental scars of her tumultuous marriage have taken their toll on Myra. In a rare moment of relaxed vigilance, someone sees Laura and Johnny, and Myra laments that she knew better. Those were "the last words she spoke for a long time" (112). After six years on the mountain, Myra becomes completely mute. She attacks a social worker from DSS who tries to inquire about the children. Laura remembers that day vividly when her mother "pulled out her hair and slobbered and screamed like a wildcat" (163).

At one foster home, Laura is assigned the task of caring for an old woman who has had a stroke. Her mouth is puckered so her words are difficult to decipher, "but not their meanness" (139). She berates Laura for her hesitancy, wondering where the family found her. Hattie laughs as she comments, "They laws, girl, you're dumb as a post, ain't you?" (130), but Laura can find no words to answer the spiteful woman.

Myra "ends the novel in stasis" (Montgomery 89) when she is committed to an institution for the mentally ill. Although Myra remains unresponsive for many years, she "exists in a world of memories" (89) about blissful times on Bloodroot Mountain. Schuster notes the "balance between the terrible and the hopeful" (35) for these Appalachians.

Shuffled among foster homes, Laura and Johnny, "silent and wide-eyed" (Greene 131) are terrified to be around people in a civilized world they do not know. Like their mother, they find it difficult to find the words necessary to interact with the strangers who come and go in their lives.

When the twins become young adults and decide to visit their mother, Johnny learns, "It's not forgetting that heals. It's remembering" (242). If Laura and Johnny can successfully navigate a life apart from the cursed elements of their family's inherent tradition of silent acceptance and rely on their own power and individual actions rather than a "large unfathomable force ... they offer the possibility of redemption to all of those who came before them" (Schuster 35).

Works Cited

Greene, Amy. *Bloodroot.* New York: Vintage, 2010. Print.
Montgomery, Jesse Ambrose. "*Bloodroot.*" *Appalachian Heritage* 39.2 (2011): 87–90. Print.
Schuster, Joseph M. "A Richness of Characters: The Fiction of Amy Greene." *Appalachian Heritage* 41.4 (2010): 29–38. Print.

Mary Ella
Necessary Lies
by Diane Chamberlain

Diane Chamberlain was a psychotherapist before she began her writing career. Her knowledge in the field of psychiatry helped give her insights for the creation of her characters. Chamberlain, who has written over twenty novels, authored *Necessary Lies,* which was published in 2013. "This powerful novel peels back the disturbing truths about the eugenics sterilization program implemented in North Carolina" (Holstine). The first and last two chapters are set in 2011, but the bulk of the story takes place in1960 on Davison Gardiner's tobacco farm in Almore, North Carolina where the Hart women are poor tenant farmers.

Social worker Jane Forrester, becomes too emotionally involved with her clients, a violation of the regulations stipulated by the Department of Public Welfare (DPW). She is particularly drawn to the plight of the Hart family, led by aging, diabetic Nonnie. Mary Ella, the quiet one who scored 70 on an IQ exam is categorized feebleminded; Ivy is a petit mal epileptic with an IQ of 80, considered dull/normal. Baby William can speak only the word "Mama." Ivy, who laments that Mary Ella and her son are "two quiet souls cut from the same cloth" (Chamberlain 12), is a beautiful wanderer, with a halo of blond hair. Mary Ella also harbors deep secrets, especially the identity of her son's father.

"Beauty and mental retardation are a dangerous combination," (78) observes Jane's co- worker, for boys are much too interested in Mary Ella while they work together in the tobacco fields. "For all her strangeness," (41) and quietude, she seems peaceful, and because of her low intelligence, illegitimate child, promiscuity, and abject poverty, the DPW has sterilized her as part of the state's Eugenics Program. This fact is known only to Nonnie, who signed the document giving permission for the procedure, yet when Mary Ella delivered her son, she was lied to about an emergency appendectomy, to explain the sutures on her lower abdomen.

Each time Jane tries to garner information, Mary Ella looks through her and does not say a word. Neighbor and fellow laborer of the Hart's, Lita contends that "William ain't right" and Mary Ella is "getting stranger by the day" (56) like her mother Violet, a schizophrenic committed to the Dorothea Dix Hospital. Lita has also been sterilized, qualifying because of her race and her five sons, all born out of wedlock.

Even though they provide minimal labor for him, Gardiner surprisingly allows the Hart's to stay in their house. Calling Mary Ella a pretty imbecile who does whatever nature tells her to do, he bestows favors on her when she goes to his home several times a week. An astute reader will correctly surmise that Gardiner is the father of her child.

After Jane reveals the secret of her sterilization, Mary Ella, who was rarely conversant in the past, is now "plum silent, all wrapped up in herself" (226). Several circumstances that put the baby's health in danger prove that among this household of women, no one is able to safely care for him. After a social worker places William in a foster home, Mary Ella refuses to speak or eat, and in a poignant response, repeatedly runs her hand over the bed where her son used to sleep. She does not initiate conversation or respond to anyone, not even her sister. When she is mobile, she is like a frozen "statue" (255); eventually she commits suicide.

The plot becomes more complex at this point when Ivy, who is secretly pregnant by Gardiner's son Henry Allen, fears the same fate of being sterilized at the time of her baby's birth and having it taken from her. She is right on one count—her infant daughter is taken from her, but before she can be examined by a physician prior to the sterilization, she and Henry Allen run away together. Fifty years later, Jane and Ivy reunite as they prepare to testify in Washington, D.C. about the injustices of the Eugenics Program. They become a collective voice on Mary Ella's behalf.

Works Cited

Chamberlain, Diane. *Necessary Lies*. New York: St. Martin's Griffin, 2013. Print.
Holstine, Lesa. "Necessary Lies." *Library Journal* 138.13 (2013). Academic Search Premier. Web.

Index